The
# Illustrator 7

Wow!
Book

*Sharon Steuer*

**The Illustrator 7 Wow! Book,**
Sharon Steuer

Peachpit Press
1249 Eighth Street
Berkeley, CA  94710
510/548-4393
510/524-2221 (fax)

Peachpit Press is a division of Addison Wesley Longman.

Book design: Barbara Sudick
Editors: Elizabeth Rogalin, Gary Pfitzer
Cover design: Barbara Sudick (art direction), Sharon Steuer (illustration)

ISBN 0-201-68897-2
0 9 8 7 6 5 4 3 2 1

Printed and bound in the United States of America.

## Dedication

*To everyone who put in the extra effort to make this update possible, especially the round-the-clock* Wow! *team: Robin, Diane, Elizabeth, Paul, Sandee and Peg. To my loving family and friends, who make everything worthwhile. To Puma and Bear for showing me that Cassie wasn't the only great cat in the world. And as always, a most special dedication to Jeff Jacoby, my love and husband, who continues to prepare the delicious, gourmet, saturated-fat-free meals which feed the on-site* Wow! *staff…but mostly, for his unwavering love and belief in me.*
**— Sharon Steuer**

*To Sharon Steuer, for giving me this opportunity — more so for being a terrific person to work with and a great friend. It was a pleasure. To my wonderful parents, Joseph and Judith Feminella for always believing in me. To John Ryan, my first computer tutor and who, along with his wife, Tracey Dinkin, have become great influences in my life. To Squeegee, my kookie-kitty. To my sweet, Chanel, who went to kitty heaven before I finished this book. I miss you. To Sam Moore. Without your love and brave heart, I would be lost. Thank you.*
**— Robin AF Olson**

# Contents

# 3

## Lines, Fills & Colors

**8**

# Important: Read me first!

## Stop the presses!

With access to the Worldwide Web, you can download updates, additions, new format plug-ins and bug fixes for current Illustrator versions via: **www.adobe.com** Please check this site regularly! This book is based on the way version 7.0.1 edits spot colors, so please make sure that you are using 7.0.1 or later. For the latest information and workarounds on known production issues, check the "Tech folder" on the *Wow!* disk and the *Wow!* website (where you'll also find *Wow!* artists' e-mail addresses and links to related websites): **www.peachpit.com/wow.html**

## Additional Illustrator training

Learning is usually accelerated by taking a good class; the *Wow!* Website (see Tip above) will include a list (and links to) facilities offering classes in Illustrator. Try the animated tutorials on the *Adobe Illustrator CD.* Also see the Training folder on the *Wow!* disk for *Zen Lessons* (that supplement *Chapter 2*) and a suggested *Illustrator Wow!* course curriculum. Suggested reading can be found in the *Publications* appendix.

This book has been designed to help you harness the enormous power of Adobe Illustrator by providing you with hundreds of pages of useful production techniques, timesaving tips and beautiful art generously shared by *Illustrator Wow!* artists nationwide. Whether you're a recent convert to Illustrator, or one of the thousands of Illustrator experts who haven't had the time to learn the newer features, this book is for you. All techniques were kept deliberately short to allow you to squeeze in a lesson or two between clients, and to encourage the use of this book within the confines of a supervised classroom.

In order to keep the content in this book tantalizing to everyone—from novice to expert—I've assumed a reasonable level of competence with basic Mac and Windows concepts such as opening and saving files, launching applications, copying objects to the clipboard, and doing mouse operations. I've also assumed that you've completed the *Adobe Illustrator Tutorial,* and understand conceptually the basic functionality of the tools.

I'd love to tell you that you can learn Adobe Illustrator by flipping through the pages of this book, but the reality is, there is no substitute for practice. The good news is, the more you work with Illustrator, the more features you'll be able to integrate into your creative process.

Use this book as a reference, a guide for special techniques, or just a source of inspiration. After you've read this book, read it again, and you'll undoubtedly learn something you missed the first time. As I hope you'll discover, the more experienced you become with Adobe Illustrator, the easier it will be to assimilate all the new information and inspiration you'll find in this book. Happy Illustrating!

Sharon Steuer

# How to use this book...

Before you do anything else, read the *Wow! Glossary* on the pull-out quick reference card at the back of the book. The *Glossary* provides definitions for the terms used throughout *The Illustrator 7 Wow! Book* (such as: ⌘ = the Command key for Mac/the Control key for Windows, or what "toggle" means).

## WELCOME TO *WOW!* FOR WINDOWS AND MAC

If you already use Adobe Photoshop 4 or later, you'll see many interface similarities to Illustrator 7. Adobe intends this version of Illustrator to create, in part, a common look and feel across Photoshop, PageMaker and Illustrator. The change should make the time you spend on learning each program much shorter (especially if you're a newcomer to all three products). Your productivity should also increase across the board once you adjust to the new shortcuts and methodologies (see "Shortcuts and keystrokes" following, and Tips on page 3).

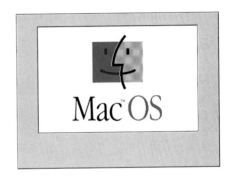

## Setting up your palettes

In terms of following along with the lessons in this book, you'll probably want to disable the "Type Area Select" option (see the red Tip on page 133). Next, I recommend you view swatches as sorted by name: hold down Option (Alt) and choose "Name" from the Swatches pop-up menu to list all Swatch views by name (see at right).

By default, Illustrator 7.0 has the habit of filling palettes with excess styles. In order to follow the lessons without these extraneous styles getting in your way, see the ReadMe in the "Custom Prefs" folder on the *Wow!* disk; it contains alternative preferences and startup files you can use to simplify your workspace. Even if you use stripped-out Startup files, Illustrator 7.0 may introduce unwanted junk into documents created in previous versions of Illustrator when opened in 7. To clear out a palette of unused styles, click on the All Swatches icon,

*With the All Swatches icon selected and the Option (Alt) key pressed, choosing "Name" from the Swatches pop-up*

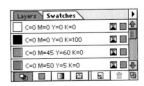

*All Swatch views now display by Name*

Choosing Select All Unused from the Swatches pop-up, then clicking the Trash icon

After deleting (and repeating select / delete)

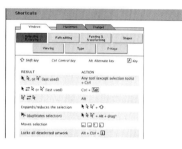

Printable shortcuts charts from Help

**For Mac: Restoring AI 6.0 prefs**

Unfortunately, this is Mac only. In General Preferences (⌘-K), "AI 6.0 Tool Shortcuts" restores:

- Control-key access to Convert-direction with Direct-select, and Add/Delete Points with the Pen.
- One-handed access to Lock/Hide functions, though slightly different from the originals: Lock ⌘-2, Unlock ⌘-Option-2, Hide ⌘-3, Show ⌘-Option-3.
- The ability to cycle units of measurement (⌘-Control-U).
- The ability to access individual locked guides (see Tip, page 21).

**Note:** *This disables Context-sensitive menus, but toggle it on and off with* Wow! *QuicKeys (text at right).*

then choose "Select All Unused" from the Swatches pop-up, and click the Trash icon to remove these unwanted extras (sometimes you'll have to repeat the select-and-delete procedure to ensure the palette is cleared).

**Shortcuts and keystrokes**

To simplify the reading of this book, keyboard shortcuts are given almost exclusively in Macintosh terminology—if you're on Windows, simply substitute **Ctrl** (Control) for ⌘, and **Alt** for Option. On the *Wow!* disk you'll find "Adam Z's Shortcuts Kit," which, along with the "Shortcuts" listing found in the Help menu, can be printed and kept tucked into the book.

Although Illustrator 7.0 introduced many improvements to keyboard navigation (such as single key tool access and Tab to hide palettes), Adobe did replace some keystrokes that were vital to efficient work flow with some that many find awkward or unusable, in particular: Lock/Unlock, Hide/Show All, Average/Join, and Average-Join in one step. However, since similarity of interface seems to be the goal at Adobe, it's likely that updates to Illustrator 7 will integrate an "Actions" palette (as Adobe has already done in Photoshop), which would give us the option to reassign keystrokes.

Since you're likely to use shortcuts only if they're efficient, awkward shortcuts aren't always included in the text. Instead, menu-routing information will be accompanied by reminders to use Context-sensitive menus, if applicable. In addition, I've included "*QK:*" (QuicKeys) keystroke alternatives to use as guides in constructing more user-friendly keystrokes, if that option is available to you. Regrettably, for the time-being, if you're on Windows, you can't customize keystrokes until either Adobe provides the tools, or QuicKeys (or another macro program) becomes available for Windows. Meanwhile, if you're hungry for shortcuts, refer to Adobe's shortcuts as listed in "Adam Z's Shortcuts Kit" on the *Wow!* disk.

Luckily, if you're a Mac user, you can immediately access the *QK:* keystrokes by installing the special version of CE Software's QuicKeys from the *Wow!* disk. If you use QuicKeys already, just install the *Wow!* keyset. (The *QK:* keystrokes are based on time-tested shortcuts from previous versions of Illustrator.) Some of these shortcuts are available even without QuicKeys, if you use the "AI 6.0 Tool Shortcuts" instead of Context-sensitive menus (see Tip at left)—but *Wow!* QuicKeys allows you to access these keystrokes *and* use Context-sensitive menus. You'll find a full listing of the *QK:* keystrokes (including some all-new shortcuts such as turning AI 6.0 Tool Shortcuts on and off) in "QuicKeys Folder" on the *Wow!* disk.

## HOW THIS BOOK IS ORGANIZED...
You'll find six kinds of information woven throughout this book—all of it up-to-date for Illustrator 7.0.1: **Basics**, **Tips**, **Exercises**, **Techniques**, **Galleries** and **References**.

**1 Basics.** *Chapter 1: Illustrator Basics* and *Chapter 2: The Zen of Illustrator* qualify as full-blown chapters on basics and are packed with information that distills and supplements your Adobe Illustrator manuals and disks. Every chapter starts with a general overview of the basics. Although these sections have been designed so that advanced users of Illustrator can move quickly through them, I strongly suggest that the rest of you read them very carefully. Please keep in mind that this book serves as a supplement to, not a substitute for, your Adobe Illustrator *User Guides* and CD-ROM.

**2 Tips.** Look to the information in the gray and red boxes for hands-on tips that can help you work more efficiently. Usually you can find tips alongside related textual information, but if you are in too impatient a mood to read a section in depth, you might just want to flip through, looking for tips that are of interest to you. The red arrows ➤, red outlines and red text found in tips (and sometimes with artwork) have been added to emphasize or further explain a concept or technique.

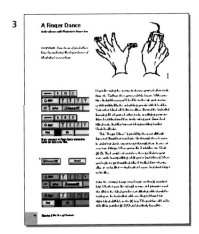

2 | **Tip boxes**
Look for these gray boxes to find Tips about Adobe Illustrator.

**Red Tip boxes**
The red Tip boxes contain warnings or other essential information.

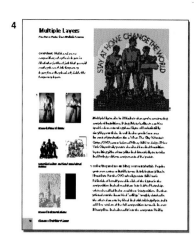

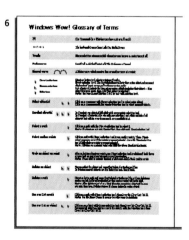

**3 Exercises.** (Not for the faint of heart.) I have included intermediate-level, step-by-step exercises to help you make the transition to Illustrator technician extraordinaire. *Chapter 2: The Zen of Illustrator* and the *Zen Lessons* on the *Wow!* disk are dedicated to helping you master the mechanics, and the soul, of Illustrator. Take these lessons in small doses, in order, and at a relaxed pace.

**4 Techniques.** In these sections, you'll find step-by-step techniques gathered from almost a hundred *Illustrator Wow!* artists. Most *Wow!* techniques focus on one aspect of how an image was created, though I'll often refer you to different *Wow!* chapters (or to a specific page where a technique is introduced) to give you the opportunity to explore a briefly-covered feature in more depth. Feel free to start with almost any chapter, but, since each technique builds on those previously explained, try to follow the techniques within each chapter sequentially. Some chapters conclude with an **Advanced Technique**, which assumes that you have assimilated all of the techniques found throughout the chapter. *Chapter 8: Masks & Special Effects* is an entire chapter dedicated to advanced tips, tricks and techniques.

**5 Galleries.** The gallery pages consist of images related to techniques demonstrated nearby. Each gallery piece is accompanied by a description of how the artist created that image, and may include steps showing the progression of a technique detailed elsewhere. *Chapter 9: Illustrator & Other Programs* consists almost entirely of gallery pages to give you the flavor of Illustrator's flexibility.

**6 References.** *Technical Notes, Resources, Publications* and *Artists* appendixes, and a *General Index* can be found in the back of this book. In addition, I will sometimes direct you to the *User Guide* or *Getting Started* when referring to specific information already well-documented in either the *Adobe Illustrator User Guide* or the *Getting Started* supplement. ✍

# Illustrator Basics

This chapter is packed with tips and techniques chosen to help you to use Adobe Illustrator with optimal ease and efficiency. Whether you're a veteran of Illustrator or a relative newcomer, you're likely to find information here that will greatly increase your productivity and help you get up to speed on the latest features. Remember, this chapter is an addendum to, not a replacement for, Adobe Illustrator's *User Guide* or *Tutorial*.

## COMPUTER & SYSTEM REQUIREMENTS

Creating artwork on the computer is wonderful and exciting. Blissfully, our computer art tools, including Adobe Illustrator, have seen great improvements in the past few years. Unfortunately, one of the sad facts about demands for better and more powerful software is that the more powerful upgrades might not run on older computers.

The minimum requirements for using Illustrator on the Macintosh is a 68030 processor with 16 MB of installed RAM, with 8 MB of RAM made available to Illustrator. You need to be running the Apple OS 7.5.1 or later. Illustrator will need a minimum of 25 MB of free space on your hard drive to install. Note that the installation medium is CD-ROM.

PC owners will need an Intel 486 processor, Windows 95, Windows NT 4.0 Workstation, or Windows NT 4.0 Server operating system, a VGA display card and 16 MB of installed RAM. To install Illustrator, you'll need a minimum 25 MB of free space on your hard drive and a CD-ROM drive.

**Don't start yet!**

Before you begin reading this book, make sure you read both "How to Use This Book," on pages xi–xiv, and the pull-out *Glossary* at the back of the book. If you are on Windows, pay special attention to these sections for help translating the Mac keyboard labels, used here, into the appropriate counterparts for Windows.

**Additional recommendations**

The minimum requirements to run Illustrator are just that: *minimum*. Anything you add will increase performance, efficiency and reduce headaches!

- 32 MB of RAM (or more)
- 8X CD-ROM Drive
- Extra hard drive space
- Removable storage device
- Video Card or extra VRAM (for 24-bit color)
- A 17"+ monitor

Also, see Adobe's *Getting Started* supplement for more on system and memory requirements for your version of Illustrator.

## WHAT'S NEW FOR MAC AND WINDOWS

As I mentioned in "How to use this book," what's *newest* about this version of Illustrator is that it has been re-designed to create a common look and feel across all Adobe programs.

The very patient Windows users will find an almost endless array of new bells and whistles in Illustrator 7. Gradients (*Chapter 5*), Layers (*Chapter 4*), Filters (*Chapter 6*), the Transform palette (page 14), and multiple levels of Undos (page 17) are just some of the wonderful changes new to Windows users.

A quick summary of what's new in Illustrator 7 (for both Mac and Windows users) follows.

### Customizable Grids

A wonderful new addition, grids can be shown behind or in front of your artwork, and will rotate along with the "Constrain Angle" (see pages 22 and 137 for more).

### Context-sensitive menus

To access Illustrator's new Context-sensitive menus while using Windows, just click the Right mouse button. Mac users can hold down the Control key and click and hold the mouse button. A menu will appear, relevant to the tool or objects you are working with, and its pertinent functions are then available to you. Some people find this a great way to learn the program, and it keeps you from continually referring to the pull-down menus.
**Note:** *On the Mac, if Control-click does not access Context-sensitive menus, see Tip, "Restoring AI 6 prefs for Mac" on page xii for details.*

### Single key tool-selection and navigation

Press "T" to choose the Type tool, "P" for the Pen tool, and so on. Choose any tool in the toolbox simply by pressing the correct key. To access hidden tools, keep striking the key until the desired tool appears. To learn the single key equivalent for tools, hold your cursor over a tool in the toolbox, and its single key shortcut will appear—if this doesn't work, enable "Show Tool Tips" in General Preferences (⌘-K). Tool Tips will also display descriptive captions for all icons and certain functions. **Note:** *Single-key navigation won't work inside a text block.*

## New Paint palettes

Gone is the simple, compact Paint palette. Now you'll find it has been subdivided into many separate tabbed palettes: Color, Swatches, Stroke, Attributes, Gradient— and even the bottom of the Toolbar! Color systems, like Pantone and Trumatch, also reside in their own, uneditable palettes (see *Chapter 3* for more on paint palettes).

## New Character palette features

You can now create type that flows vertically and works with some multinational font character sets. For more about type, see *Chapter 7*.

## More file formats

Illustrator 7 can open many file formats, thus improving your flexibility in working with other programs and other platforms. See "Image Formats" later in this chapter, and *Chapter 9* for more about working with other formats.

Web designers can now export artwork in JPEG and GIF89a format. See *Chapter 10* for more on Illustrator and the web. ↻

## WORKING WITH POSTSCRIPT OBJECTS
### Anchor points, lines and Bézier* curves

Adobe uses its own language, called "PostScript," to describe mathematically each of the objects that you create in Illustrator. Instead of using pixels to draw shapes, Illustrator creates objects made up of points, called "anchor points." They are connected by outlines (which can be curved or straight) called "paths," and are visible if you work in Artwork viewing mode (View: Artwork). The PostScript language describes information about the location and size of each path, as well as each path's dozen or so attributes, such as its fill color, and its stroke

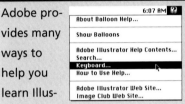
* Named after the software engineer who pioneered its use, Pierre Bézier

## How to Allocate RAM (for Mac)

Just because your computer has a lot of RAM (memory), that doesn't mean Illustrator has enough *allocated* to it (Adobe allocates a preset minimum amount of RAM). To improve the speed of many of Illustrator's functions, you'll want to increase the memory allocation. *Single* click the Illustrator icon when the program isn't running, and ⌘-I to adjust the "Minimum" and "Preferred" sizes. Remember to reserve enough RAM for your computer to run the system, and any other applications you'll want open simultaneously.

## Illustrator on your screen

Illustrator images on your computer screen are displayed at approximately 72–96 pixels per inch (ppi) depending on your platform and your monitor. Don't worry if your illustrator objects or text appear "jaggy" on the screen, since, as long as you print to a PostScript printer, you can print at the maximum resolution of that printer; this is called "device-dependent resolution."

weight and color. Because you are creating objects, you'll be able to change the order in which the objects stack upon each other. You'll also be able to group objects together so they can be selected as if they were one object, and even ungroup them later, if you wish.

Although you can now work in Illustrator while previewing the path in full color, in many cases you'll find that editing your image in Artwork mode (which displays the paths in black outline) provides greater accuracy and greatly speeds up the time it takes for Illustrator to redraw the computer screen.

If you took geometry, you probably remember that the shortest distance between two points is a straight line. In Illustrator, this rule translates into each line being defined by two anchor points which are created by clicking with the Pen tool.

In mathematically describing rectangles and circles, Illustrator computes the center, length of the sides or radius, based on the total width and height you specify. For more complex shapes involving freeform curves, Adobe Illustrator allows you to use the Pen tool to create Bézier curves, defined by nonprinting "anchor" points (which literally anchor the path at that point), and "direction" points (which define the angle and the depth of the curve). To make these direction points easier to see and manipulate, Illustrator connects each direction point to its anchor point with a nonprinting direction line, also called a "handle." The direction points and handles are visible when you're creating a path with the Pen tool or editing the path with the Direct-selection tool. While all of this might sound complicated, and could involve some initial awkwardness, manipulating Bézier curves can prove quite intuitive.

### More about Bézier curves

If you're new to Bézier curves, you should go through the Adobe *Tutorial* lessons. For some Bézier fine-tuning, I have included some "Zen" practice lessons in the "Training" folder on the *Wow!* disk.

Many graphics programs include Béziers, and learning to master the Pen tool, though challenging at first, is very important. Friskets in Painter, paths in Photoshop, and the outline and extrusion curves of many 3D programs all have at their base a Bézier curve.

The key to learning Béziers is to take your initial lessons in short doses and stop if you get frustrated. Designer Kathleen Tinkel describes Bézier direction lines as "following the gesture of the curve"; this artistic view should help you to create fluid Bézier curves.

**And finally, some rules about Bézier curves:**
- The length and angle of the handles "anticipate" the curves which will follow.
- The length of handles are equal to approximately $\frac{1}{3}$ the length of the curve, if it were straightened.
- Place anchor points on either side of an arch, and not in between.
- The fewer the anchor points, the smoother the curve will look, and the faster the curve will print.
- Adjust a curve's height and angle by dragging the direction points, or grab the curve itself to adjust its height. ⌣

**WATCH YOUR CURSOR!**
Illustrator's cursors change to indicate not only what tool you have selected, but also which function you are about to perform. If you watch your cursor, you will avoid the most common Illustrator mistakes.

**If you choose the Pen tool:**
- **Before you start,** your cursor displays as the Pen tool with "×" indicating that you're starting a new object.

- **Once you've begun your object,** your cursor changes to a regular Pen. This indicates that you're about to add to an existing object.

- **If your cursor gets close to an existing anchor point,** it will change to a Pen with "∧" indicating that you're

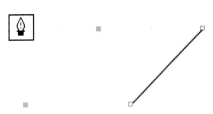

*Clicking with the Pen tool to create anchor points for straight lines*

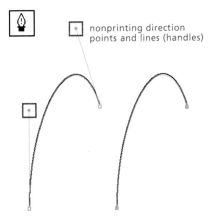

nonprinting direction points and lines (handles)

*Click-dragging with the Pen tool to create anchor points and pulling out direction lines for curves*

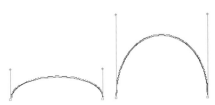

*When direction handles are short, curves are shallow; when handles are long, curves are deep*

*The length and angle of the handles determine the gesture of the curves*

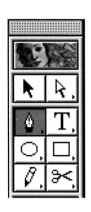

Starting an object

Adding a point

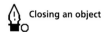
Closing an object

Creating a corner (over an existing point)

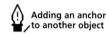
Adding an anchor to another object

*Basic cursor objects options for the Pen tool, "P"*

## Correcting common mistakes

**Avoid these common mistakes:**

- If you try to deselect by clicking outside of your object while you still have the Pen tool, you'll scatter extra points throughout your image, which can cause problems later. If you're aware that you *did* click by mistake, choose Undo. To check for and remove stray points, choose Artwork mode, look for "x"s (other than in the centers of ovals or rectangles) and choose Edit: Select Stray Points, then delete the selected points.

- If you try to delete an object that had been selected by the Direct-selection tool, only the selected point or path will be deleted. Since what remains of the object will now be fully selected, delete again to remove the entire object.

about to click on top of the last anchor point. If you click-drag on top of that anchor point, you'll redraw that curve. If you hold the Option key while you click-drag on top of the point, you'll pull out a new direction line, creating a corner (like the petals of a flower). If you click on top of the point, you'll collapse the outgoing direction line, allowing you to attach a straight line to the curve.

- **If your cursor gets close to an end anchor point of an object,** it will change to a Pen with "o" to indicate that you're about to "close" the path. If you do close the path, then your cursor will change back to a Pen with "×" to indicate that you're beginning a new object.

- **If you use Direct-selection to adjust the object as you go,** then make sure that you look at your cursor when you're ready to continue your object. If it's still a regular Pen, then continue to place the next point, adding to your object. If the Pen tool has "×" (indicating that you are about to start a new object), then you must redraw your last point. As you approach the last anchor point, your cursor will change to a Pen with "/". Click and drag over this last point to redraw the last curve. To form a corner on the point as you draw, hold down your Option key to click-drag out a new direction line.

### Bézier-editing tools

The group of tools you can use to edit Illustrator paths are called Bézier-editing tools. To access these tools, click and hold on the Scissors or Pen tool and drag to select one of the others. (To learn about *filters* that edit, see *Chapter 6.*)

- **The Scissors tool** cuts a path where you click by adding two disconnected, selected anchor points exactly on top of each other. To select just one of the points, deselect the object, then click with the Direct-selection tool on the spot where you cut to select the upper anchor point and drag it to the side to see the two points better. If your path was open when you cut it with the Scissors tool, then the paths will be split in two so you can see each path, on either side of the cut, separate from the other.

- **The Knife tool** slices through all unlocked visible objects and closed paths. To use the Knife tool, simply drag across the object you want to slice, then select the object(s) you want to move or delete (also see top Tip).

- **The Add-anchor-point tool** adds an anchor point to a path at the location where you click.

- **The Delete-anchor-point tool** deletes an anchor point when you click *directly* on the point.

- **The Convert-direction-point tool** lets you convert an anchor point in an already drawn path from a smooth curve to a corner, from a corner to a smooth curve, or from a smooth curve to a hinged curve (two curves hinged at a point). To convert a curve to a corner, click on the anchor point. To convert a corner to a smooth curve, click-drag on the anchor point counterclockwise to pull out a new direction line (or twirl the point until it straightens out the curve). To hinge a smooth curve, grab the direction point itself and drag it to the new position.

### Geometric objects

The Oval (aka Ellipse), Rectangle, Polygon, Spiral and Star tools create objects called "geometric primitives." These objects are mathematically described symmetrical paths that are grouped with a nonprinting anchor point, which indicates the center. Use the centers of the geometric objects to "snap-align" them with each other, or with other objects and guides. You can create these geometric objects numerically or manually. The Polygon, Spiral and Star tools were once *filters* in a Plug-in Toolbox. Now you can access them as hidden tools from the Oval tool in the Toolbox. (See *Chapter 2* for exercises in creating and manipulating geometric objects, and see the Tip, next page.)

## A more precise slice
Use any selected *path* to slice through all visible unlocked objects—choose Object: Path: Slice.

## To change your object...
To make changes to a path, click on it with the Direct-selection tool, which displays all anchor points and the direction handles on either side of a selected curve. Adjust the length and angle of a curve by grabbing and dragging points, direction handles or the curve itself. If you select an object but don't see direction handles:
- Deselect it, then try again.
- If you're in Preview mode, be sure to click on the *path itself* or switch to Artwork mode. Or, deselect the Area Select option in General Preferences.

**Note:** *Only* curves *have handles!*

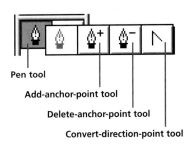

Pen tool

Add-anchor-point tool

Delete-anchor-point tool

Convert-direction-point tool

## The hollow "Snap-to" arrow
As long as "Snap to point" is enabled in General Preferences, you can grab objects from any path or point and drag until they *snap* to a guide or other object; the arrow will turn hollow.

☒ Snap to point

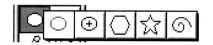

- **To create a geometric object with numeric input,** select the desired geometric tool, move your cursor into the image window and click to establish the upper left corner of your object. Enter the desired dimensions in the dialog box, and click OK. To create the object numerically from the object's center instead, Option-click in your image window. Or, double-click on the tool first, switching the tool mode to show "+" in the center, which indicates that the object will be drawn from its center. Holding down the Option key in this case will draw the object from the corner.

- **To create a geometric shape manually,** select the desired geometric tool, and click-drag to form the object from one corner to the other. To create the object from the center, hold down the Option key and drag from the center outward (keep the Option key down until you release the mouse button to ensure the "draw from center"). Alternatively, press the letter key for that tool ("N" for ellipse, "M" for rectangle) until "+" shows in the center, indicating that the object will be drawn from the center. Holding down the Option key in this case will draw the object from the corner. Holding down the Rectangle tool allows you to switch to the Rounded Rectangle tool. Once you have drawn the geometric objects, you can edit them exactly as your other hand-drawn paths. ↻

## GROUPING & SELECTING OBJECTS
### To group, or not to group...

Many object-oriented programs (that is, programs that create objects, such as Illustrator and CorelDraw) provide you with a grouping function so you can act upon multiple objects as if they were one. In Illustrator, though, you don't have to group objects or parts of objects to act on them as a unit; you merely have to select them. But, since grouping objects together places all the objects on the same layer, you don't want to group objects unless you actually need to (for more information on layers and re-ordering objects, see *Chapter 4*).

So when do you want to group objects? Group objects when you need to select them *repeatedly* as a unit. Take an illustration of a bicycle as an example. Use the Group function (⌘-G): to group the spokes of a wheel, next group the two wheels of the bicycle, then group the wheels with the frame (⌘-Shift-G ungroups). We'll continue referring to this bicycle below:

### Selecting within groups

- **With the Direct-selection tool.** Click on a point or path with the Direct-selection tool to select that point or portion of the path. If you click on a spoke of a wheel, you'll select the portion of the spoke's path you clicked on.

- **With the Selection tool.** Click on an object with the Selection tool to select the largest group containing that object. In our example, it would be the entire bicycle.

- **With the Group-selection tool.** Use the Group-selection tool to select subgroupings. First, click with the Group-selection tool to select the entire spoke path. The second click will result in the entire wheel, the third will be the two wheels, and the fourth will be the entire bicycle. **Note:** *Once you've selected objects with the Group-selection tool, if you want to grab and move them, you must change to one of the other selection tools. If you click again with Group-selection tool, you'll be selecting the next group up!*

- **See the "Finger Dance" lessons in Chapter 2.** This section includes a variety of selection exercises.

### Averaging & Joining

Two of Illustrator's most useful functions are Average and Join (both found under the Object:Path menu). In essence, averaging allows you to align selected *points*. (To align *objects*, use the Align palette.) To average, use the Direct-selection tool to marquee-select or Shift-select any number of points belonging to any number of objects. Then use the Context-sensitive menu to Average (or see

## If you can't group...

If you try to group objects and get the message "Can't make a group of objects that are within different groups":

- Make certain that the objects that you wish to group are fully selected.
- Cut the objects.
- Use Paste In Front or Paste In Back (⌘-F or ⌘-B) to paste the objects back into your image in the exact same location (see page 78 for specifics on this).
- While the objects are still selected, select Group (⌘-G).

Selection tool

Direct-selection tool

Group-selection tool

## Efficient ungrouping

Remember, if all you want to do is select an object within a group, you don't need to ungroup it; just use the Direct-selection tool to select it. If you *do* actually want to ungroup, select the group by using the regular Selection tool and repeat Ungroup (⌘-Shift-G) as many times as you wish to remove levels of grouping. For instance, with the example of the bicycle (used at the left), selecting the entire bicycle and typing ⌘-Shift-G the first time would remove the last grouping applied; typing it four times would remove all of the grouping.

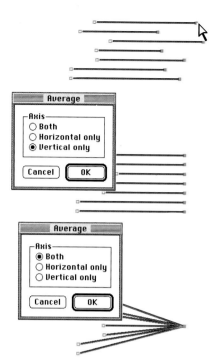

*Using the Average command to align selected endpoints vertically, then choosing "Both"*

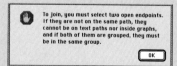

## Joining warning

If you get an error message that you can't join points, do the following—in addition to the conditions in the warning:

> To join, you must select two open endpoints. If they are not on the same path, they cannot be on text paths nor inside graphs, and if both of them are grouped, they must be in the same group.
>
> OK

- Make sure that you've selected only *two* points (no third stray point selected by mistake?).
- Make sure that you've selected *endpoints*, not midpoints.

the *Wow! Shortcuts Chart*) to align the selected points horizontally, vertically or along both axes.

Whereas the Average command can be performed on any number of points, you can only perform Join on two open endpoints. Use the Context-sensitive menu to Join (⌘-J) open endpoints. This function will operate differently depending on the objects:

- **If the two open endpoints are exactly on top of each other,** then Join will open a dialog box asking if the join should be smooth (a curved Bézier anchor with direction handles) or a corner (an anchor point with no handles). Both points will fuse into one point.

- **If the two open endpoints are *not* exactly on top of each other,** then Join will create a straight line joining the two points. If you attempt to join two points to fuse as one but you don't get the dialog box, then you have merely added an adjoining straight line! Undo and see "Averaging & Joining" below.

- **If you select an open path** (in this case, you don't need to select the endpoints), then Join will close the path.

- **If the two open endpoints are on different objects,** then Join will connect the two paths into one.

**Averaging & Joining in one step.** Press ⌘-Option-Shift-J (*QK:* ⌘-Option-J). The join forms a corner if joining to a line, or a hinged curve if joining to a curve. ◡

### GRAPHING & CHARTING

Through the Graph tool, Illustrator allows you to create charts and graphs in nine different styles. The interface isn't designed for those who are new to charts or graphs, so if you intend to use this tool, I suggest you thoroughly read the graph chapter in the *User Guide* and then experiment with the various Graphs & Graph Designs provided by Adobe in the Samples folder. Also, please keep in mind that the purpose of a chart or graph is clear communication of numeric information as a visual aid. No matter how beautiful or slick an illustration is, if it doesn't present your information clearly, it's bad design.

Before you begin, set a default chart or graph style by double-clicking on the Graph tool and choosing the style you want. To actually produce your graph, use the Graph tool very much like the Rectangle tool: either click-drag to create a rectangular object from corner to corner, or hold down the Option key and click with the tool to specify numerically the dimensions of your graph.

After you establish the dimensions, the Graph dialog box will open, awaiting your input of numeric data. Enter labels and numbers by highlighting the desired cell and typing into the entry line along the top. Tab to enter text in the next horizontal cell. You must look carefully in the *User Guide* to determine how you should enter data for the specific graph style you want.

**Note:** *Unfortunately, it's too easy to enter text accidentally into the wrong field; so be meticulous. Just about the only correction strategy available while you're entering data is clicking Transpose to transpose horizontal and vertical data.*

You can also import data saved in "Tab-delineated" text format. Any word processing, spreadsheet or charting program should let you save or export numbers and labels into text that has been separated by Tabs (to indicate that text elements are related) and Returns (to indicate a new set of related text elements).

To change the style of an existing graph, select the entire graph with the Selection tool and double-click on the Graph tool in the Toolbox. Choose another style and click OK. Be aware that, because different chart and graph styles require different types of data, each chart cannot necessarily be translated to all other formats.

To reaccess a graph's numeric data, use the Selection tool to select your graph and choose Object: Graphs: Data. But before you try to alter your numeric data, make sure you have saved your graph (there is no Cancel command in the data entry, though you can, of course, ⌘-Z).

## Maintaining "graphness"

If you want to continue to work with your graph numerically, *don't*, under any circumstances, ungroup your graph; it will make numerical data changes impossible. To avoid losing the special graph formatting, follow these special precautions:

- Use the Selection tool to select the entire graph for changes in style. Once your graph is selected, 1) Double-click the Graph tool to change the graph style; 2) Choose Object: Graphs: Data to change numeric data; or 3) To apply shaped design elements, see "Customizing graph designs" in this section.
- Use the Group-selection tool to select a category of data, then restyle or recolor as desired.
- Use the Type tool or Direct-selection tool to select and change individual text elements.
- Use the Direct-selection tool to select individual elements to change their styling.

## When you *do* ungroup

Once you're *completely* finished numerically adjusting a graph, you may wish to delete some objects. Select the graph (with the Selection tool) and use Ungroup (⌘-Shift-G). No longer part of an editable graph, the objects can now be deleted.

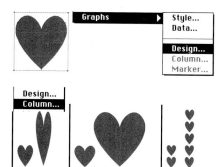

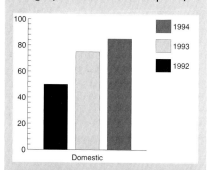

*Defining a design; using the heart to create columns vertically scaled; uniformly scaled; forming a repeating design*

## Using graphs as templates

Many designers use the Graph tool to plot points and generate the scale and legend. They can create an illustration that uses the placement of the graph as a guide (see *Chapter 4* for help in locking the graph for use as a template).

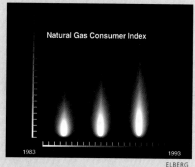

*Eve Elberg used the bar graph above as a template to plot the basic points in this illustration. For the glowing effect, she used blends and gradients (see **Chapter 5**).*

## Customizing graph designs

Being able to insert design elements into a graph is a snazzy but much overused aspect of the graphing feature. Illustrator allows you to define graph designs, which can be used as substitutes for rectangular column bars and line markers. Using the "scaling" option, you can take a heart-shaped design and incorporate it into a graph by stretching (vertically scaling) or enlarging (uniformly scaling) the heart to the correct height. A variant of this technique allows you to define a portion of the heart to be scaled (called the "Sliding" Design). By using the "repeating" option, you can get the hearts to stack on top of each other until they reach the correct height.

Defining a graph design element works much the same way as defining a pattern design (see *Chapter 3*). After creating the object(s) you wish to use as a design element, place a rectangle to enclose your design (with no fill or stroke) behind that element (choose Object: Arrange: Send To Back), select the rectangle with its design and choose Object: Graphs: Design. In the dialog box, click New and name your design. To apply the design, use the Selection tool to select the graph, choose Object: Graphs: Column and select the desired method of fitting your design to the column size. You can also use design elements to serve as "markers" (indicating plotted points) for line and scatter graph styles. Follow the above procedure but choose Object: Graphs: Marker.

In speaking with the art departments at some of the nation's busiest newspapers and periodicals, I discovered that even though they often finish their charts and graphs in Illustrator, most use other programs to translate numbers into graphics. Included on the *Wow!* disk, however, is the shareware premiere of Chronchart, a Mac shareware application, created by Eric Jungerman for the *San Francisco Chronicle*. Chronchart works with Microsoft's spreadsheet Excel to take any subset of your information (including stipulations such as "the 30 most recent sales over $1000") and transform it into graphs and charts editable by Illustrator. ↻

## TRANSFORMATIONS

Moving, scaling, rotating, reflecting and shearing are all operations that transform selected objects. Always begin by selecting what you wish to transform. If you're not happy with the transformation you've just applied, use Undo before applying a new transformation—or you'll end up applying the new transformation on top of the previous one.

In Illustrator, you can perform all transformations manually (see *Chapter 2* for exercises), or through a dialog box for numeric accuracy for specifying the distance, degree, number of steps, percentage or angle. From the dialog box, you can also decide whether lines will be scaled, whether to transform a copy of the object and, if appropriate, whether selected objects, patterns that fill the objects, or both, will be transformed. (For more about transforming patterns, see Tip on page 74.)

Illustrator remembers the last transformation you performed, and keeps those numbers in the appropriate dialog box until you transform differently or restart the program. This means that, if the last time you scaled an image numerically, you chose not to scale the line weights, the next time you scale, manually or numerically, your line weights will not be scaled.

### Moving

In addition to manually grabbing and dragging objects, you can numerically specify a new location: Double-click on the Selection arrow in the Toolbox (there's even a Preview option!). For help determining the distance you wish to move, click-drag with the Measure tool the distance you wish to calculate. Then *immediately* open the Move dialog box to see the measured distance loaded automatically and click OK (or press Return).

### Basic Transformation tools

For scaling, rotation, reflection and shearing of your objects, you can click (to manually specify the center about which the transformation will occur), then grab

## Scaling objects to an exact size

- *The transformation palette way:* Type the new width or height in the palette and press Return.
- *The "proxy" way:* Create a "proxy" rectangle the size of your image, then from the upper left corner of the proxy, Option-click to create another rectangle in the target dimensions. Then with your proxy selected, click with the Scale tool in the upper left and grab-drag the lower right to match the target. (Hold Shift to scale in only one dimension.) Delete these rectangles, select your objects, double-click the Scale tool and apply the settings.

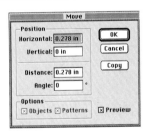

*Double-click the Selection tool to access Move*

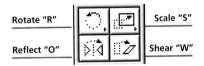

## Transform again

Illustrator remembers the last transformation you performed—from simple moves to rotating a *copy* of an object. Press ⌘-D (or Context-sensitive menu "Transform again") to repeat the effect.

*The selected area indicated in red*

*Direct-selected and dragged wing objects*

HESS

*For Eric Hess's "Soaring Hearts Futons" logo, he roughly Direct-selected, then with Reshape he marqueed as indicated above, and dragged)*

your object to transform it. (For practice with manual transformations, see *Chapter 2*.)

To transform your objects numerically, you can specify how the transformation will affect the selected objects:

- **Double-click on a transformation tool** to access the dialog box. This allows you to transform the objects numerically, originating from an object's center.

- **Option-click on your image with the transformation tool** to access the dialog box to transform your objects numerically, originating from where you clicked.

- **Click-drag on your image with a transformation tool** to transform the selected objects, originating from the center of the group of selected objects.

### The Transformation palette

From this palette you can determine numeric transformations that specify an object's width, height, location on the document and how much it will be rotated or sheared. The Transformation palette that ships with Illustrator 7.0 is a bit odd: you *can* repeat a transformation (⌘-D) once the numbers have been applied, but after you apply the transformation for the first time, the information in the palette is not retained, so you can't refer back to it. To maintain your numeric input, apply transformations through the transform tools discussed above.

### More Transformation tools—Reshape & Twirl

The new Reshape tool is quite different from the other transformation tools. Start by Direct-selecting the paths you wish to reshape. Next, choose the Reshape tool from the Scale tool pop-up, (or press "S" until it appears). With this tool, marquee or Shift-select all points you wish to affect, then drag the points to reshape.

Using the Twirl tool (from the Rotate tool, or "R"), click-drag or Option-click to transform (for details see "GeoTools by Scott McCollom" on the *Wow!* disk). ↺

## WORKING WITH PALETTES

Illustrator's palettes are accessible via the Window menu. Each palette is unique, but many share common features:

- **Docking tabbed palettes to save desktop space.**
  A delight for those of us who don't have a great expanse of desktop real estate, you can now reduce the space palettes require by docking the palettes together into smaller groups. Do this by grabbing the palette tab and drag it to another palette to dock it. You can also drag a tab to the *bottom* of a palette to stack palettes vertically. There's a custom docked palette setup for you in the Startup File on the *Wow!* disk.

- **You can make most palettes smaller or larger.**
  If there's a sizing icon in the lower right corner, click and drag it to shrink/expand the palette (the Gradient palette won't expand if it's docked with Colors). Some palettes also have a pop-up menu offering additional "Options." Click the square on the top right bar of the palette to shrink all palettes docked together down to just title bars. Click the right square again and the palette will re-expand. See also the Tip "Teeny tiny palettes" at right.

- **You must select your object(s) first; then you can make changes to the style.** With your objects selected, you can select any box in the palette containing text (click on the label or in the box) and type. If you're typing something that has limited choices (such as a font or type style), Illustrator will attempt to complete your word; just keep typing until your choice is visible. If you're typing into a text field, use the Tab key to move to other text fields within the palette.

- **IMPORTANT: When you're finished typing into palette text fields, you must press Return (or Enter).** This action signals to Illustrator that you are ready to enter text somewhere else or resume your illustration.

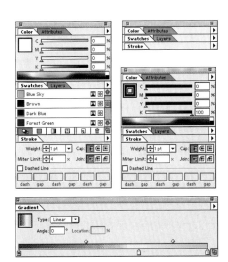

*Modes of expansion for docked palettes; lower figure is Gradient palette alone and expanded*

### Teeny tiny palettes

Double-click on the tab name, or the space to the right of the tab, to cycle through expanded and collapsed views of that palette.

### Palette be gone!

Just press Tab to hide the palettes and toolbar, then Tab to toggle them visible again. If you'd rather keep the toolbox and hide the other palettes just use Shift-Tab!

### Typing numbers into palettes

To use the current unit of measurement, type the number, and Tab to move to the next text field, or Return. To use another unit of measurement, *follow* the number with "in" or " (inch), "pt" (point), "p" (pica), or "mm" (millimeter) and Return. To resume typing into an *image* text block, press Shift-Return. (*Tip from Sandee Cohen:* Type *calculations* in text fields!)

## Easy default styling

Select an object styled the way you want your next object to be. Illustrator automatically resets the default to style the next object identically. A real time-saver!
**Note:** *This doesn't work for type.*

## If you can't see a new style...

If you're trying to make style changes, but nothing seems to change on the screen, make sure:

- your objects are selected.
- you are in Preview and not Art-work mode.

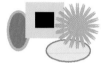

*The original objects*

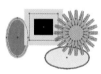

*Objects selected, and the bottom of the toolbox indicating that differing styles are selected*

Objects will remain unchanged unless you actively choose new settings →

Typing "1" (Return), or choosing a stroke weight from the pop-up, sets stroke weight for only those selected objects that already have strokes

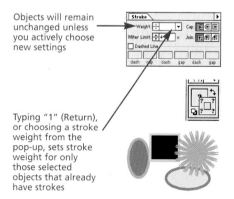

*The objects after setting a stroke weight of 1*

- **You can edit selective characteristics on multiple objects.** With palettes, you can set one specific style for all selected objects without affecting any other characteristics. For example, your selection might contain multiple objects, one with no stroke, and the rest with outlines of different colors and weights. If, in the Stroke palette, you set the stroke weight to 1 (point) and leave the other choices unchanged, this will set the stroke weight of all objects that have strokes to 1 point, but it won't add strokes to unstroked objects, and won't affect the colors of any strokes. You can use this same technique to change assorted text blocks to the same typeface while maintaining differences in type sizes and other formatting.

- **The new way to fill or stroke an object**
  You can toggle between a selected object's fill or stroke by clicking on the icons near the bottom of the Toolbar (see example on this page) or simply by pressing the "X" key. You can then choose the stroke or fill color you want from the Color or Swatches palette by dragging the color swatch onto the selected object or the icons on the toolbar, or by adjusting the sliders. You can also use the Eyedropper tool while in the Color palette. Use the "/" key to set the stroke or fill to None for any selected object(s). See *Chapter 3* for more information on color. ↻

## WORKING SMART
### Saving strategies

Probably the most important advice I can give you is to save (⌘-S) every few minutes or so. Whenever you make a substantial change to your image, use File: Save As from the File menu and give your image a new name.

Especially since Illustrator files are relatively small in size and save fairly quickly, it's much more time efficient to save incremental versions of your image than it is to reconstruct an earlier version all over again. Back up your work at least once a day before you shut down. Just think to yourself, "If this computer never starts up again, what will I need?" Develop a backup system using disks, Zip or

Jaz drives, SyQuests, DATs (digital audio tapes), opticals or CDs so you can archive all of your work. I suggest using a program such as Dantz's Retrospect, so you can automatically add new and changed files to your archives.

I believe in archiving virtually everything and have finally developed a file-naming system that actually helps me keep track of my working process—simplifying my recovery of a working version if necessary. My system involves three components. First, start with a meaningful description of your current image ("hearts compound") and second, add a numerical notation of the version ("1.0"). Keep your numbering system consecutive regardless of the label throughout the entire project. Keep the number in a sequence decimally when you make an incremental change to your image ("1.1, 1.2, 1.3…"). Change to the next numeric sequence when you make a substantive change ("2.0"). Don't start numbers at 1.0 for each phase of the project or you'll be unable to figure out which came first: "Sky 1.0" or "Heart 1.0." If, instead, the labels are "Sky 1.0" and "Heart 4.0," then the creation order is self-explanatory. Lastly, add a suffix to indicate its file type (.ai for Illustrator, .psd for Photoshop, .eps for Encapsulated Postscript file). Also, make sure that you keep all files in a named and dated folder that distinguishes them from other projects. For saving in other formats, see top Tip, page 25, *Chapter 9* and *Chapter 10*.

### Multiple Undos

Most programs give you one chance to undo your last move. Illustrator 7 allows up to 200 levels of undo, but will only hold the user-specified number of undos in a low-memory situation. When it needs to purge levels of undo to regain memory, Illustrator will remove all levels beyond what you've selected as your minimum. In File: Preferences: Units & Undo you can set the number of levels of undo to a number less than 200. This number will be the most levels saved in low-memory situations. I suggest 20 to 30 levels is usually adequate and keeps you aware that you should still save frequently.

Save *(saves your file to disk)*, **Save As** *(for saving the current document with a new name and/or format)*, **Save a Copy** *(for leaving the current document as is, while saving a copy),and* **Revert** *(for reverting to the previous saved version)*

### If you don't save or back up...

**...programs crash.**

And whatever you've done since the last time you saved will be gone forever. Programs are most likely to crash if it's been a long time since you last saved, so, at the very least, save whenever you take a break, whenever you're about to print and before you perform a memory-intensive task, such as switching programs, using a filter or transforming a large file.

**...hard drives crash.**

When you purchase a hard drive, there will be a statistic (called the "mean failure rate") that estimates the average time (in hours) that it will take for this drive to fail. It might be longer, it might be shorter, but it *will* fail (i.e., crash). Sometimes you will be able to recover files, but eventually the drive will fail for good and take your life's work to the grave.

Even after you save a file, your Undos (and Redos) are still available, making it possible to save the current version, undo it to a previous stage and then save it, or continue working from an earlier state. Having 20 to 30 undos available in each of multiple documents should come close to the experience of having infinite undos! (Be aware, though, some actions, such as Preference settings, might be not be undo-able). ⌣

## CHANGING YOUR VIEWS

### Preview and Artwork

To control the speed of your screen redraw, learn to make use of the various Preview and Artwork modes. Choose from the View menu, or press ⌘-Y to go from Artwork to Preview and ⌘-Y again to return to Artwork. To use Preview Selection, press ⌘-Shift-Y, which leaves everything in Artwork mode except the object(s) currently selected. From the View menu, you can also hide and show grids and guides. (For info on Preview and Artwork modes for individual layers, see *Chapter 4*.) ⌣

## ZOOMING IN & OUT

Illustrator provides many ways to zoom in and out:

- **With the Zoom tool.** Click to zoom *in* one level of magnification, hold down the Option key and click to zoom *out* one level. Or, click-drag to define an area, and Illustrator will attempt to fill the current window with the area that you defined.

- **From the View menu.** Choose Zoom In/Out, Actual Size or Fit in Window (see "Zippy zooming" tip at left).

- **By using the shortcut commands for Zoom.** With any tool selected, use ⌘-hyphen (think "minus to zoom out") and ⌘-+ (think "plus to zoom in").

- **Through Context-sensitive menus.** This new way to zoom in and out also lets you change views, undo, and show or hide guides/rulers/grids. With nothing selected, hold down your Control key (Mac), or Right mouse button (Windows) to access these options.

**Note:** *This is only accessible with "AI 6.0 Tool Shortcuts" disabled in General Preferences (see "How to use this book" for more on AI 6.0 Tool Shortcuts).*

### New Window

Before Illustrator allowed editing in Preview, New Window was an essential feature. Although Illustrator now allows editing in Preview, New Window is still extremely useful. This allows you to display different views of your current image simultaneously. You can separately zoom each window in or out, resize them, have edges hidden or visible, or set different *layers* to be hidden or locked, in Preview or Artwork (see "Hide Edges/Show Edges" below, and see *Chapter 4* for more on layers). Most window configurations are saved with the file.

### New View

New View allows you to save your current window viewpoint, remembering also your zoom level and which layers are hidden, locked or in Preview mode. Custom views are added to the bottom of the View menu to easily recall a saved view (see *Chapter 4* for more info on views).

### Hide Edges/Show Edges

If looking at all those anchor points and colored paths distracts you from figuring out what you need to do with selected objects in your current window, choose View: Hide Edges (⌘-H, or Context-sensitive menu), and ⌘-H again to Show Edges (see Tip at right).

### Snappy New Window Controls

As in Photoshop, you'll see three small icons at the very bottom of the toolbox. One is always selected; this is the default by which Illustrator will display your window. Choose from (starting at the far left) Standard Screen (desktop showing around the edges of your file), Full

## Many ways to copy an object

- Press ⌘-C to copy the object to the Mac Clipboard so it can be pasted into another document or program supporting "Post-Script on the Clipboard."
- Grab the object and hold down the Option key as you transform it or drag it to another location.
- Click the Copy button in any Transformation dialog box.
- In the Layers palette, Option-drag the dot representing the selected objects from one layer to another. (See *Chapter 4* for more on layers.) Or, drag-copy the layer to the new layer icon to copy the contents of the entire layer.
- "Drag and drop" selected objects from one document to another, or to other programs supporting drag and drop.

## Don't forget about your edges!

If you're used to Photoshop's Hide Edges command, be forewarned: Once you hide your edges (⌘-H), all subsequent selected shapes will also have invisible handles and paths, which can cause confusion if you forget you issued the command! If you can't seem to select something, check to see if you need to toggle to Show Edges.

You don't have to wait for Illustrator to finish redrawing the Preview before you pull down the next menu or perform another task. You can interrupt Illustrator from redrawing the image by typing ⌘-. (period). This standard Mac interrupt command will switch from Preview to Artwork.

For Mac users who miss direct access to Page Setup, use the *Wow!* QuicKeys set on the *Wow!* disk for this and other shortcuts. See "How to use this book" for more on QuicKeys and *QK:* shortcuts.

The *User Guide* discusses the "Adobe Illustrator Startup" file. This file lives in your Plug-ins folder and loads information, such as which colors, patterns, graph design elements and gradients will be available the next time you open Illustrator. The *Wow!* disk contains customized Startup files (one with minimum swatches, for example). Place the startup document you want to use in the plug-ins folder. For details on how to create your own Startup documents for loading your personal application preferences automatically, see the *User Guide*. Remember: bigger Startup files slow the program considerably.

Screen with Menu (file window visible but confined to the center of the screen with no desktop showing; you can access your menu bar) and Full Screen (same as Full Screen except menu bar cannot be accessed). Toggle between the views by pressing the "F" key. ↺

## SETTING UP YOUR PAGE

The truth is, controlling your page and printing options is much more difficult than it ought to be. After I explain the different metaphors, please return to the Adobe *User Guide* to get the specific details.

Double-click on the Hand tool to fit your image to your current window. A box with a solid black outline representing the size of your Artboard defines the parameters of your final image. A dotted line indicates the margins of the printer which is currently selected.

### Document and Page Setup

Document and Page Setup, in previous versions of Illustrator, were separate entities. In Illustrator 7, they're combined and can be reached by pressing ⌘-Shift-P. The Document Setup will appear first. Once you're in Document Setup, you'll be able to go to Page Setup.

Use Document Setup to set the size and orientation of the artboard, split long paths, adjust output resolution and more.

Use Page Setup if you want to change the selected printer and page orientation. Select your printer from the Paper pop-up menu, and choose portrait or landscape orientation (*QK:* Option-P accesses Page Setup directly).

For Mac, change the Reduce or Enlarge option to scale your image in relation to Page Setup. This is a terrific way to scale something quickly to see how it looks when printed out smaller or larger. A 4" line of a 4-point weight, printed at 25% reduction (the maximum you can reduce), will print as a 1", 1-point line. However, because Page Setup only scales your image in relation to the current printing setup, it will not affect the size of the image when placed into another program or another image. Use

View: Hide Page Tiling to hide the dotted lines. Use the Page tool to click-drag the dotted-line page parameters around the Artboard; only objects within the dotted line will print to your printer (see Tip at right for more).

## The Artboard

Think of the Artboard as the final image size. To change Artboard size, choose File: Document Setup. To match the artboard to your current printer, enable Use Page Setup and choose from one of the pop-up presets, or set the size up to 120" x 120" (which switches your paper size to "Custom"). Why might you want your Artboard to be a different size from that of your current printer? Commonly, you might want to create a large image that you'll eventually print to an imagesetter, but it first needs to be proofed to your laser printer. If this is the case, choose Page Setup to reduce the image size to fit your current printer. Another option is to "tile" your image onto pages which you can physically paste together to simulate the larger page size. See the *User Guide* for details on the various options for printing tiled pages.

## Rulers, Ruler Guides and Grids

From the View menu, toggle Illustrator's Show/Hide Rulers (⌘-R), or use the Context-sensitive menu (as long as nothing in your document is selected). The rulers will be set to the unit of measurement in Document Setup.

In previous versions of Illustrator, the ruler origin was in the lower right corner of the image. In Illustrator 7.0, the ruler origin (where 0,0 is) is in the *lower left* corner of your image. To change the ruler origin, grab the *upper left* corner (where the vertical and horizontal rulers meet) and drag the crosshair to the desired location. The zeros of the rulers will then reset to the point where you release your mouse (to rezero the ruler, *double-click* the upper left corner). But beware, resetting your ruler origin will realign all new patterns.

To create vertical or horizontal ruler guides, click-drag from one of the rulers into your image. A dotted-line

### Resetting the page margins

If you have been adjusting the page margins with the Page tool, you might find it difficult to return the margins to the exact default positioning. To reset the defaults, open Page Setup and select the alternate page orientation. Click OK, reopen Page Setup and choose the correct orientation; the margins will reset to the default position.

### Changing measurement units

To set units of measurement for rulers, palettes and some dialog boxes/filters, choose File: Document Setup (⌘-Shift-D). To set units for *new* documents, change units in General Preferences.
**Note:** *For now, for Mac users only, press ⌘-Control-U to cycle through the different units of measurement (only available with "AI 6.0 Tool Shortcuts" enabled in General Preferences (⌘-K). See page xii for more on these special shortcut options).*

### Quick access to locked guides!

Currently, also for Mac users only: hold Shift-Control and click-drag on a guide to move it. Shift-Control-*double-click* turns the guide into a selected object that can be deleted (with "AI 6.0 Tool Shortcuts" enabled in General Preferences, see page xii for more on these options).

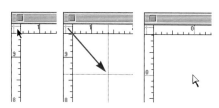

*Grabbing and dragging the ruler corner to re-center the ruler origin (zero point)*

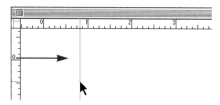

*Clicking inside the ruler and dragging into your image to create a vertical or horizontal guide*

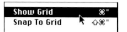

## Whiter whites / blacker blacks

If your whites or blacks seem to be taking on an undesirable color cast, look to your color management software (see text at right) as the possible source of the problem. See the color management software documentation for help in adjusting or disabling your color management.

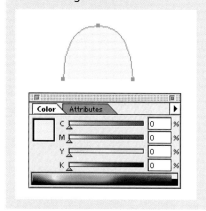

guide will appear where you release your mouse. Guides are automatically locked after you create them, so the easiest way to correct a mistake in placing a new guide is to Undo (this can also reset a moved ruler origin). You can lock and unlock guides with the Context-sensitive menu. You should note that locking or unlocking guides affects every open document. (For help turning objects into custom guides, see pages 96–98 and 164.)

New to Illustrator 7 is the long-awaited Grid function. To view grids, either select View: Show Grid or use the Context-sensitive menu. You can adjust the color, style of line (dots or solid) and size of the subdivisions of the grid from File: Preferences: Guides & Grid.

As with guides, you can also enable a "snap to" grid function. This is very helpful for doing accurate object and text placement and is handy when doing web page design (see *Chapter 10* for more). You can toggle "Snap To Grid" on and off by choosing View: Snap To Grid. See the Tip on page 137 for more on grids.

**IMPORTANT:** *If you adjust the x and y axes in File: Preferences: General: Constrain Angle it will affect the drawn objects and transformations of your grid, as they will follow the adjusted angle when you create a new object. This is great, however, if you're doing a complicated layout requiring alignment of objects at an angle.* ⌣

### COLOR IN ILLUSTRATOR

Consumer-level monitors, which display color in red, green and blue lights (RGB), cannot yet be made to match four-color CMYK (Cyan, Magenta, Yellow, Black) inks printed onto paper. Therefore, you must retrofit our current technology with partial solutions, starting with calibrating your monitor.

Some programs (such as the "Gamma" utility installed with Photoshop) provide you with some degree of control over the way your monitor displays colors. In addition, Illustrator 7 ships with a CMS (Color Management System) that for some will help keep the colors on-screen closer to the color you output. ColorSync (Mac) and Kodak Digital Science Color Management (Windows) are the two systems (please see the *User Guide* for information on installing and using these systems and the Tip on page 22).

In addition to this software calibration, methods of hardware calibration are available that actually adjust the beams of the cathode-ray tube emitting the RGB lights. Generally, the larger the monitor, the more likelihood that colors will vary in different areas of the screen. Monitor color is also affected by the length of time your monitor is on and the ambient light in your workroom.

To assist you in matching the color on the screen to printed colors, compare Illustrator's custom color libraries (such as TruMatch and Pantone) by choosing Window: Swatch Libraries: Specific Library with a coordinated swatchbook of colors (you must purchase this separately). You can now work towards matching your display with colors based on actual four-color printed samples. A different option is to use a four-color printed chart book, like Agfa's *PostScript Color Process Guide*, which provides preprinted samples combining the process colors in 5% increments, organized by the percentages of CMYK inks mixed together. See the *Resources* appendix for contact information on these companies (Agfa, TruMatch and Pantone and others). ↻

### Working In RGB, CMYK and HSB (Oh my!)

Illustrator now gives you the added flexibility of being able to work and print out of RGB, CMYK and HSB. This is a mixed blessing in that vibrant RGB colors cannot be accurately captured in print and can result in muddy printed color. If you work in print, just work in CMYK!

The big positive aspect of being able to work in RGB is that these colors are great for creating artwork for on-screen display. See *Chapter 10* for more on RGB.

### Multiple color models—all in one document!

What?! Unlike Photoshop, which requires that you select a color model to work in before it allows you to begin

CMY Color Model          RGB Color Model

*CMY (Cyan, Magenta, Yellow) **subtractive** colors get darker when mixed; RGB (Red, Green, Blue) **additive** colored lights combine to make white*

## Trapping issues

Continuous-tone, antialiased bitmapped images naturally form "traps" to hide misregistration of CMYK inks, but hard, crisp PostScript edges are a registration nightmare. Some products, such as Island Graphics' IslandTrapper, used for this book, can globally trap pages. If you know the exact size and resolution of your final image, you can rasterize Illustrator files (or specific objects) into bitmaps by using Object: Rasterize, or rasterize in Photoshop (see *Chapter 9*).

If you don't wish to rasterize:

• Construct your images so that overlapping shapes having common inks form natural traps (see page 64).

• Set individual colors to Overprint in the Attributes palette.

• Globally set blacks to overprint (Filter: Colors: Overprint Black).

• See the *User Guide* for details on setting traps in *solid* objects using Object: Pathfinder: Trap.

• For trapping patterns and gradients, see Tip on page 64.

Although computers can make conversions from CMYK to RGB (and vice versa) seem as simple as a menu command, such conversion will often result in muddy colors. If you plan on rasterizing, convert your file in Photoshop where you'll have greater control over ink density, UCR and GCR separations and more. Consult with your service bureau and printer for detailed directions based on your job specifications.

If you plan to print in CMYK and see an  "Out Of Gamut Warning"in the Color palette, take this as a caution that the current color is out of the range of printable colors. Either switch your color mode to CMYK from the Color pop-up, or click on the "closest approximation box" next to the gamut warning for an RGB or HSB color approximation. Switching to CMYK mode will allow you to see the actual values of the plates.

Adobe's PostScript 3 language is full of new features that improve printing time, deliver "truer colors" and provide "WebReady printing." For details on PS3, refer to Adobe's "White Paper" on PS3 from the web at: www.adobe.com

working on your document, Illustrator 7.0 allows you to work in multiple color models at the same time! Especially if you work in print (I just can't say this enough) be very careful to always check your objects to make certain they are in the appropriate (and similar) color model before you output your work. Do this by choosing File: Document Info and reviewing the relevant options there. Check the Adobe website for future changes in this methodology and "dot releases" as they become available.

### Color Systems, Styles and the New Web Palette

In addition to mixing color in RGB, HSB and CMYK, you can also select colors from other color matching systems or the new 216 color "web-safe" palette. Focoltone, Dicolor, Toyo, Trumatch, and Pantone libraries or the Web palette can be accessed by choosing Window: Swatch Libraries: then the specific color system you wish to work with. Keep in mind that you now open color libraries as separate uneditable palettes.

In previous versions of Illustrator, styles and colors in any open document were automatically listed and accessible to all other open documents. This is no longer the case! In order to access styles in another document, you must choose Window: Swatch Libraries: Other Library, then choose the Illustrator file you wish to access the styles from. This opens a new palette with that document's swatches. To store a swatch from an open library into your current document, just drag the swatch from *its* library palette to your Swatches palette. To avoid printing problems later, if you then decide to change the color recipe—make sure to change its name as well! (For details on 7.0 printing issues, see Sandee Cohen's "Color Output Issues.txt" on the *Wow!* disk.) ↵

### IMAGE FORMATS
### Earlier Illustrator formats

FreeHand, Canvas, CorelDraw and a number of 3D programs allow you to save images in older Illustrator formats. You might also have a document created directly in an earlier version of Illustrator. Instead of double-clicking its icon, drag it onto an Illustrator alias or open an older format file from within Illustrator by choosing File: Open (⌘-O) and selecting the document you want to open. If it's a file you plan to work on or open again, use Save As to save a copy in the current Illustrator format.

### EPS (Encapsulated PostScript)

EPS is a universal format, meaning that a wide variety of programs support importing and exporting images in EPS format for printing to PostScript printers. In most programs, when saving an image in EPS format, you can choose to include a Preview (the Preview is an on-screen PICT or TIFF representation of your image; an EPS image placed in another program without a Preview will print properly, but can't be viewed). To import an EPS image into Illustrator, choose File: Place (see *Chapters 4 and 9* for examples and more about EPS).

### Other image formats

Illustrator 7 supports a wealth of file formats (such as JPEG, TIFF, PICT, PCX, Pixar and Photoshop). If you choose to Place these formats, you can choose whether these files will remain *linked* or will become *embedded* "image objects" (see *Chapter 9* for specifics on linking and embedding, and *Chapter 10* for details on web-related formats). If you choose Open, most of these become embedded. See the *User Guide* and Adobe *Read Me* files for listings of supported formats that shipped with version 7.0, and check Adobe's website (www.adobe.com) for additional file format plug-ins. You can also open and edit PDF (Acrobat format) documents and "raw" Postscript files directly from within Illustrator. (For more on file format issues, see *Chapter 9*.) ⌣

### POSTSCRIPT PRINTING & EXPORTING

When you're ready to print your image (to a laser or inkjet printer, imagesetter or film recorder), you should use a PostScript printing device. Adobe owns and licenses

**When to choose "Save As"**

First and foremost, use Save As to save incremental versions of your image while you work (see "Saving strategies," page 16, and "Exporting Illustrator to other programs," *Chapter 9*). From Save As you can also choose to save in a variety of formats. Since you'll lose editing capability (and certain features, such as layers) with other formats, use them if (and only if) you plan to open your image in a program that cannot understand your current version of Illustrator. Save in Acrobat PDF (Portable Document Format) for faxing, sending to clients who don't have Illustrator, or publishing on the Web. For PDF details see the guide provided with the Acrobat Reader on the *Wow!* disk.

**Sharing styles cross documents**

Although this may change in future updates, Illustrator 7.0 won't let you access "Library" styles (see "Color Systems," opposite page) from an *open* document, nor can you add new styles to a Swatches palette by pasting or dragging and dropping objects containing new styles (though, see page 125, step 4!). Check Adobe's website (www.adobe.com) for possible updates, and see Sandee Cohen's "Color Output Issues.txt" on the *Wow!* disk, and the *Wow!* website (www.peachpit.com/wow.html).

Although you might prefer to view the better on-screen look of a TIFF image while you work, when preparing a file for final printed output, I suggest that you include only bitmaps that are *linked* EPS files (see *Chapter 9* for details on *linked* versus *embedded*, and the Tip, "Swapping placed files," on page 181). When you're ready to "Save As" in EPS (before sending the file to your printer or separator), enable the "include placed images" option. This does not actually embed EPS images into the file, but makes them print more easily (be aware, in 7.0, *TIFF* files *will* become embedded with this option). Lastly, also include the actual EPS bitmapped images along with your Illustrator file, just in case the printer/separator needs them as well.

Get into the habit of proofing all your images to a laser printer to gauge whether your image will take a long time to print. The higher your printing resolution, the longer your PostScript image will take to print. Based on your laser test, if you know that your image will require hours to print, you might be able to arrange for your service bureau to print your image overnight or on a weekend to save extra charges.

the PostScript language, making PostScript printers somewhat more expensive than non-PostScript printers. Some companies produce PostScript-compatible printers or provide PostScript emulation. Although Illustrator images sometimes print just fine to these printers, at other times you might run into problems. In general, the newer the PostScript device, the faster and less problematic your printing will be. PostScript Level 2 and Level 3 printers provide better printing clarity, and even some special effects, such as Illustrator 7's new integration of PostScript Level 3's "smooth shading" technology (which should greatly enhance gradients and reduce banding problems). Lastly, the more memory you install in your printer, the quicker your text and images will print. For crucial jobs, you must develop good relations with your service bureaus, and get into the habit of running test prints to identify possible problems. (Also see the Tip "Proofing your prints" at left.)

## Correcting & avoiding printing problems

Adobe acknowledged some output problems with the shipping version of Illustrator 7.0; so make certain you're using the latest version! Check the Adobe website (www.adobe.com) for the latest update. Also for more help, see the Tip "To link or not to link..." at left, Sandee Cohen's "Color Output Issues.txt" on the *Wow!* disk, and the *Wow!* website (www.peachpit.com/wow.html).

## More about controlling the size of your files

The major factors that can increase your file size are the inclusion of image objects, Path Pattern and Ink Pen objects, complex patterns, a large number of blends and gradients, and linked bitmapped images. Although linked bitmaps can, in themselves, be large, the same image embedded as an image object is significantly larger. If your Illustrator file *does* include linked images, and you need to save the entire file in EPS (for placement and printing, in other programs), you'll have the option "Include Placed Images." I highly recommend this option, as it will attach placed images to your Illustrator file and make printing from page layout programs and film recorders much more predictable (be sure to see top Tip at left). However, since including placed images will further increase the file size, wait until you've completed an image and are ready to place it into another program before you save a copy with placed images embedded. Whether or not you choose to embed linked images, you *must* collect all of the files that have been linked into your Illustrator documents and transport them along with your Illustrator file. Illustrator makes your task easier if you choose File: Document Info: Linked Images, which outputs a text file of all images in your document. Press Save to create a text file that can be filed for future reference; it will also give your service bureau a record of the images needed to produce the job.

### Printing speed

A related, but even more crucial factor to take into consideration when creating an image is understanding what elements make an image take longer to print. Special effects, such as transforming or masking placed images, or using complex patterns, or a slew of patterns or a gradient, or path patterns or ink pen are the worst culprits for increasing file size and, thus, printing time.

If you're going to place bitmaps into your Adobe Illustrator file, you'll greatly reduce your printing time if you perform all scaling and transformations of the bitmaps *before* placing it into Illustrator. Another reason to scale your bitmapped images before placing them in Illustrator is to ensure that the pixel-per-inch resolution of the images is 1.5 to 2 times the size of the line screen at which the final image will be printed. For instance, if your illustration will be printed at 2" x 2" in a 150-line screen, then the resolution of your bitmapped image should not exceed 300 pixels per inch at 2" x 2". Talk to your service bureau and print shop before you make these decisions. ⌣

## Saving time and space

**Note:** *Before you attempt to minimize the size of your file, make certain that you're working on a copy.* To minimize the size of your file, first remove all your unused colors and patterns. Open the appropriate palette, click the All Swatches icon, choose "Select all unused" from the Swatches pop-up menu, then click the Trash icon to delete. (You may have to repeat the select and delete process to remove *all* the excess colors.) You should also minimize the time it takes to print an Illustrator file, even if it's been placed into another program, such as QuarkXPress or PageMaker (for details on saving for export, see the "Exporting Files" in *Chapter 9*). If you've scaled or rotated an Illustrator image once it's been placed into another program, note the numeric percentages of scaling and the degrees of rotation. Next, reopen the file in Illustrator, perform the identical scale or rotation, then place this pre-transformed version back into the other program, making sure to rezero the scaling and rotation for this already transformed image. **IMPORTANT:** *Be certain to scale line weight, objects and pattern tiles when you perform these transformations in Illustrator (see page 13).*

# The Zen of Illustrator

2

**Zen:** *"Seeking enlightenment through introspection and intuition rather than scripture."**

You're comfortable with the basic operations of your computer. You've conquered the Adobe Illustrator *Tutorial*. You've committed enough hours to Illustrator to be familiar with how each tool in the palette (theoretically) functions. You even understand how to make Bézier curves. Now what? How do you take all this knowledge and turn it into a mastery of the medium?

As with learning any new artistic medium (such as engraving, watercolor or airbrush), learning to manipulate the tools is just the beginning. Thinking and seeing in that medium is what really makes those tools part of your creative arsenal. Before you can determine the best way to construct an image, you have to be able to envision at least some of the possibilities. The first key to mastering Illustrator is to understand that Illustrator's greatest strength comes not from its myriad tools and functions but from its extreme flexibility in terms of how you construct images. The first part of this chapter, therefore, introduces you to a variety of approaches and techniques for creating and transforming objects.

Once you've got yourself "thinking in Illustrator," you can begin to *visualize* how to achieve the final results. What is the simplest and most elegant way to construct an image? Which tools will you use? Then, once you've begun, allow yourself the flexibility to change course and try something else. Be willing to say to yourself: How else can I get the results that I want?

* Adapted from *Webster's New World Dictionary of the English Language*

The second key to mastering Illustrator (or any new medium) is perfecting your hand/eye coordination. In Illustrator, this translates into being proficient enough with the "power-keys" to gain instant access to the tools and functions through the keyboard. With both eyes on the monitor, one hand on the mouse, and the other hand on the keyboard, an experienced Illustrator user can create and manipulate objects in a fraction of the time required otherwise. The second part of this chapter helps you to learn the "finger dance" necessary to become a truly adept power-user.

The ability to harness the full power of Illustrator's basic tools and functions will ultimately make you a true master of Adobe Illustrator. Treat this chapter like meditation. Take it in small doses if necessary. Be mindful that the purpose of these exercises is to open up your mind to possibilities, not to force memorization. When you can conceptualize a number of different ways to create an image, then the hundreds of hints, tips, tricks, and techniques found elsewhere in this book can serve as a jumping-off point for further exploration. If you take the time to explore and absorb this chapter, you should begin to experience what I call the "Zen of Illustrator." This magical program, at first cryptic and counterintuitive, can help you achieve creative results not possible in any other medium.

# Building Houses

*Sequential Object Construction Exercises*

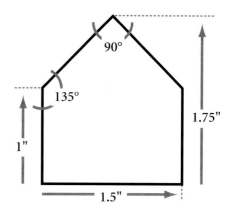

**Overview:** *Explore different approaches to constructing the same object with Illustrator's basic construction tools.*

**1**

**2**

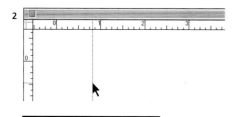

*Dragging out a guide from the Ruler, and choosing Window: Show Info to open the Info palette if it's not open before you begin*

**3**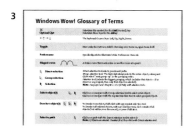

**4**

**Hint:** *Hold down the Shift key to constrain movement to horizontal/vertical direction. For more modifier key help, see the end of this chapter for the "Finger Dance" lesson.*

This sequence of exercises explores different ways to construct the same simple object, a house. The purpose of these exercises is to introduce you to the flexibility of Illustrator's object construction, so don't worry if some exercises seem less efficient than others. In File: Preferences: Units & Undo, set Inches for Ruler units (so you can use the numbers provided and the measurements above). And read through the recommendations below for preparing your working environment.

**1 Work in Artwork mode.** Doing so keeps you from being distracted by fills or line weights and lets you see the centers of geometric objects (marked by "×").

**2 Use Show Rulers and Show Info.** Choose Show Rulers from the View menu (⌘-R) so you can "pull out" guides. Use the Info palette to view numeric data as you work (I arrived at these numbers just this way!), or ignore the numeric data and just draw the houses by eye.

**3 Read through the *Wow! Glossary*.** Please make sure to read *How to use this book* and the *Glossary* pull-out card.

**4 Use "modifier" keys.** These exercises use Shift and Option (Alt) keys, which you must hold down until *after* you release your mouse button. If you make a mistake, choose Undo (⌘-Z) and try again. Some functions are also accessible from the Context-sensitive menu.

**Exercise #1:**

*Use Add-anchor-point tool*

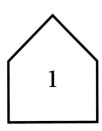

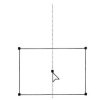

**1 Create a rectangle and a vertical guide.** Create a wide rectangle (1.5" x 1") and drag out a vertical guide that snaps to the center.

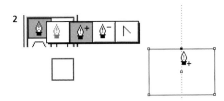

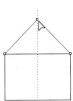

**2 Add an anchor point on the top.** Use the Add-anchor-point tool to add a point on the top segment over the center guide.

**3 Drag the new point up.** Use the Direct-selection tool to grab the new point and drag it up into position (.75" for a total height of 1.75").

**Exercise #2:**

*Make an extra point*

**1 Create a rectangle, delete the top path and place a center point.** Create a wide rectangle (1.5" x 1"). With the Direct-selection tool, select the top path and delete it. With the Pen tool, place a point on top of the rectangle center point.

**2 Move the point up.** Double-click on the Selection tool in the Toolbox to open the Move dialog box and enter a 1.25" vertical distance to move the point up.

**3 Select and join the point to each side.** Use the Direct-selection tool to select the left two points and join (⌘-J) them to the top point. Repeat with the right two points.

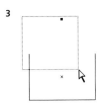

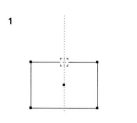

1

2

3

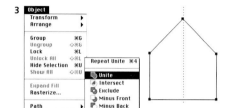

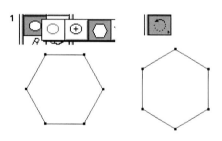

1

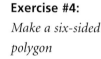

2

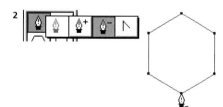

3

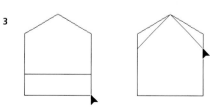

## Exercise #3:
*Rotate and unite*

**3**

**1 Create two rectangles, one centered on the other.**
Create a wide rectangle (1.5" x 1") and drag out a vertical guide snapping it to the center. With the Option key down, click with the Rectangle tool (Option-click) on the center guide (on the top segment). Enter 1.05" x 1.05".

**2 Rotate one rectangle.** Double-click the Rotate tool to rotate the new rectangle around its center and enter 45°.

**3 Select and unite the rectangles.** Marquee-select both shapes and choose Object: Pathfinder: Unite.

## Exercise #4:
*Make a six-sided polygon*

**4**

**1 Create a six-sided polygon.** With the Polygon tool selected, click once and enter 6 sides and a .866" radius. Then double-click the Rotate tool, and enter 30°.

**2 Delete the bottom point.** With the Delete-anchor-point tool, click on the bottom point to delete it.

**3 Move the two bottom points down, then the two middle points.** Use the Direct-selection tool to select the bottom two points. Then grab one of the points and Shift-drag in a vertical line (down .423"). Lastly, Direct-select, grab and Shift-drag the middle two points down vertically into position (down .275").

**Exercise #5:**

*Use Add Anchor Points filter in a three-sided polygon*

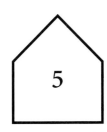

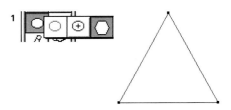

**1 Create a three-sided polygon.** With the Polygon tool selected, click once and enter 3 sides, and 1.299" for the Radius.

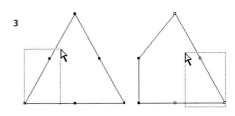

**2 Use the Add Anchor Points filter.** With the polygon still selected, choose Object: Path: Add Anchor Points. (Mac users: don't miss the top Tip on page 119!)

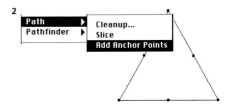

**3 Average the left two points, then Average the right two points.** Direct-select the left two points and Average them along the vertical axis (Context-sensitive: Average, or Object: Path: Average, or *QK*: ⌘-L), then repeat for the right two points.

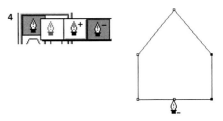

**4 Delete the bottom point.** With the Delete-anchor-point tool, click on the bottom point to delete it.

**5 Move the top point down.** Use the Direct-selection tool to select the top point, then double-click on the Selection tool itself in the Toolbox to open the Move dialog box and enter a −.186" vertical distance.

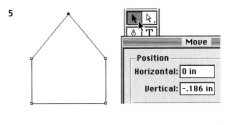

**6 Slide in the sides towards the center.** Use the Direct-selection tool to click on the right side of the house and drag it towards the center until the roofline looks smooth (hold down your Shift key to constrain the drag horizontally). Repeat for the left side of the house. Alternatively, select the right side and use the ← key on your keyboard to nudge the right side towards the center until the roofline looks smooth. Then, click on the left side to select it, and use the → key to nudge it towards the center. (If necessary, change your Cursor-key setting in Preferences: Keyboard Increments.)

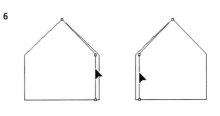

**1**

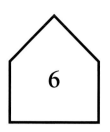

## Exercise #6:
*Cut a path and*
*Paste In Front*

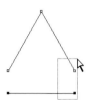

**2**

**1 Cut, paste, then move the bottom of a triangle.** With the Polygon tool selected, click once and enter 3 sides, and .866" for the Radius. With the Direct-selection tool, select and cut the bottom path to the Clipboard (⌘-X). Choose Edit: Paste In Front (⌘-F), then grab the bottom path and drag it into position (down .423").

**2 Create the sides and move middle points into place.** Direct-select the two right points and join them (⌘-J), then repeat for the left two points. Finally, select the two middle points, and grab one to drag *both* up (.275").

## Exercise #7:
*Join two objects*

**1**

**1 Make two objects.** Click once with the Polygon tool, enter 3 sides and a .866" Radius. Zoom in on the lower left corner and, with the Rectangle tool, click exactly on the lower left anchor point. Set the rectangle to 1.5" x 1".

**2**

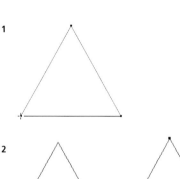

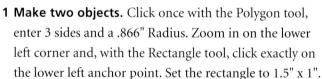

**2 Delete the middle lines and join the corners.** Direct-select marquee the middle bisecting lines and delete. Select the upper-left corner points and Average-Join (hold down Option while choosing Object: Path: Join, or *QK:* ⌘-Option-J) to average and join simultaneously. Select and Average-Join the upper right points.

**3**

**3 Drag the top point down.** Grab the top point, hold the Shift key and drag it into position (down .55").

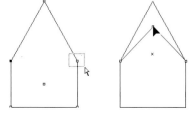

**Exercise #8:**

*Use Add Anchor Points filter, then Option-Join*

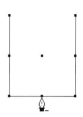

**1 Make a tall rectangle, delete top path, add anchor points, remove bottom point.** Create a tall rectangle (1.5"x1.75") and delete the top path. Choose Add Anchor Points (Object: Path) and use the Delete-anchor-point tool to remove the bottom point.

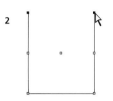

**2 Select and Average-Join the top points and move middles into position.** Direct-select the top two points and Average-Join (see Exercise #7, step 2). Then Direct-select the middle points, grab one, and with the Shift key, drag them both into position (up .125").

**Exercise #9:**

*Reflect a Pen profile*

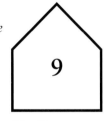

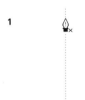

**1 Create a house profile.** Drag out a vertical guide, then reset the ruler origin on the guide. To draw the profile, use the Pen tool to click on the guide at the ruler zero point, and Shift (to constrain your lines to 45° angles) and click to place the corner (.75" down and .75" to the left) and the bottom (1" down).

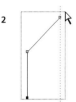

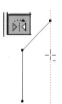

**2 Reflect a copy of the profile.** Select all three points of the house profile, and with the Reflect tool, Option-click on the guide line. Enter an angle of 90° and click Copy.

**3 Join the two profiles.** Direct-select and Join (⌘-J) the bottom two points. Then Direct-select the top two points and Average-Join (see Exercise #7, step 2).

# A Classic Icon

*Five Ways to Re-create Simple Shapes*

**Overview:** *Finding different ways to construct the same iconic image.*

McSHANE, ADIGARD / M.A.D.

1

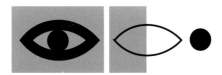

*The Artwork view of the original logo*

*The original logo, constructed from a stroked line and a solid circle*

You can construct even the simplest of iconic images in myriad ways. Patricia McShane and Erik Adigard of the M.A.D. graphics firm designed this classic logo for the *Computers Freedom & Privacy* annual conference, which addresses the effects of computer and telecommunications technologies on societal and personal freedom and privacy. This simple iconic representation of an eye is a perfect example of how you can explore different ways to solve the same graphics problem.

1 **First, construct your logo in the way that seems most logical to you.** Everybody's mind works differently, and the most obvious solutions to you might seem innovative to the next person. Follow your instincts as to how to construct each image. But if design changes require you to rethink your approach (for instance, what if the client wanted a radial fill instead of the black stroke?), then try something slightly, or even completely, different.

Viewed in Artwork mode, the original *Computers Freedom & Privacy* logo is clean and elegant with a minimum number of anchor points and lines. The M.A.D. team constructed the eye from a stroked line (made with the Pen tool) and a filled, black circle.

**2 Make the outer eye shape.** Create the solid black, almond-shaped object any way you wish: Try drawing it with the Pen tool like M.A.D. did, or maybe convert an oval into the correct shape by clicking on the middle points with the Convert-direction-point tool in the Pen tool pop-up (or cycle to this tool by pressing "P").

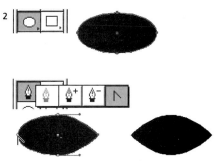
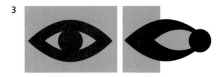

*One way to create the back of the eye*

**3 Try using solid objects.** Starting with your base object, construct the eye with overlapping solid objects. Scale a version of the outline for the green inset and place a black circle on the top.

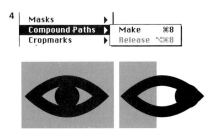

*Constructing the logo with three solid objects*

**4 Try making a compound object.** Use the objects that you created in the previous version to make a compound object that allows the inner part of the eye to be cut out. Select the outer black outline and the inner green inset and choose Object: Compound Paths: Make (⌘-8).

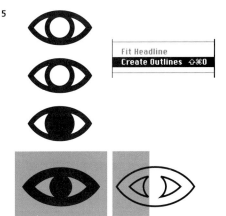

*Constructing the logo from an outer compound object and an inner solid circle*

**5 Try making the eye from a symbol font.** Included on the *Wow!* disk is a sample international symbols font from Image Club called "Mini Pics International." The character "W" is an eye very close to our icon. First, load your Mini Pics font (see your operating system manual for loading fonts). Choose the Mini Pics font from the Character palette (⌘-T), then click with the Type tool and type the character W. Next, click on a Selection tool (this selects your type as an object) and press ⌘-Shift-O or, choose Type: Create Outlines. This command converts the letter into a compound object different from the one you made in version 4 (above), with three objects cut out of the outline. Since the eye you're trying to make doesn't have a dark solid center, use the Direct-selection tool to select and delete the center compound object. Then try to match the original eye by adjusting the remaining compound paths with the Direct-selection and Scale tools.

Converting and transforming this symbol font may be a convoluted way to create such a simple shape, but the technique is certain to come in handy.

*The same logo constructed from a text object converted to an outline, then scaled*

# Zen Scaling

**Note:** *Use the Shift key to constrain proportions.* ***Zen Scaling*** *practice is also on the* ***Wow!*** *disk.*

**1 Scaling proportionally towards the top**  Click at the top, grab lower-right (LR), drag up

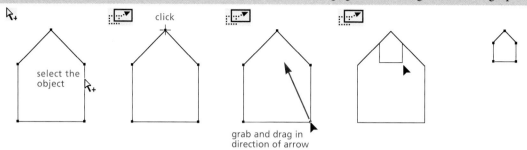

select the
object

click

grab and drag in
direction of arrow

**2 Scaling horizontally towards the center**  Click at the top, grab LR, drag inwards

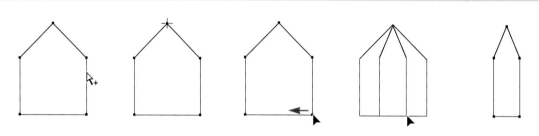

**3 Scaling vertically towards the top**  Click at the top, grab LR, drag straight up

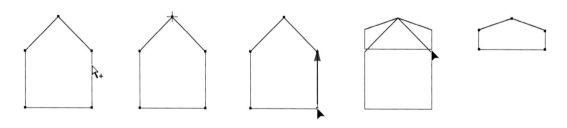

**4 Scaling vertically and flipping the object**  Click at the top, grab LR, drag straight up

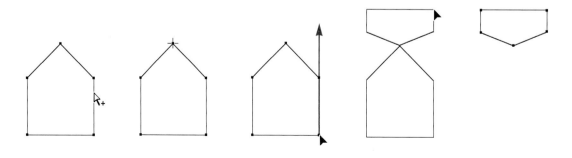

# Zen Scaling *(continued)*

**Note:** *Use the Shift key to constrain proportions.* **Zen Scaling** *practice is also on the* **Wow!** *disk.*

## 5 Scaling proportionally towards lower-left (LL)  Click LL, grab upper-right, drag to LL

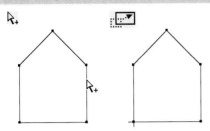 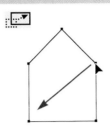 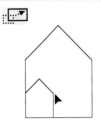

## 6 Scaling horizontally to the left side  Click LL, grab lower-right (LR), drag to left

## 7 Scaling vertically towards the bottom  Click center bottom, grab top, drag down

  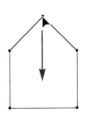 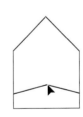 

## 8 Scaling proportionally towards the center  Click the center, grab corner, drag to center

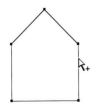   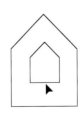 

*Or, to scale about the center, use the Scale tool to click-drag outside the object towards the center*

# Zen Rotation ⟲

**Note:** *Use the Shift key to constrain movement.* **Zen Rotation** *practice is also on the* **Wow!** *disk.*

**1 Rotating around the center**   Click in the center, then grab lower-right (LR) and drag

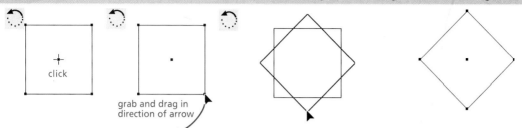

click

grab and drag in
direction of arrow

*Or, to rotate about the center, use the Rotate tool to click-drag outside the object towards the center*

**2 Rotating from a corner**   Click in the upper left corner, then grab LR and drag

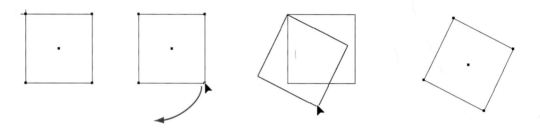

**3 Rotating from outside**   Click above the left corner, then grab LR and drag

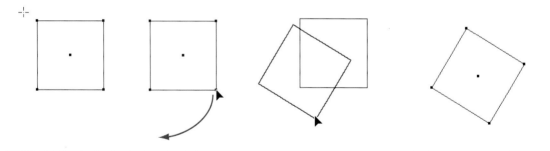

**4 Rotating part of a path**   Marquee points with the Direct-selection tool, then use Rotate tool

*Marquee the forearm with Direct-selection tool*     *With the Rotate tool, click on the elbow, grab the fingers and drag it around*

# Creating a Simple Object Using the Basic Tools

**Key:** *Click where you see a* RED *cross, grab with the* GRAY *arrow and drag towards* BLACK *arrow.*

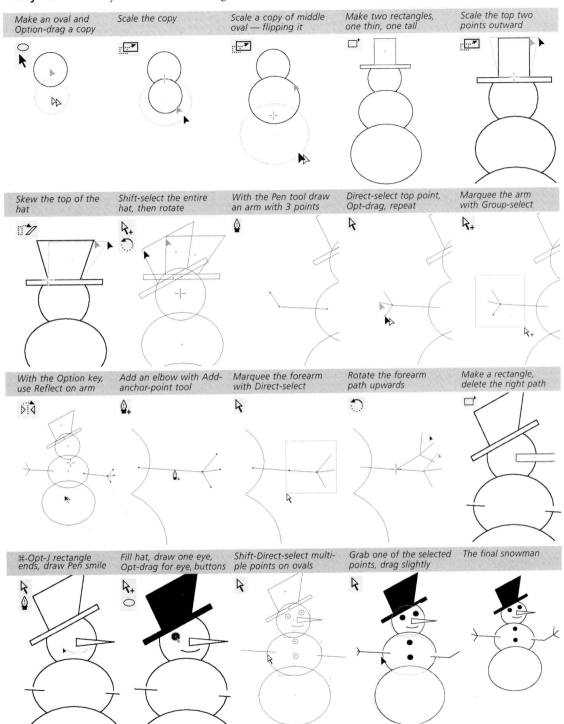

Make an oval and Option-drag a copy

Scale the copy

Scale a copy of middle oval — flipping it

Make two rectangles, one thin, one tall

Scale the top two points outward

Skew the top of the hat

Shift-select the entire hat, then rotate

With the Pen tool draw an arm with 3 points

Direct-select top point, Opt-drag, repeat

Marquee the arm with Group-select

With the Option key, use Reflect on arm

Add an elbow with Add-anchor-point tool

Marquee the forearm with Direct-select

Rotate the forearm path upwards

Make a rectangle, delete the right path

⌘-Opt-J rectangle ends, draw Pen smile

Fill hat, draw one eye, Opt-drag for eye, buttons

Shift-Direct-select multiple points on ovals

Grab one of the selected points, drag slightly

The final snowman

# A Finger Dance

*Turbo-charge with Illustrator's Power-keys*

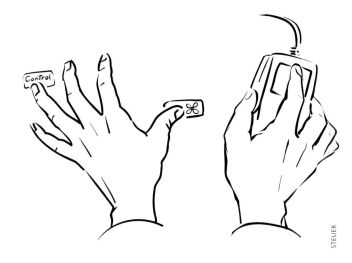

**Overview:** *Save hours of production time by mastering the finger dance of Illustrator's power-keys.*

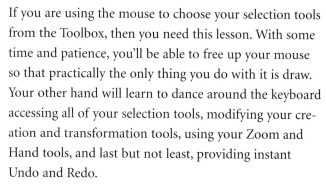

Find a summary of Finger Dance power-keys on the pull-out quick reference card.

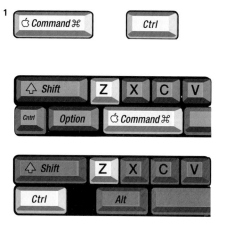

If you are using the mouse to choose your selection tools from the Toolbox, then you need this lesson. With some time and patience, you'll be able to free up your mouse so that practically the only thing you do with it is draw. Your other hand will learn to dance around the keyboard accessing all of your selection tools, modifying your creation and transformation tools, using your Zoom and Hand tools, and last but not least, providing instant Undo and Redo.

This "Finger Dance" is probably the most difficult aspect of Illustrator to master. Go through these lessons in order, but don't expect to get through them in one or even two sittings. When you make a mistake, use Undo (⌘-Z). Try a couple of exercises, then go back to your own work, incorporating what you've just learned. When you begin to get frustrated, take a break. Later—hours, days or weeks later—try another lesson. And don't forget to breathe.

**Rule #1: Always keep one finger on the ⌘ key (CTRL for Windows).** Whether you are using a mouse or a pressure-sensitive tablet, the hand you are not drawing with should be resting on the keyboard, with one finger (or thumb) on the ⌘ key. This position will make that all-important Undo (⌘-Z) instantly accessible.

**Rule #2: Undo if you make a mistake.** This is so crucial an aspect of working in the computer environment that I am willing to be redundant. If there is only one key combination that you memorize, make it ⌘-Z, Undo.

**Rule #3: The ⌘ (Ctrl) key turns your cursor into a selection tool.** In Illustrator, the ⌘ key does a lot more than merely provide you with easy access to Undo (⌘-Z). The ⌘ key will convert any tool into the selection arrow that you last used. In the exercises that follow, you'll soon discover that the most flexible selection arrow is the Direct-selection tool.

**Rule #4: Watch your cursor.** If you learn to watch your cursor, you'll be able to prevent most errors before they happen. And if you don't (for instance, if you drag a copy of an object by mistake), then use Undo and try again.

**Rule #5: Pay careful attention to *when* you hold down each key.** Most of the modifier keys operate differently depending on *when* you hold each key down. If you obey Rule #4 and watch your cursor, then you'll notice what the key you are holding does.

**Rule #6: Hold down the key(s) until after you let go of your mouse button.** In order for your modifier key to actually modify your action, you *must* keep your key down until *after* you let go of your mouse button.

**Rule #7: Work in Artwork mode.** When you are constructing or manipulating objects, get into the habit of working in Artwork mode. Of course, if you are designing the colors in your image, you'll need to work in Preview, but while you're learning how to use the power-keys, you'll generally find it much quicker and easier if you are in Artwork mode.

### Remove "Easy Access"! (Mac)

When you're using Illustrator, you must take the Apple program called *Easy Access* out of the Extensions folder (in the System folder). Although *Easy Access* was developed as an aid to mouse movements for people with limited manual mobility, it interferes with Illustrator's normal functioning. If you have limited manual dexterity, try using QuicKeys to simplify menu selection, keystrokes and object creation.

**Note:** *Before you begin this sequence of exercises, choose the Direct-selection tool, then select the Rectangle tool and drag to create a rectangle.*

**1 Finger Dance (⌘)** Grabbing a selected object and moving it

**2 Finger Dance (⌘)** Deselecting an object, selecting a path and moving it

**3 Finger Dance (⌘-Shift)** Moving a selected object horizontally

**4 Finger Dance (⌘-Shift)** Deselecting an object, selecting a path and moving it horizontally

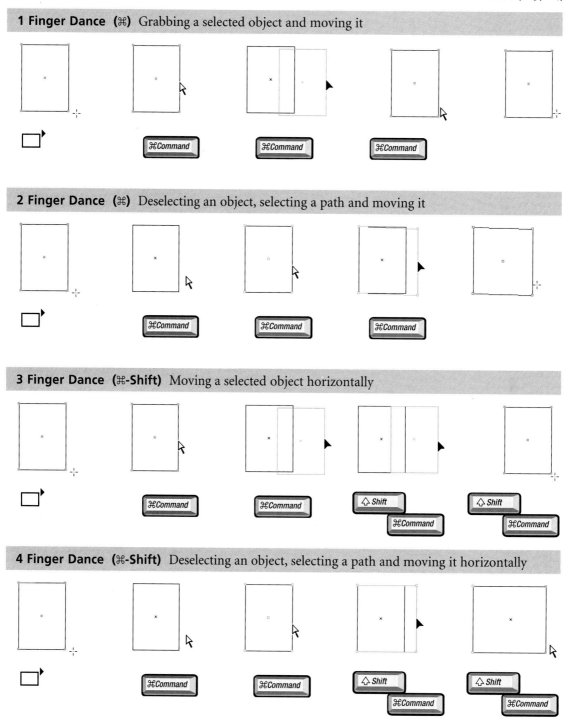

**Note:** *Before you begin this sequence of exercises, choose the Direct-selection tool, then select the Rectangle tool and drag to create a rectangle.*

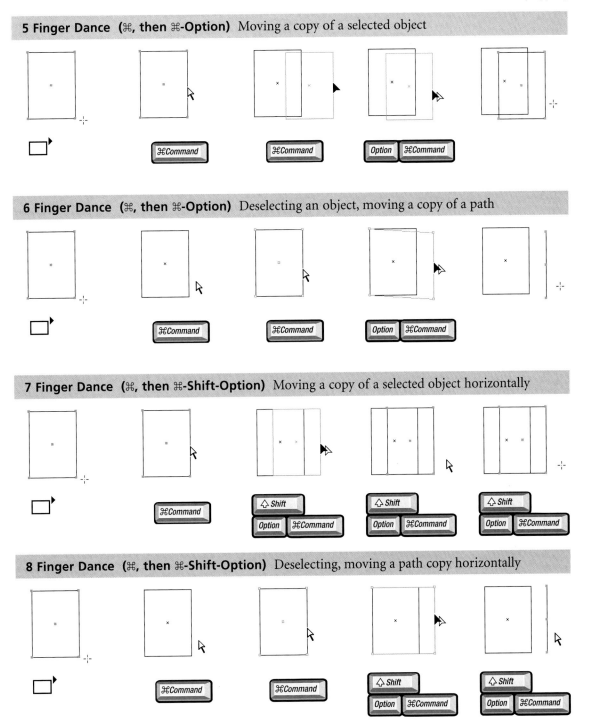

**5 Finger Dance** (⌘, then ⌘-Option) Moving a copy of a selected object

**6 Finger Dance** (⌘, then ⌘-Option) Deselecting an object, moving a copy of a path

**7 Finger Dance** (⌘, then ⌘-Shift-Option) Moving a copy of a selected object horizontally

**8 Finger Dance** (⌘, then ⌘-Shift-Option) Deselecting, moving a path copy horizontally

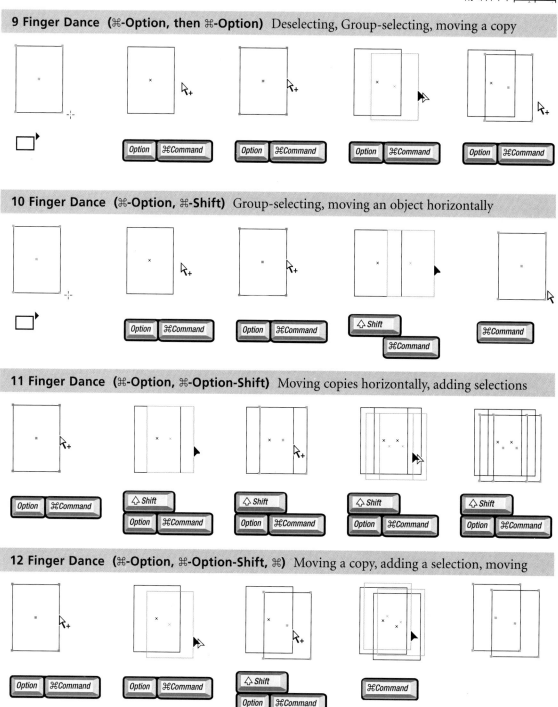

**9 Finger Dance** (⌘-Option, then ⌘-Option) Deselecting, Group-selecting, moving a copy

**10 Finger Dance** (⌘-Option, ⌘-Shift) Group-selecting, moving an object horizontally

**11 Finger Dance** (⌘-Option, ⌘-Option-Shift) Moving copies horizontally, adding selections

**12 Finger Dance** (⌘-Option, ⌘-Option-Shift, ⌘) Moving a copy, adding a selection, moving

# Lines, Fills & Colors

3

Lines, fills and colors are at the core of creating with Adobe Illustrator. The Adobe manuals and tutorials explain the rudiments of constructing simple objects, so this chapter will instead focus on techniques for going beyond the basics. If you look carefully, you'll discover that virtually all the techniques in this chapter are used (as basics) in combination with some of the flashier techniques found in the chapters that follow. Illustrator, mixed with a healthy dose of careful observation and attention to detail, can help you create quick, simple and elegant images without any of the fuss or muss of complex tricks or special effects.

With Illustrator 7, the number of tools and palettes needed for creating lines, fills and colors has increased.

## Goodbye, Old Paint palette...

With Illustrator 7's new look comes a new way to work with color and styles. The once self-contained Illustrator 5/6 Paint palette (Mac version only) has been divided up into separate Color, Swatches, Stroke, Attributes and Gradient palettes. Thankfully, these palettes "dock"—by dragging the tabbed part of the window and connecting it to another palette. This way they don't take up quite so much valuable desktop space. You can also set fill and stroke using the bottom of the toolbar. (See Tip at right and pages 15–16 in *Chapter 1* for more on palettes.)

The way you work with palettes has also changed, including the addition of "drag and drop" of colors (and sometimes styles) from one palette to another. Future

### Illustrator's new paint palettes

- **The Color palette** is for mixing colors, and for changing color modes from the palette pop-up (or Shift-click the Color ramp). See the *Chapter 10* warnings and tips for working in RGB.
- **The Swatches palette** contains a default set of color swatches, gradients and patterns. Select the first icon on the bottom left to show all swatches. (See the *Quick Reference Card* for more on this palette.) Create a new default by using a custom Start-up file (see red Tip on page 48).
- **The Stroke palette** lets you set line, cap, miter and dash styles of a stroke (see page 49 for more on this palette).
- **The Gradient palette** lets you set gradient styles for fills (see *Chapter 5*).
- **Custom Color Library palettes** are accessible through Window: Library: Other and choose any *unopened* document to access its styles (updates may let you access open documents).

updates to Illustrator are likely to alter the specifics of working with these palettes, so make sure to check the Adobe website regularly for updates and announcements.

### And, a CMYK color caution...

In Illustrator 7.0, objects filled with CMYK Process colors are not updated when the CMYK swatch is changed—even if the CMYK swatch was stored in the Swatches palette! If you intend to adjust the colors that objects are filled or stroked with, you must store each color as a Spot color *before* you style objects with that color. To set a color to Spot, double-click on its name in the Swatches palette to open Swatch Options. There you can set Spot Color and CMYK from the pop-ups. Swatch Options will also allow you to adjust the specific color recipe, and as long as the color is defined as Spot, all objects colored with that spot color will be updated as you adjust the colors. Clicking OK will apply the changes globally.

The only problem with defining colors as Spot is that you'll have to be extremely careful about color separations. Check File: Separation Setup to globally convert Spot to Process, or alert your service bureau to this issue.

### More tools and palettes

Two cool Illustrator tools are the Eyedropper (which *picks up* line, fill and color styles) and the Paint-bucket (which *deposits* line, fill and color styles). These two tools offer some extremely useful shortcuts for copying styles from one object to another, or even to pick up color from any bitmapped image object. Click on an object with the Eyedropper to set the default styling for your next object, or click on an object with the Paint-bucket to fill it with the current styling. You can toggle between the two tools by pressing the Option key.

My favorite use of the Eyedropper is to copy a style from one object to another. Select the object you would like to change, choose the Eyedropper tool, and double-click on an object with the style you like. *Voilà!* Your selected object is now styled to match the object you double-clicked on, including dashes, line weights or custom fills. By default, both the Eyedropper and Paint-bucket tools copy the complete styling of an object, but double-clicking on either of the tools in the Toolbox allows you to customize the settings for both. Oddly enough, the settings that control what is deposited into an object when you *double-click* with the Eyedropper are the settings you have chosen for the *Paint-bucket*.

One of the aspects of Illustrator that seems mysterious to newcomers is the way path lines end. I'm the first to encourage you to work in Artwork mode, but you may discover someday that, although the lines seem to contact perfectly in Artwork mode, they visibly overlap in Preview. The solution is now found in the Stroke palette. Access it by choosing Window: Show Stroke.

By selecting one of the three Caps styles for your line endings, Illustrator lets you determine how the endpoints of your selected paths will look. The first (and default) choice is called a Butt-cap, which causes your path to stop at the end anchor point. Butt-caps are essential for creating exact placement of one path up against another. The middle choice is the Round-cap, which rounds the endpoint in a more "natural" manner. Round-caps are especially good for softening the effect of single lines or curves, making them appear slightly less harsh and computery. The final type is the Projecting-cap, which can extend lines and dashes half of the stroke weight beyond the end anchor point. You should also know that in addition to determining the appearance of path endpoints, Caps styles also affect the shapes of dashed lines.

You can also adjust the corners in an angled path if they appear too flat, or stick out too far behind the anchor points. The default Miter-join with a limit of 4 usually looks just fine, but if you want to round or bevel your corners, simply choose the Round or Bevel-joins. Each line weight has a particular Miter-limit at which the joins will switch from blunt to pointy; the thicker the line, the higher the limit will be. Miter-limits can range from 1 (which is always blunt) to 500.

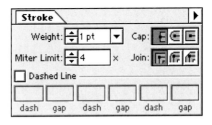

The Stroke palette

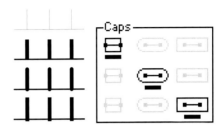

The same lines shown first in Artwork, then in Preview with Butt-caps, Round-caps and Projecting-caps

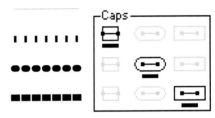

A 5-pt dashed line with a 2-pt dash and 6-pt gap shown first in Artwork, then Preview with a Butt-cap, Round-cap and Projecting-cap

A path shown first in Artwork, then in Preview with a Miter-join, Round-join and Bevel-join

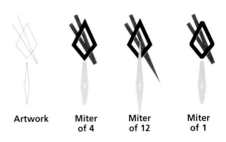

Artwork    Miter of 4    Miter of 12    Miter of 1

Objects with 6-pt strokes and various Miter-limits, demonstrating that the angles of lines, as well as weight, affect Miter-limits

# Simply Realistic

*Realism from Geometry and Observation*

**Overview:** *Re-create a mechanical object using and altering the Rectangle or Oval tools; place all inner enclosed objects while finding the right values; add selected highlights and offset shadows and reflections.*

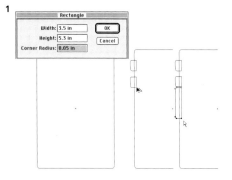

Creating and adjusting rounded rectangles to construct the basic forms

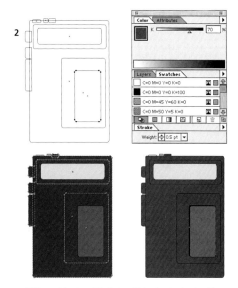

Filling objects with tints of black, stroked with a .5-pt, 100% black line

Many people believe the only way to achieve realism in Illustrator is with elaborate gradients and blends, but this illustration by Patrick Lynch proves that artistic observation is the real secret. For his *Manual of Ornithology* (with Noble S. Proctor, for Yale University Press), Lynch needed equipment illustrations to aid in birdwatching, so he took this opportunity to learn Adobe Illustrator.

**1 Re-creating a mechanical object with repeating geometric shapes, by altering copies of objects.** Most artists find that close observation, not complex perspective, is the most crucial aspect to rendering illustrations. To focus your attention on the power of basic shapes, choose a simple mechanical device to render. Experiment with the Oval, Rectangle and Rounded Rectangle tools to place the basic elements. Especially with mechanical devices, components often tend to be similar; thus, look for opportunities to adjust a copy of an object, rather than create another that might not align perfectly. For his personal stereo/radio knobs, Lynch dragged a copy of one knob (holding Option-Shift), stretched it by selecting one end with the Direct-selection tool and dragged it down (with the Shift key), creating a sequence of knobs with the same height, but different widths.

**2 Using tints to fill the objects.** Select all your objects and choose a .5-pt black stroke from the Stroke and Color palettes. Then select an object (or set of objects), set the Fill to Black and Option-click on the New Swatch icon to name it "Black" and set the Color Mode to Spot Color. Click OK and create a tint using the Tint slider in the Colors palette. Continue to fill and adjust the tints for individual objects until you are happy with the basic value structure. Lynch used percentages from 10–80%, with the majority of the objects being 80% black.

**3 Creating a few carefully placed highlights.** Look closely at your object and decide where to place selected highlights. Start with a couple of thin, lighter-tinted lines, making sure to choose Round-caps for the lines (in the expanded Stroke palette). In a couple of instances, place shorter and slightly heavier lines of an even lighter tint on top of the first lines. For lines that follow the contour of your object, select part of your object's path with the Direct-selection tool and copy and Paste In Front that part of the path. Use your cursor-keys to offset the contour and use the Eyedropper to double-click on one of your highlight lines to set the contour with the highlight line style. If you need to trim contours, use the Scissors tool and delete the unwanted portion of the path. Lastly, using a light tint as a fill, with no stroke, create a small circle at the confluence of two lines (try leaving a small gap between the lines and the circle). Option-drag the circle if you wish to place it in other locations. For his highlights, Lynch used lines varying in weight from .5 to 2 points, in tints from 0 (white) to 50%, and five carefully placed white circles.

**4 Creating shadows and transparencies.** Follow the same procedure as above, but this time use darker tints to create shadows and transparencies. Make sure to offset shadows behind the object, especially if the shadows have solid fills. ☺

3

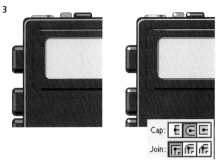

*Carefully placing a few lighter-tinted, filled circles and lines with Round-caps for highlights*

4

*Creating text and LED numbers, then offsetting objects and giving offsets a darker gray tint*

*Making subtle changes in value to create the illusion of transparency*

*The Artwork view of the final illustration*

# Combining Circles
*Cutting and Joining Overlapping Objects*

**Overview:** *Design an illustration using overlapping objects; cut and remove overlaps and join objects.*

LINO BOY'S MOTTO: "I AM HIGHLY RESOLVED!"

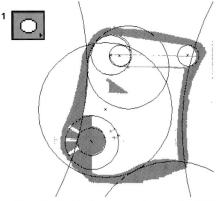

Using the Oval tool to trace circles over the PICT template

Selecting an object and locking everything else, then using the Scissors tool to cut overlaps

The first cut section, selecting pairs of anchors after moving the excess paths out of the way, then Average-Joining the pair

Adobe Illustrator is a flexible enough program to accommodate many different illustration styles. Mark Fox has always designed using a compass to draw perfect circles, an unusual drawing style that translates easily to computer illustration. Use this technique to join any two objects, but don't forget also to look at filters (*Chapter 6*).

**1 Placing your objects.** Fox scanned a sketch he made with his compass, saved it as a PICT, and opened it as a template (see pages 80–83 for template lessons, or to auto-open your scan as a template, see the ReadMe in the "Templates" folder on the *Wow!* disk). Create your objects without worrying about how they overlap. Holding down the Shift key, Fox traced circles with the Oval tool.

**2 Cropping the objects, removing the excess and joining the objects.** To lock all *unselected* objects, select one object, hold Option and choose Arrange: Lock (or *QK:* ⌘-Shift-Option-2). With the Scissors tool, click on the path where this object will overlap and join with others. Then choose Arrange: Unlock All (*QK:* ⌘-Option-2) and repeat the above procedure for other objects to be joined. After selecting and deleting excess paths, Direct-select each pair of points you want to join (one pair at a time), and Average-Join them by holding Option and choosing Arrange: Join (or *QK:* ⌘-Option-J). 🌀

## Gallery: Mark Fox/BlackDog

*Mark Fox's whimsical design style hasn't visibly changed since his transition from ink and compass to Adobe Illustrator. The sketch to the right above for "Horse of a Different Color" shows Fox's notations for compass centers, as well as the circles. Although most people rely primarily on the Pen tool when drawing in Illustrator, Fox creates all his logos by cutting and joining rectangles and circles—occasionally using the Pen tool (for straight lines) and the Rotate tool.*

# A Variety of Lines

*Overlapping Lines to Form Roads and Rails*

**Overview:** *Use sequences of Copy and Paste In Front to create variations in line styles to form highways and railroads.*

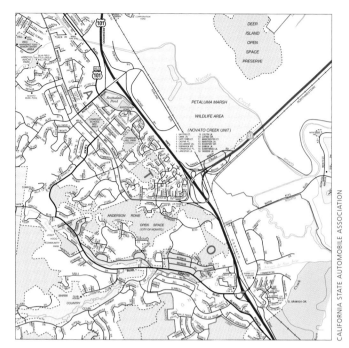

1

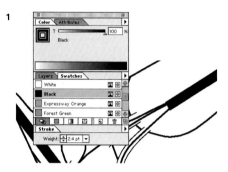

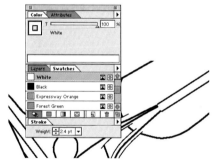

*The black outline and white knockout styles*

2

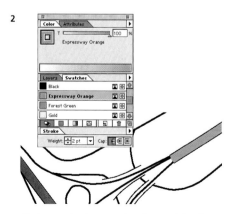

*Custom spot colors are stored as swatches in the Swatches palette.*

You can create many special effects by varying line styles (see "Lisa Jackmore's Dashing Dashes" in the "Tips & Techniques" folder on the *Wow!* disk). The California State Automobile Association (CSAA) uses overlapping line styles in its road maps to represent streets, highways and even railroad tracks.

**1 Creating the black outline and the white "knock-out."** Using the Pen tool, create curves or lines, making sure you're in Preview mode (⌘-Y toggles between Art-work and Preview modes) so you can work in color. Direct-select all the objects you wish to convert into road map highways. In the bottom of the Toolbox, make sure Fill is active (press "X" to toggle Fill and Stroke), press "D" then "/" (D sets your default Fill to white and Stroke to 1-pt black, then / sets the fill to None). In the Stroke palette, set the stroke weight to 2.4-pt. Keep the paths selected, although as you work you can use View: Hide Edges (⌘-H) to hide or show path selection outlines.

Copy the selected objects and choose Edit: Paste In Front (⌘-F) to paste a copy exactly on top of the original objects. Change the copied objects to a white, 1.6-pt stroke, which will automatically "knock out" colors underneath in the printing process.

**2 Pasting another copy in front and styling it in a color.** The next step is again to choose Edit: Paste In Front, style this copy in a color at a 2-pt line weight and check Overprint in the palette, which allows for a .2-pt trap between the black outline and white knockout.

**3 Pasting a final black line down the center of the highway.** To create the dividing lines on the highway, use ⌘-F to paste another copy in front and style the line with a black, .4-pt stroke.

**4 Creating the black line for the railroad, then pasting a dashed-line copy in front for railroad ties.** Create a new curve or line and set the stroke to .3-pt black. The crossties will be created by overlaying this original with a 3-pt dashed line. With the .3-pt line selected, choose Copy, then ⌘-F. Double-click the Stroke palette tab to cycle the palette to the expanded viewing option. Give this new line a stroke of 3 points, then, in the bottom section of the palette, click on the box labeled "Dashed." To create the railroad crossties, click in the first text box labeled "dash" (this creates the solid portion of the dash), type ".3" (meaning points) and use the Tab key to move to the next text field to specify a gap of 14. Press Return or click outside the palette to apply the final changes. If you want to re-enter new numbers, make sure your cursor is actively blinking in the text box before you type.

### Overprinting blacks and knocking out whites

The Attributes palette allows you to check "Overprint" when you assign any fill or stroke. Or, to specify *global* parameters for overprinting blacks, choose Filter: Colors: Overprint Blacks. And remember, white automatically knocks out all colors underneath.

### From one spot to another

Select a swatch that approximates the color you want, click the New Swatch icon, then double-click the new swatch to rename/redefine.

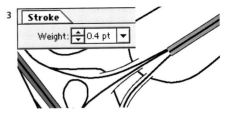

The black line down the center of the highway

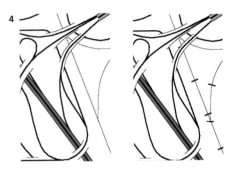

The railroad base alone and the crosstie dashes

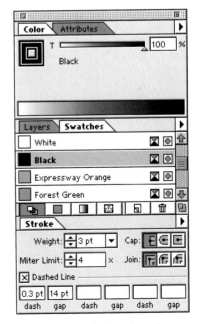

Setting dashes in the Swatches palette

**Chapter 3** *Lines, Fills & Colors*   **55**

# Isometric Systems

*Cursor-keys, Constrain-angles & Formulas*

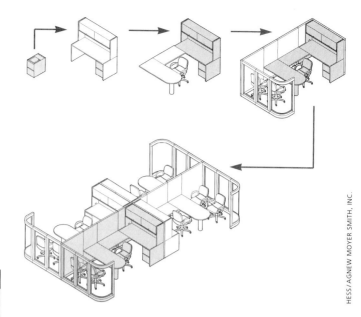

**Overview:** *Create detailed views of an object from front, top and side; use an isometric formula to transform the objects; set "Constrain-angle" and "Cursor key" distance; use cursor-keys with snap-to-point to adjust and assemble objects.*

## Stubborn snapping-to-point

Sometimes if you try to move an object over slightly, it will annoyingly "snap" to the wrong place. If this happens, move it away from the area and release. Then regrab the object at the point from which you'd like to align it and move it so that it snaps into the correct position. If you still have trouble, zoom in. As a last resort, you can disable "Snap to point" in General Preferences.

1

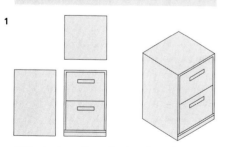

*Separate views, then after transformations*

2

*Scaling, skewing and rotating*

Technical illustrations and diagrams are often depicted in isometric perspective, and Adobe Illustrator can be the ideal program both for creating your initial illustrations and for transforming them into this perspective. The artists at Agnew Moyer Smith (AMS) created and transformed the diagrams on these pages using their three-step perspective. For both the initial creation and manipulation of the isometric objects in space, AMS custom-set "Cursor key distance" and "Constrain angle," and made sure that "Snap to point" was enabled—all from Preferences: General and Keyboard Increments.

**1 Creating detailed renderings of the front, side and top views of your object to scale.** Before you begin a technical illustration, you should choose a drawing scale, then coordinate the settings in General Preferences to match. For instance, to create a file drawer in the scale of 1 mm = 2", set the ruler units to millimeters and "Cursor key" distance to .5 mm, and make sure that the "Snap to point" option is enabled. With these features enabled and matching your drawing scale, it's easy to create detailed views of your object. With your ruler units set to the correct scale, choose Window: Show Info to keep easy track of your object sizing as you work. If a portion of the real object is inset 1" to the left, you can use the ← cursor-key to move the path one increment (.5 mm) further left. Finally, snap to point will help you properly fit together and assemble your various components. Select and group all the components of the front view. Separately group the top and side so you'll be able to easily isolate each of the views for transformation and assembly. AMS renders every internal detail, which allows them to view "cut-aways" or adjust individual elements, or groups of elements, such as opening a drawer.

2 **Using an isometric formula to transform your viewpoints.** The artists at AMS created and transformed the diagrams on these pages using their three-step process, which is fully demonstrated on the *Wow!* disk. To transform your objects, double-click on the various tools to specify the correct percentages numerically. First, select all three views and scale them 100% horizontally and 86.6% vertically. Next, select the top and side, shearing them at a −30° angle, and then shear the front 30°. Lastly, rotate the top and front 30° and the side −30°.

3 **Assembling the top, front and side.** With the Selection tool, grab a specific anchor-point from the side view that will contact the front view, and drag it until it snaps into the correct position (the arrow turns hollow). Next, select and drag to snap the top into position. Finally, select and group the entire object for easy reselection.

4 **Using the constrain-angle and cursor-keys to adjust objects and assemble multiple components.** Look at the Movement chart to determine the direction in which to move. Try using the Direct-selection tool to select a portion of the object, setting the constrain-angle to 30° (or −30°), then using the ← and → cursor-keys to slide your selection along that isometric axis. Or, use the Selection tool to select entire objects and snap them into position against other objects.

### More isometric formulas
Find the AMS isometric formula (along with a two-step method by Dan Swanson) on the *Wow!* disk. You'll also find AMS's formula for reversing their three-step method.

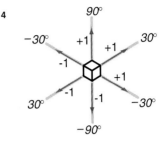

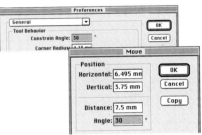

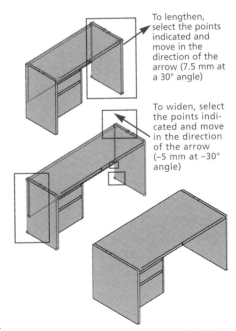

To lengthen, select the points indicated and move in the direction of the arrow (7.5 mm at a 30° angle)

To widen, select the points indicated and move in the direction of the arrow (−5 mm at −30° angle)

*Transforming one object into the next, by Direct-selecting the appropriate anchor points and using the Move command, or by setting and using custom constrain-angle and cursor-keys*

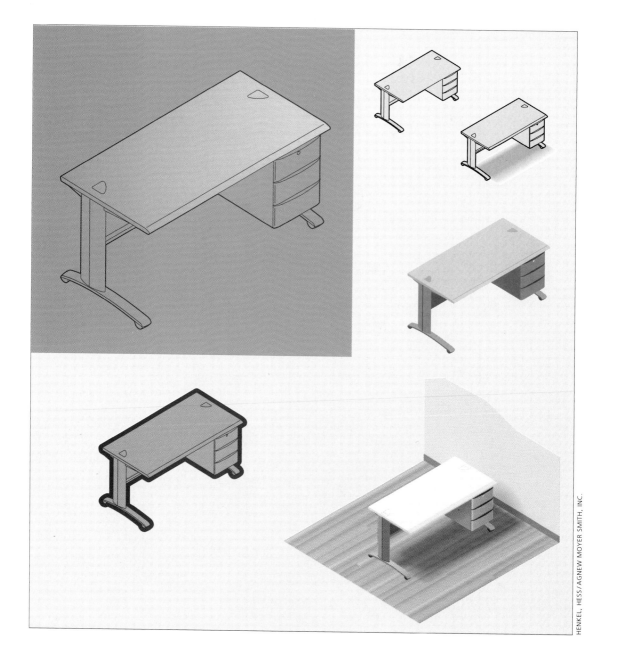

## Gallery: Rick Henkel, Kurt Hess / Agnew Moyer Smith, Inc.

*Creating a technical illustration in Illustrator may save you time over traditional graphic methods, but the real time savings lies in producing variations on a theme. Agnew Moyer Smith's artists use Illustrator because it provides so much flexibility in altering an illustration after construction of objects is complete. These different presentations of desks for Steelcase office furniture demonstrate how dramatically different the visual effect can be just by altering the stroke and fill styles of an object and its immediate surroundings. The shadow on the wood floor was set to the Overprint option.*

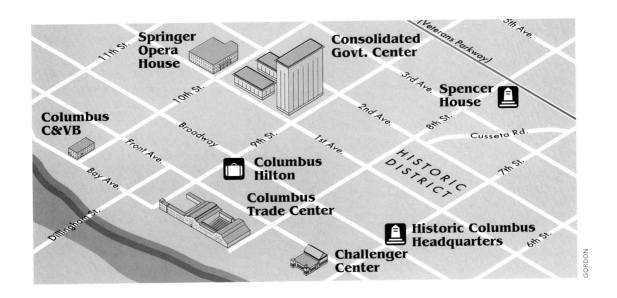

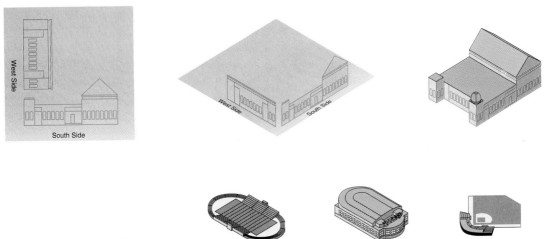

## Gallery: Steven Gordon

*For this map of Columbus, Georgia, cartographer Steven Gordon compiled building information from aerial photographs, postcards, sketches and architectural drawings. Gordon began by drawing the building sides and roofs, the street grid, and positioning the street names. All elements were rotated 45°. Building roofs and the streets and their names were scaled 100% horizontally and 57.74% vertically. All building sides were scaled 57.74% horizontally and 100% vertically. The west-side shapes were rotated 30°; the south-side shapes were rotated −30°. The two sets of shapes were then fitted together to compose the building. Gordon found that while isometric formulas work correctly for perpendicular sides and flat, horizontal roofs, the formulas could not produce the curved walls, domes and pitched roofs of buildings like those to the right; those shapes were drawn by hand. Gordon applied the Round-join to all building lines to avoid spikes at corners (see page 49).*

# Customizing Color

*Custom Labels for Making Quick Changes*

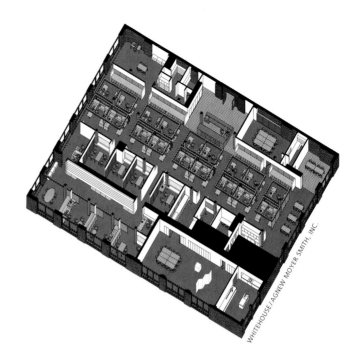

**Overview:** *Define custom spot colors; type labels for the colors; select and edit colors and objects.*

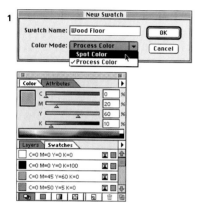

**1**

*Creating a spot color*

**2**

# Wood Floor

*A typed custom label*

# Wood Floor
### Wood Floor

*Setting the type style to a thin, black outline with the correct custom fill; and the final typed label at actual size*

When you need to store dozens of color swatches, it is essential to develop a more organized method of storing colors than the Swatches palette provides. Designers at Agnew Moyer Smith (AMS) invented a clever system using colors to label different categories of objects, allowing the designers to isolate and change the spot colors easily, as well as enabling them to make global changes to any category of objects filled with a given color.

**1 Creating custom colors.** In the Colors palette, start by setting the CMYK sliders to create the color you want to use. In the Swatches palette, Option-click on the new swatch icon. Give your color a name that will signify the type of object you plan to fill with the color, and choose "Spot" from the Color Mode pop-up. Bob Whitehouse of AMS used labels such as "Wood Floor," "Computer" and "Phones" to label the colors he wished to use in his illustration above. To help in the selection of reliably reproducible colors, Whitehouse used the Agfa *PostScript Process Color Guide* to look up the color he actually wanted and then entered the percentages of CMYK indicated. (For more about color consistency, see page 22.)

**2 Typing a label for each of the colors.** After you have created a spot color swatch, use the Type tool to type a label for the color on the side of your illustration. If you want the labels to print, place the type within the page margins. If you don't want the labels to print, then place the type outside the margins or in a nonprinting layer (see *Chapter 4* for more on layers). Choose a selection tool and click on the text block if necessary to activate the baseline of the type. To make the label useful, style it identically to the objects to be created using the like-named custom color. For instance, for the label "Wood Floor," Whitehouse chose a .33-pt black stroke and filled the type with the custom color "Wood Floor."

**3 Repeating the procedure for all colors and labels.** Create colors for each object to be styled differently, and make labels for all your objects. Whitehouse needed to create dozens of custom Spot colors, properly labeled, for each type of object included in his floor plan.

**4 Changing color definitions as necessary.** The spot color system makes it easy to change definitions of colors. From the Swatches palette, double-click on the color you want to change to open Swatch Options, where you can make changes to the color recipes. Click OK to apply the changes to all objects containing that color.

**5 Using the labels to find all like objects.** To find all like objects, for instance, "Wood Beams," click on the name in your list and choose Edit: Select: Same Fill Color to select all wood beams in your illustration. Once selected, you can reposition or recolor them all together.

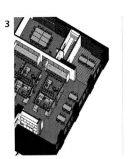

Close-up and zoomed-out views of the illustration with the labels

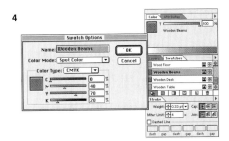

Double-clicking on a spot color swatch in the Color palette to open its dialog box

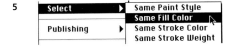

Selecting the label, then using Edit: Select: Same Fill Color to find the objects

**Spot colors for four-color-process jobs**

Illustrator 7.0 does not update objects when you re-define a Process color, nor allow tints of Process colors. Instead, you may want to define all swatches as Spot colors. Just make certain that you've enabled "Convert to Process" options when generating separations.

# Organizing Color

*Arranging an Artist's Palette of Colors*

**Overview:** *Work with color swatches to choose initial colors; make adjustments to, and rename, custom colors; save a palette of your custom colors.*

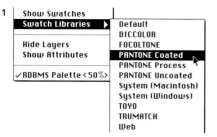

Opening one of the Pantone color palettes

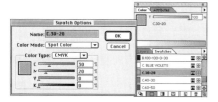

*Respecifying and renaming custom spot colors to form an orderly, accessible palette*

## Moving multiple sliders

With the Shift key down, if you grab one color slider you'll move all colors together. Grabbing the right-most slider gives the greatest control. Drag to the right to 100% to saturate the color fully. Drag left to desaturate.

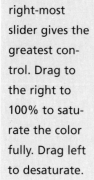
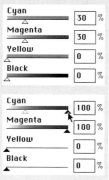

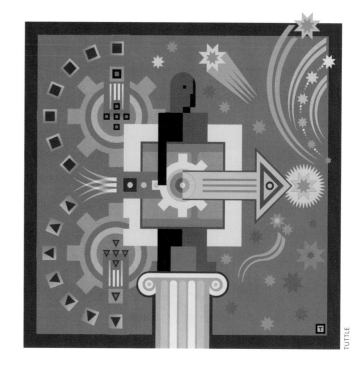

As any colorist knows, a well-organized palette can go beyond providing you with mere colors; it can facilitate the creative process. Progress Software Company's product signature color is the deep Pantone Violet #2685, so when art director Deborah Hurst commissioned artist Jean Tuttle to create a series of illustrations for a "family" of Progress sales literature, they worked closely to develop a limited palette that would feel related to the signature color. Tuttle developed a method to organize the colors so she could work with them in an intuitive manner.

**1 Using swatches of printed colors to choose ranges of colors with which to work.** As I mentioned in *Chapter 1*, color on the screen is not a reliable predictor of the color you will get in print. Therefore, start with one of the computer-to-print color matching systems to choose your initial colors. With art director Hurst in Boston, and Tuttle in Dobbs Ferry, New York, the two used the Pantone color system to choose swatches of color to consider for the palette. Once they had agreed upon the general color scheme, Tuttle could open the

Pantone color palette (Window: Swatch Libraries) and gain access to the computer version of the colors from within Illustrator. For each color she was considering, Tuttle put a square filled with that color into a document. After she pulled the basic colors she wanted, she could close the Pantone palette—leaving her with just the colors she had chosen for her palette.

Tuttle renamed each color in her palette based on five color groupings: Blues, Purples, Blue Violets, Red Violets and Accents. Because Illustrator lists custom colors alphabetically, Tuttle preceded each color grouping by a letter that would force Illustrator to group the colors as she wished. Using a process color matching book as a guide, Tuttle then rounded off the CMYK percentages for each individual color, incorporating the color formulas in the name (B.50-50, for example, would be Purples: 50% Cyan / 50% Magenta) and created variants on each of the colors as well, saving each color swatch into her palette. To visually separate the color groupings as they list in the Swatches palette, she created a series of white colors to use purely as name placeholders—for example, one white was named "B. Purples" (because there's a space before the "P," it lists ahead of the numbered purples in the list) —making sure that each of these white custom colors used as a label was placed into a square in the palette as well. To develop your custom set of swatches, select each palette object, Option-click on the new layer icon to specify the name, and choose "Spot" from Color Mode (see Tip on page 61).

## 2 Accessing and tinting colors with your palette.
Another benefit to using spot colors in your palette is that you can easily specify tint percentages for any color. Just select the color and adjust the Tint slider in the Colors palette or type in a percentage in the text box. For each illustration Tuttle produced for this series, she had access to her entire set of colors and their tints. With this palette, Tuttle was able to create a "smoky blue" color environment to use for the entire family of illustrations.

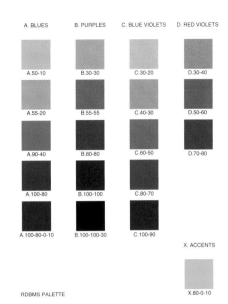

A chart made of the custom colors for future access to the full palette, including a rectangle for each white made as a name placeholder

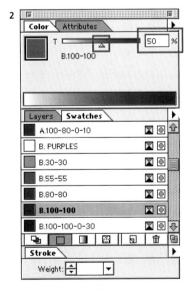

Specifying a tint of a custom color

### Tints will "stick" until changed
The tint percentages of your last selected object will set the tint of your next fill and stroke color, unless you manually change them.

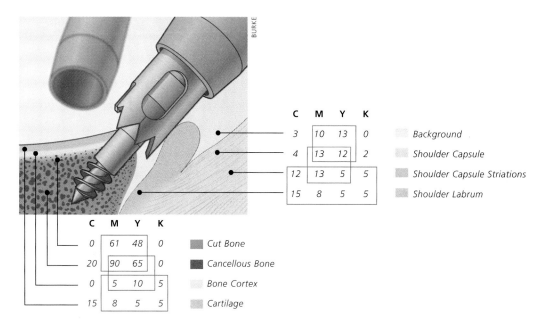

## Gallery: Christopher Burke

*When printed using the CMYK four-color process, Adobe Illustrator's smooth, crisp edges can be a registration nightmare. Even the slightest misregistration of inks can create visually disturbing white gaps between colors. So, although you shouldn't have to worry about what happens to your illustration once it's completed, the reality is that in this phase of computer graphics evolution, you still have to help your printer along. "Trapping" is a technique of printing one color over the edge of another—usually achieved by creating overprinting strokes that overlap adjacent objects. However, work-around solutions exist; Christopher Burke, for example, constructs the colors in his images in such a way as to ensure "continuous coverage" for at least one (preferably two) of the color plates in every region of his image. As long as adjacent objects share at least 5% of at least one color, no white gaps can form, and trapping will naturally occur! (Also see the Tip below and on page 23.) This method of keeping just enough in common between adjacent colors allows Burke to maintain a full-spectrum palette. (The background of the image is an Illustrator drawing rasterized in Photoshop and placed back into Illustrator as an EPS—see Chapter 4 for placing EPS images, and Chapter 9 for more on rasterizing Illustrator images.)*

### Manual trapping of gradients and pattern fills

Since you can't style strokes with gradients or patterns, you can't trap using the Pathfinder Trap filter either. To trap gradients and patterns manually, first duplicate your object and stroke it in the weight you'd like for a trap. Then use Object: Path: Outline Path to convert the stroke to a filled object, which you should fill in the same style as the object you'd like to trap. Lastly, enable the Overprint Fill box in the Attributes palette. If necessary, use the Gradient tool to unify gradients across objects (page 108), and manually replicate pattern transformations.

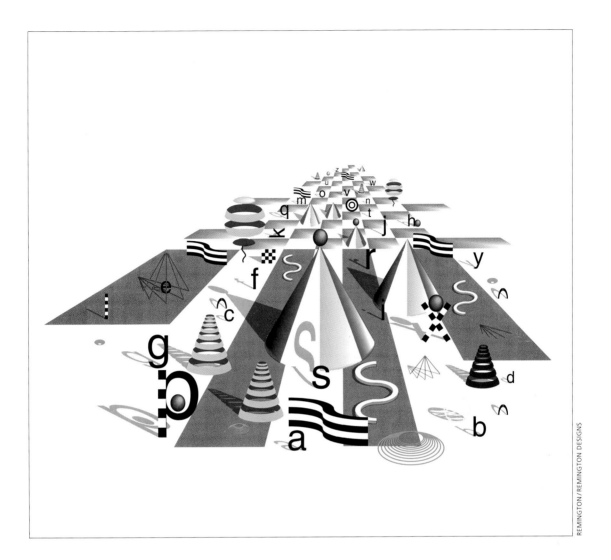

## Gallery: Dorothy Remington / Remington Designs

*Color printers are notoriously unpredictable in terms of color consistency, so Dorothy Remington developed a method to increase consistency from proof to final output. When Remington constructs an image, she freely chooses colors from any of the CMYK process color models (Pantone Process, TruMatch, Focoltone and Toyo) that come with Illustrator, provided that she has the matching color swatchbooks. When she sends the computer file to the service bureau for proofing, as well as for final output, she also sends along the color swatches representing colors used in the image. Remington asks the service bureau to calibrate the printer to match the enclosed swatches as closely as possible. Although requesting such special attention might result in a small surcharge, it can save you an immense amount of time (in back-and-forths to the service bureau) and expense in reprinting the image because colors did not turn out as expected.*

### Gallery: Hugh Whyte/Lehner & Whyte

*To celebrate Letraset's distribution of a new Pantone line of blacks, Hugh Whyte was commissioned to produce a thematic illustration for Letraset to silk-screen on T-shirts. The beauty of using the Pantone custom colors was that when he had them printed to positive separations, the films were perfectly registered for the different screens in silk-screening. The printer could then mix the inks to Whyte's exact specifications using the Pantone swatchbook to match.*

## Gallery: Jeffrey Barney / Barney McKay Design

*When Santa Anita Park decided to produce a commemorative poster, Jeffrey Barney chose this 1930s-style illustration to reflect the park's period elegance. The color proofs needed to match the actual colors used at the park, to be of large enough format to view at near poster size, and to be consistent with the colors that would result from the printing process. Given these parameters, Barney decided to calibrate all of his work against Iris prints (see the* Resources *appendix). He therefore had his computer monitors professionally calibrated to match the prints. He also regularly brought the prints to the park and made color notes directing himself how to alter each color. In Illustrator, Barney created a set of custom spot colors labeled by name, so as he adjusted the CMYK formula for each color, all occurrences of that color, and corresponding tints, would automatically update (for more about tints, see page 60). Finally, after he proofed the final Iris prints, the service bureau matched the color separations to them.*

# Brush Strokes

*Making Realistic Marks with the Brush*

**Overview:** *Set the Brush tool to the desired range of widths; trace or draw your composition; select and group brush drawing; optionally, make a slightly different version to copy and paste on top of the original; make final adjustments.*

**1**

*The original sketch in red Conté crayon*

*The PICT scan opened as an Illustrator template*

Creating spontaneous painterly and calligraphic marks is a wonderful recent addition to Illustrator. As long as you have a graphics tablet and a pressure-sensitive, pen-like stylus, Illustrator's Brush tool can literally sense the pressure you apply and vary your strokes accordingly. For this portrait of Gregory Sloan Jacoby, I was able to use Illustrator's Brush tool with Wacom's ArtZ tablet to create a loose, brush-and-ink style, limited edition print.

**1 If you'll be working from a source, prepare your template.** Although you can draw directly into the computer, if you want to trace a sketch or a photograph, you'll need to prepare your template. For Gregory's portrait, I used AppleScan software to scan a 4" x 6" tight sketch at 400% at 75 pixels per inch and opened it as a template in Illustrator. (See *Chapter 4* for template help.)

**2 Setting your brush preferences and drawing.** Instead of actually creating painterly lines, Illustrator's Brush tool creates filled objects that appear to be variable weight lines. So unless you're experimenting with effects, set a solid color fill in the Color palette with no stroke.

Double-click on the Brush tool to open the Paintbrush Options dialog box. Experiment with the different settings until you find ranges that are comfortable for you. (Unfortunately, if you don't have a pressure-sensitive tablet, your brush stroke options will be limited.) Then draw. Make adjustments to colors or brush preferences as necessary. For Gregory's portrait, I initially worked with rather large strokes, so in the Options dialog box, I used a range of 1 to 6 points, with Round-caps and Round-joins (similar in concept to the Caps and Joins, page 49).
**Note:** *With the Pencil tool, lowering the Curve Fitting Tolerance settings in Preferences: General results in more points; higher results in fewer. This adjustment doesn't seem to affect the Brush tool.*

**3 Cleaning up extra points.** Objects created with the Brush tool will always need some cleaning up. The more extra points and oddly positioned points you have, the more irregular the image will appear when printed and the longer the image will take to print (some objects with too many points might not even print at all). Use the Delete-anchor-point tool to remove excess points interfering with the smoothness of curves, and use the Direct-selection tool to adjust the placement of anchor points and direction of curves.

**4 Experimenting with your image.** The first portrait I completed looked too clean, so I saved the version and kept experimenting, making slight adjustments using the Direct-selection tool to redraw a few of the lines. Since I liked parts of both versions, I selected and grouped each (⌘-G), then tried to combine the two, accidentally creating an offset that I liked. The softer brush effect in the final image is a result of this offset.

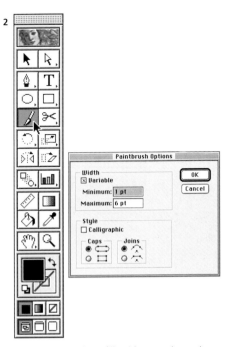

*Setting Paint Style to fill, with no stroke, and double-clicking the Brush tool to set options*

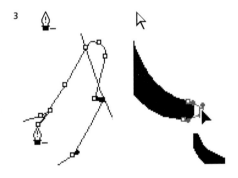

*Eliminating extra points with the Delete-anchor-point tool and adjusting curves with the Direct-selection tool*

*Pasting a second, slightly altered version over the first version*

## Gallery: Lyuda Lavrentyeva

*Lyuda Lavrentyeva used the Brush tool with a pressure-sensitive tablet and the Pantone NEC color matching system to create this loose, vivid image. Her working method incorporates many techniques demonstrated elsewhere in the book, such as creating the darker line drawing on a locked upper layer while adding the broad patches of color underneath (see page 84). Lavrentyeva also used a number of filters, including Pathfinder: Soft to blend colors, Pathfinder: Unite to join objects, and the Select: Select Same Fill filter to help her make global color changes. (See* Chapter 6 *for more on filters, including the Stylize: Calligraphy filter.)*

LAVRENTYEVA

## Gallery: Jen Alspach

*For this natural, ink-pen-like Illustrator drawing, Jen Alspach used the Wacom ArtZ tablet to trace one of her scanned horse photos (placed as an EPS custom template; see page 80–81). Alspach used a number of different tools to create a diversity of line texture, beginning with the Brush tool's Calligraphic option set to 120 to trace over the photo. After deleting the EPS template, she switched the Brush tool to a variable line weight between .5 and 3 to form some of the contouring lines, set the Pencil tool at 1, .5 and .125 to create the scratchy texture, and set the Brush tool's Calligraphic option at 45. Finally, Alspach created blends to complete the background (see* Chapter 5*).*

ALSPACH

MORENO

## Gallery: Cheryl Moreno

*With just pen and ink, Cheryl Moreno's delightful figures and "doodles" jump off the page. Until recently, Moreno would carefully use Illustrator's Pen tool to trace her spontaneously drawn calligraphic figures. Now that she has discovered the Brush tool and a Wacom tablet, Moreno is able to eliminate the sketch-and-scan phase.*

MORENO

# Intricate Patterns

*Designing Complex Repeating Patterns*

STEUER

**Advanced Technique**

**Overview:** *Design a rough composition; define a pattern boundary and place behind everything; use the box to define guides; place small lines to use as registration while dragging; define and use the pattern.*

1

*Arranging objects into a basic design*

*Placing a confining rectangle (defining the pattern tile), guides and registration lines*

## Pattern tiles into objects

To retrieve a pattern tile, just drag the pattern swatch onto your work area. To convert an applied pattern fill into editable objects, choose Object: Expand Fill.

**Note:** *Expand Fill won't work on very complex patterns, like this one.*

Included with Illustrator are many wonderful patterns for you to use and customize, and the *User Guide* does a good job of explaining pattern-making basics. But what if you want to create a more complex pattern?

A few simple guidelines and registration marks can help you minimize what could be a painstaking process of trial and error. With some essential help from author and consultant Sandee Cohen, I was finally able to come up with a method that allowed me to experimentally design an intricate tile that would print properly as a repeating pattern. This fabric and wallpaper pattern was created for an upcoming children's book by Matt Lake.

1 **Designing your basic pattern, then drawing a confining rectangle and guides.** Create a design that will allow for some rearrangement of the elements. Be aware that you cannot make a pattern tile from objects filled with gradients, rasterized or placed images, or other patterns. Use the Rectangle tool to draw a box around the part of the image you would like to repeat. This rectangle defines the boundary of the pattern tile. Send the rectangle to the back of the page or to the bottom drawing layer (if you would like help with layers, see *Chapter 4*). This

boundary rectangle, which controls how your pattern repeats, *must* remain an unstroked, unfilled, nonrotated, nonskewed *rectangle*. Next, make sure that the "Snap to point" option is enabled (in General Preferences), then choose Show Rulers and pull out the guides to snap to each side of the rectangle (your cursor turns hollow as it snaps). Make sure you've selected the Lock Guides option (see pages 21 and 96 for more on guides).

Next, you need to create small lines that will help you to move objects while maintaining registration. On each of the guides, use the Pen tool to draw the lines outside of the pattern in a color not used in the pattern. These registration marks will help you to align elements as you move them from corner to corner.

**2 Developing the repeating elements.** In order for the pattern to repeat properly, you must place copies of any elements extending beyond the bounding rectangle in the area butting up against the overlapping object. For instance, if an object extends below the rectangle, you must place a copy of the continuing part of the object into the upper portion of the pattern. So, for the grass in the jungle pattern to repeat properly, I selected grass in front of the tiger and used Group (⌘-G) for easy reselection. In order to align the grass properly, I selected the bottom right horizontal registration mark with the grass that was to be moved. I grabbed the registration mark, and then, while holding down the Option and Shift keys (the Option key leaves the original, while the Shift constrains the dragging to vertical and horizontal movements), dragged a copy until it snapped into position along the upper horizontal guide. If you make a mistake, try again. (See "A Finger Dance" in *Chapter 2* for practice with Shift, Option and other modifier keys.)

**3 Weaving your repeating objects in front of or behind others.** One way to make a pattern interesting is to weave elements on top of some objects and behind others. After placing your copy of the repeating element

2

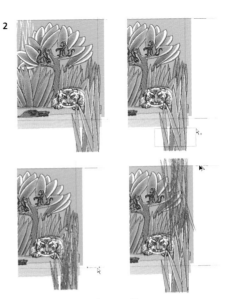

*Moving grasses up into position*

3

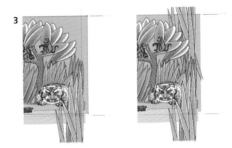

*Cutting the copied grass and using Paste In Front to place it in front of the sky*

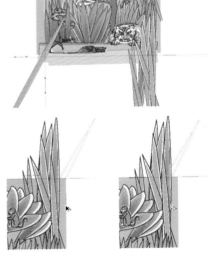

*Weaving diagonal grasses through the pattern*

4

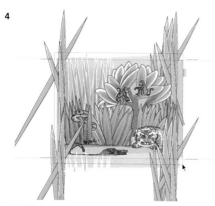

## Controlling patterns

Enable "Transform pattern tiles" in General Preferences to reset the default to transform patterns along with their objects. You can also transform patterns in any of the dialog boxes (with or without the object itself). To *manually* move, rotate, scale or skew the pattern tiles *alone*, start your transformation and hold down the "~" key as you drag (or use the cursor-keys). Relocate the ruler origin to set where the next pattern will begin. (For info about Path Patterns see *Chapter 6*.)

## Speeding redraw with patterns

When your pattern-filled object is in position, put it on a separate layer set to Artwork mode (for help with layers see *Chapter 4*), or even rasterize it (see page 124).

into its properly registered position, and while it's still selected, cut that copy to the Clipboard (⌘-X). Then choose an object or objects in your composition that you can easily Paste In Front of (⌘-F) or Paste In Back of (⌘-B). For the jungle, I cut the grass copy, then selected the blue sky and chose Paste In Front, which placed the copy in front of the blue sky but behind all other elements. Other grasses, such as the diagonal blades, needed to be on top of some grass while behind others. I used a combination of Paste In Front and Paste In Back with such elements to increase the complexity of the weaving.

4 **Testing your pattern.** When you're ready to test your pattern (to see if you like what you've done so far), first clear out your palette of excess styles (see "How to use this book," page xi). Next, make sure that all the objects and layers that you'll need are visible and unlocked (Object: Show All/Unlock All, or *QK:* ⌘-Option-3/⌘-Option-2), select your pattern elements (including the bounding rectangle), and either choose Edit: Define Pattern to name your pattern, or drag your selection to the Swatches palette (double-click the swatch later to customize its name). Then create a new rectangle and select the pattern as your fill from the Swatches palette to see how your pattern repeats within a filled object. If you redesign the pattern tile, and then wish to update the pattern swatch with those changes, select your pattern elements again, but this time Option-drag the elements onto the pattern swatch you made before.

5 **Simplifying and scaling your final pattern.** The larger and more complex your pattern is, the more difficult and time-consuming it will be to print. When you finally get a pattern you like, do your best to minimize its size. (If you used the Brush tool, see page 68, this chapter, for deleting excess points; see *Chapter 6* for filters that can simplify your piece.) Finally, from the Pattern dialog box, select unused patterns and delete them. Make sure you save this smallest possible version of the file with a new name.

STEUER

## Gallery: Sharon Steuer

*A reduced version of the final pattern (tile prescaled to 52%). In the original pattern tile, I used the Brush tool (see pages 68 through 71), multiple layers to separate the colored elements (see Chapter 4), and the Blend tool (see Chapter 5) to create the color transitions in the sky and leaves.*

# Templates & Layers

4

## Layer palette navigation

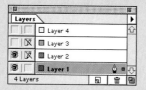

- To hide a layer, click its Eye icon. Click again to show it.
- To lock a layer, click in the box to its left (a Crossed-out Pencil displays). Click again to unlock.
- To select contiguous layers, Shift-click on one layer, then the other. To select or deselect *any* layers ⌘-click in any order.
- To open Layer Options, Double-click on a layer (see next page).
- To select all objects on a layer, Option-click on the layer name.
- To toggle lock/view options between only the current layer and all other layers Option-click on the appropriate icon.
- To move objects from one layer to another, see Tip on page 88.
- To duplicate a layer, grab and drag it to the New Layer icon.

See the *Quick Reference Card* for more layers shortcuts.

Used wisely, layers can dramatically reduce printing and screen redraw time, and improve organization of complicated artwork, thereby increasing your productivity.

If you're a Windows user, layers are among the most powerful features new to you—although if you use Photoshop 3 or beyond, they'll look familiar. If you're a Mac user already knee-deep in layers, you'll find that, while some operations take getting used to, there are a number of most welcome additions.

Alongside the new updating readout that displays the current number of layers you'll find New Layer and Trash icons. Click the New Layer icon to add a layer in numeric sequence, or Option-click New Layer to set Layer Options (such as naming your layer) as you add the layer. Or, make a New Layer Below (⌘-click) or Above (⌘-Option-click) the current layer. Click the Trash icon to delete selected layers. (To delete without a warning message, grab the layers, hold Option, and drag to the Trash.)

## The layers mindset

Try to think of layers as sheets of clear acetate, stacked one on top of the other, allowing you to separate dozens of groups of objects easily. You can rearrange the stacking order of the layers, lock, hide or copy layers, and move objects from one layer to another.

By default, the Layers palette (Window: Show Layers) always starts with one layer, though you can add as many layers as you wish. You're only restricted by how much memory you have available.

### Maximizing Layer Options

Double-click a Layer name to set Layer Options to:

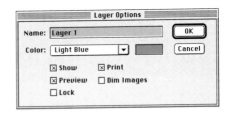

- **Name the layer.** In complicated artwork, naming layers keeps your job, and your brain, organized.

- **Change the layer's color.** A layer's color determines the selection color for paths and anchor points. Adjust the layer color so selections stand out against artwork.

- **Show/Hide layer.** This option functions the same as the Show/Hide toggle, which is accessed by clicking the Eye icon (see Tip on previous page). By default, hiding a layer will set it to *not* print (please also see Tip, page 90).

- **Preview/Artwork mode.** Controlling which layers are set to Preview/Artwork is essential to working with layers. If objects on certain layers are more easily edited in Artwork mode, or are slowing down screen redraw (such as patterns and gradients), you'll want those layers in Artwork, while photos used as templates will have to be in Preview mode. This option performs the same action as ⌘-clicking the Eye icon (see middle Tip, page 81).

- **Lock/Unlock layer.** This option functions the same as the Lock/Unlock toggle, which is accessed by clicking to the left of the layer (see Tip on previous page).

- **Print/Suppress printing.** Enabling or disabling this option allows you to override the default that sets visible layers to print, and hidden layers to not print. Also see Tip on page 90, and Technique on pages 92–93.

- **Dim Images.** Enable this for template use (see below).

### The Layers pop-up menu

The first set of functions in the Layers pop-up are: New Layer, Duplicate layer, Delete Layers, New Layer Above (with Option key) and New Layer below (with ⌘) and

---

### Setting multiple Print Options

With multiple layers selected (see Tip, opposite), double-click on one of the selected layers. This will access Layer Options for all selected layers. Leave a checkbox "gray" or blank to maintain different settings for the selected layers. For a practical application demonstrating this, see pages 92–93.

### Objects on different layers

Here are three ways to move a group of objects from one layer to the top of objects in another:
- Reorder the layers (see page 81).
- Move the bottom objects to the top layer (see Tip, page 88).
- Cut the bottom objects, select the topmost object and Paste In Front (⌘-F) with Paste Remembers Layers *off* (see "Paste In Front, Paste In Back," page 78).

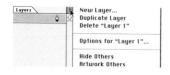

New Layer...
Duplicate Layer
Delete "Layer 1"

Options for "Layer 1"...

Hide Others
Artwork Others

## To select *all* objects

Unlock and show all layers, then unlock and show all objects (from the Object menu, or *QK:* ⌘-Option-2, ⌘-Option-3), *then* press ⌘-A to Select All.

## A good habit for old jobs

Before you begin working on an unfamiliar file, choose Object: Show All (*QK:* ⌘-Option-3) to show any hidden objects, and check to be sure that all layers you intend to print are set to print (see "Print/Supress Printing," previous page).
— *Robin AF Olson*

## Powerful for print production

You can use layers to separate print production marks and notes. For instance, use separate layers for the die tracing, blueline (or keyline), type, printer remarks, and one each for any linked or embedded art. Because you can toggle Hide / Show layers by deselecting or selecting the Eye icon on the Layers palette, you can hide certain layers when you want to proof your file from within Illustrator. (See the Tip "WYSIWYG Layers?" on page 90 for details on when layers print, or don't print.)
— *Robin AF Olson*

Options—all of which can be performed via layer icons, or Layer Options (discussed earlier in this chapter). Hide Others, Artwork Others and Lock Others all perform actions on unselected layers. Merge Layers is available when two or more layers are selected, and will place all *visible* objects on the top layer—and delete hidden ones!

Paste Remembers Layers is a great feature (one of my favorites): when off, pasted objects go into the selected layer; when on, objects remember their layers in exciting ways… (see pages 92–93 for more details).

## WHERE HAVE ALL THE TEMPLATES GONE?

One of the layer substitutes that Illustrator always provided was the Template layer. Sadly for some, these templates must now be created using layers. See the ReadMe file in the "Templates folder" on the *Wow!* disk for auto-templates, and see pages 80–81.

## CONTROLLING THE STACKING ORDER OF OBJECTS

Though the Layers palette is a relatively new addition, Illustrator has always provided a powerful and flexible environment to manage the stacking order of objects. The seemingly straightforward commands Hide, Show, Lock, Unlock (now in the Object menu), Paste in Front, Paste in Back, Bring to Front, Send to Back and the new Bring Forward and Send Backward (from the Object: Arrange menu) offer considerable control over Illustrator objects. Even though you can now benefit fully from the layer options, the original secret powers are still well worth learning. (See the Tip, page 79, on Bring to Front/Send to Back, Bring Forward/Send Backward.)

## Paste In Front, Paste In Back (⌘-F, ⌘-B)

Illustrator doesn't merely bring or send an object in front of or behind all other objects when you choose Paste In Front or Back; it positions the object *exactly* in front of or behind the object you select. The second and equally important aspect is that the two functions paste objects that are cut (⌘-X) or copied (⌘-C) into the exact same location—in relation to the *ruler origin.* This ability applies from one document to another, ensuring perfect registration and alignment when you copy and use Edit: Paste In Front / Back (⌘-F / ⌘-B). These functions apply only when the "Paste Remembers Layers" option in Layers pop-up is *disabled.* See pages 92–93 for a practical application of this option, and the *Wow!* disk for exercises in reordering objects using pasting and layers.

## Lock / Unlock All (Object menu, or *QK:* ⌘-2 / ⌘-Opt-2)

When you're trying to select an object and you accidentally select an object on top of it, try locking the selected object and clicking again. Repeat as necessary until you reach the correct object. When you're done with the task, choose Object: Unlock All to release the locked objects. **Warning:** *You can use the Direct-selection tool to select and lock objects that are part of a group (see page 8 for more on grouping)—but if you select an unlocked object in the group with the Group-select or other selection tools, the locked objects can become selected, making it too easy for them to be transformed accidentally or even deleted. Hidden objects, of course, will stay hidden even if you select other objects in the same group.*

## Hide / Show All (Object menu, or *QK:* ⌘-3 / ⌘-Opt-3)

An alternate approach for handling objects that get in the way is to select them and choose Object: Hide Selection, which hides them—even in artwork mode. Use Show All on hidden objects, by choosing Object: Show All.

Hidden objects won't print but may reappear if you export them to other programs, or upon reopening. 🌀

---

### Bring Forward / Bring to Front and more...

Within a layer, *Bring Forward* stacks an object on top of the object directly above it. *Bring to Front* moves an object in front of all other objects on its layer. Logically, *Send to Back* sends an object as far back as it can go in its stacking order. *Send Backwards* sends an object behind its closest neighbor.

---

### If you can't select an object...

If you have trouble selecting an object, check the following:

- Is the object's layer locked?
- Is the object locked?
- Are the edges hidden?
- Is the "Area select" box disabled (in General Preferences)?

If you keep selecting the wrong object, try again after you:

- Switch to Artwork mode.
- Zoom in.
- Hide the selected object; repeat if necessary.
- Lock the selected object; repeat if necessary.
- Choose View: Preview Selection to preview *only* your selected object, so you know what you're about to lock, hide or edit.
- Put the object on top in another layer and hide that layer, or select Artwork for that layer.
- Use the Move command (Option-click on the Selection arrow in the Toolbox) to move selected objects (you can move them back later) a set distance.

**Note:** *See page 18–19 for more on hiding edges and zooming.*

---

### Hide or lock all *except*...

To hide all *but* selected objects, choose Object: Hide Selection with the Option key down (or *QK:* ⌘-Shift-Option-3). To lock all *but* selected objects, choose Object: Lock with the Option key down (or *QK:* ⌘-Shift-Option-2).

# Tracing a Scan

*Creating Custom Templates for Tracing*

STEUER

**Overview:** *Scan a photo; place it into its own layer in Illustrator and set layer options; tint the photo for easier tracing; trace the photo in a layer above using a variety of tools.*

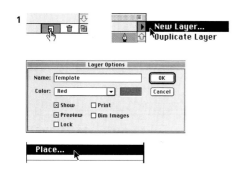

*Option-clicking on the icon or selecting from the pop-up to create a new layer, setting layer options, then placing the scan*

Illustrator now allows you to place grayscale or color images to use as templates. Because images placed for template use are not intended for final printing, you can tint these placed images from within Illustrator.

For its mail-order catalogue, Exposures wanted to reproduce a tooled-leather daguerreotype case from the Smithsonian Institution's collection. With only a color snapshot to work with, Exposures commissioned me to produce the black-and-white line version they needed to create the molds for the new leather cover (artist's rendering shown above). Using Illustrator's layers functions, I traced over a tinted grayscale version of the scanned photo to re-create the original relief image as line art.

**1 Scanning and placing the image into a custom layer.**
Scan the image you wish to use as a tracing template as grayscale and save it in TIFF format. For the Exposures project, I optimized the low contrasts of the relief by scanning the photo in only 16 levels of gray (4-bit). In Illustrator, open the Layers palette to see "Layer 1," in which you'll create your line illustration. Option-click on the New Layer icon in the Layers palette (or choose New Layer from the palette arrow pop-up) to name the layer "Template" and enable your view and print options, but don't lock it. Click OK to apply these layer options. Then, select File: Place to place the scan into your Template layer. (To change options later, double-click on the layer name.)

**2 Tinting the scan.** With your scan selected, choose Filter: Colors: Adjust Colors. Choose RGB from the Color Mode pop-up, and enable Convert and Preview, then adjust the RGB sliders to tint your photo so it's a different color from the Illustrator path lines you'll be drawing with. IMPORTANT: *Only use Adjust Colors on images intended for on-screen use, and that won't go to final output. Use Photoshop (or other high-end photo manipulation program) on images intended for pre-press output.*

**3 Reordering the layers.** Grab the Template layer and drag it below Layer 1 so the photo will be underneath your future line drawing. Now lock the template (click to the right of the Eye to show the Crossed-out Pencil) and click on Layer 1 to make it the active layer for drawing.

**4 Tracing with geometric tools.** Examine your photo template. If you see objects that are almost symmetrical, use a Rectangle or an Oval tool to trace an approximation of that object, then use the transformation tools (Rotate, Scale, Reflect and Skew) to adjust the object to fit the photo better. Lastly, use the Direct-selection and Pen tools to reshape and redraw paths. For instance, I started the wavy borders surrounding the flowers with a rounded rectangle and used the Oval tool to approximate the circular flower pods. In both of these cases, I used transformation tools on the objects, redrew sections with the Pen tool, and used the Direct-selection tool to adjust the paths.

**5 Using the Pen and Brush tools to draw freeform objects.** For creating objects constructed of fluid lines and curves, use the Pen tool. When you are drawing squiggly or calligraphic marks, use the Pencil tool. I used the Pen tool to create all flowers and leaves, and the Pencil tool only for the squiggly centers of the flowers.

2
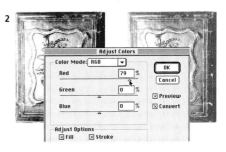
*Original scan, then tinted using Filter: Colors: Adjust Colors (choosing RGB, Preview, Convert)*

3

*Moving the Template layer below Layer 1, then locking the template and activating Layer 1*

4
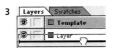

*Using the Direct-selection tool to adjust paths drawn with the Oval and Pen tools*

5

*The final line illustration*

**Previewing one layer at a time**
To toggle a layer between Preview and Artwork mode, ⌘-click the Eye.

Preview   Artwork

**Jiffy-quick *Wow!* templates**
The "Templates" folder on the *Wow!* disk includes "instant" templates with ReadMe instructions.

# Digitizing a Logo
*Controlling Your Illustrator Template*

BARRY / ROSENWACH

**Overview:** *Scan a clean, enlarged version of your artwork; place the art as a template in Illustrator; analyze the curves of the template; trace the template; hide the template for adjustments; copy the finished illustration and paste it into a new document.*

You can easily use Illustrator to re-create traditional line art with the computer—easily, that is, if you know the tricks. Years after Rick Barry rendered the Breeders' Cup logo in black and white using traditional methods, he re-created it digitally in order to produce colorized versions. One version, using gradients, is shown above (for more about gradients, see *Chapter 5*).

1 **Preparing a large, clean scan.** Select a high-contrast image to re-create in Illustrator. Scan the image as black-and-white "line art" at 75 pixels per inch (ppi), but enlarged to 200–400%, and save it in TIFF format. An image scanned at 1" x 1" at 300 ppi contains the same number of pixels as a 4" x 4" scan at 75 ppi. Since that 75 ppi image would appear four times larger when viewed in Illustrator, this gives you more flexibility to zoom in and work on the tiny details of your artwork. Although the original logo was not very big, Barry had a "stat" produced at 12" wide and scanned it into the computer. Since his scanning software didn't permit adjusting the pixel-per-inch ratio, Barry scanned at 300 ppi and used Photoshop to set the image to 75 ppi without changing the actual number of pixels (*not* "Resampling") before using it as a template in Illustrator.

**Note:** *Don't be concerned if you encounter 72 ppi (the resolution of your screen)—72 or 75 ppi is fine for templates.*

1

*Scanning a large, clean version of your artwork*

**2 Setting up the TIFF as a template.** Hold down your ⌘ key and choose "New Layer Below" from the Layers pop-up menu, then name the layer "Template" and set your Options. Next use Edit: Place to choose your scan, thus placing it into the Template layer. Now lock the template and click on Layer 1 to make it the active layer for drawing.

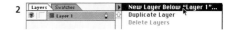

**3 Adjusting the page size for the large template.** A large template will bleed over the edges of a standard paper size, so an easy way to make the template appear smaller while you work is to adjust Page Setup (File: Document Setup). Set the reduction to 25% and click OK.

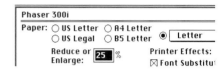

*The large template bleeding over the page*

*Adjusting Page Setup so the image fits within the page margins*

**4 Tracing the template.** Look at the entire template and compare it to the original you have scanned. Are any of the curves or lines misrepresented in the template? Remember that the template is just a guide; if a discrepancy exists, follow the original. Working first in Artwork mode (from the View menu), use the Pen tool to trace your template (for help with the Pen tool, see page 4). Place the minimal number of points necessary to complete the object, and don't be too concerned with how closely you're matching the contour. Then, zoom in close (with the Zoom tool, drag to marquee the area you wish to inspect) and use the Direct-selection tool to make adjustments to the length and angle of the direction lines until the Bézier curves properly fit the template.

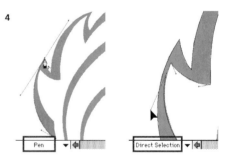

*Using the Pen tool to draw curves and using the Direct-selection tool to adjust the curves (for info on Illustrator's cursors which change to reflect your action, see page 6)*

**5 Adjusting your views.** As your image develops, view it in both Artwork and Preview modes, zoom in and out as necessary, and click the Eye icon in the Layers palette to control whether your template layer is hidden or visible.

**6 Scaling the final.** To place the finished illustration into another program, save the original, then choose Select All (⌘-A), copy the image and paste into a new document. With the logo still selected, double-click the Scale tool to scale the final to meet your specific needs, making sure that you enable "Scale line weight." 

*Hiding the template to make final adjustments*

# Layering Colors

*Coloring Black-and-White Images with Layers*

**Overview:** *Create your black out-lines; set up layers in Illustrator for the colors inside the lines and other layers for background elements; place black-and-white art into the upper layer; color the image; group outlines with their colors.*

The background for the illustration, created in the bottom two layers

An outline sketch

*EPS Format*
- Preview: None / 1-bit IBM PC / ● 1-bit Macintosh
- Encoding: ● ASCII / Binary
- OK / Cancel
- ☒ Transparent Whites

Choosing the "Transparent Whites" option when saving in EPS format

While the most obvious way to trace placed images in Illustrator is to put the image to be traced in a locked lower layer and use an upper layer to trace the new Illustrator objects, in some cases you'll want your tracing layer to be *below* a placed image. When illustrating a three-ringed circus for a Ringling Brothers Barnum & Bailey International Program, Michael Kline placed his sketches with the whites transparent into a locked upper layer so he could add color using Illustrator while maintaining a hand-sketched look.

**1 Setting up your Illustrator layers.** In Illustrator, create enough layers for the various background elements in your image. (For help making layers, see pages 80–83.) Assign each layer a different color to help keep track of which objects will be in each layer (selected paths and anchor points will be color-coded to match their layer). Then create the background of your illustration in these layers. When the background is ready, create at least two additional top layers for the figures you will be coloring. For his circus illustration, Kline established four layers— using the bottom layer ("Layer 4") to create the background itself and "Layer 3" to create the objects that would be directly on top of the background.

**2 Sketching or scanning a black-and-white drawing.**
Scan a hand-drawn sketch or draw directly into a bit-mapped program. Save it as an EPS file, with a black-and-white preview (1-bit) and the "Transparent Whites" option. Kline drew figure sketches with a soft pencil on rough paper, scanned them, then saved them individually as transparent, 1-bit, black-and-white EPS files.

The scanned drawing placed into Layer 1

**3 Placing your drawings into the top layer.** From the Layers palette, make the top layer active (click on the layer name) and use the Place command (from the File menu) to place one of your drawings into the top layer. Then, lock the layer (click in the box to the right of the Eye icon).

**4 Coloring your drawings.** You must tell Illustrator in which layer you will be drawing by activating and unlocking the second layer (to the left of the layer you should see the Eye and no Crossed-out Pencil). Now, using filled colored objects without strokes, trace *under* your placed sketch. To view the color alone, hide the top layer.

The colorized drawing with the line drawing visible and the line drawing hidden

**5 Grouping your drawing with its colors.** When you're finished coloring the first figure, select the placed EPS with the objects that colorize that figure and group them together. The colored, grouped figure will now be on the top layer, where you can easily reposition it within your composition. 🖐

The drawing and the underlying color before and after being grouped together

### Switching layers by selecting an object
If you are creating or editing objects with a number of layers unlocked, you don't have to use the Layers palette to switch your active layer. When you select an object from an unlocked layer, the layer that the selected object is on automatically becomes your new active layer. The next object you create will use the same paint style as the object you had selected and will be placed on that new active layer.

Moving the grouped, colorized figure around the composition

# Multiple Layers

*Creating a Poster from Multiple Sources*

**Overview:** *Sketch and scan a composition; set up basic layers in Illustrator for the objects you will create; place art into temporary layers; trace the placed art; delete the temporary layers.*

**1**

*Scanned photos of figures*

*Assembled collage and hand-traced sketch scanned*

*Scanned background photos*

Multiple layers can be a lifesaver when you're constructing complex illustrations. Using these layers to isolate or combine specific elements will simplify your tasks substantially and save you an immense amount of production time. When The City Volunteer Corps (CVC) commissioned Nancy Stahl to design a New York City subway poster, she saved time and frustration by creating pairs of template-and-artwork layers for tracing and arranging various components of the poster.

**1 Collecting and assembling source materials.** Prepare your own source materials to use as tracing templates in Illustrator. For the CVC subway poster, Stahl took Polaroids of herself posed as each of the figures in the composition and scanned them into Adobe Photoshop, where she scaled them, and moved them into position. She then printed out the assembled "collage," roughly sketched in the other elements by hand and, with tracing paper, created a line version of the full composition to use as an overall template. She then scanned it into the computer.

Finally, Stahl scanned a number of photos showing different buildings in New York City's skyline for individual placement and tracing in Illustrator.

**2 Setting up illustration layers.** Before you begin to import any photos or drawings, take a few moments to set up layers to help you isolate the key elements in your illustration. (For help making layers, see pages 80–83.) For the subway poster, before she actually started her Illustrator image, Stahl set up separate layers for the background, the type, and the buildings that would make up the skyline, as well as one layer for each of the figures and a final layer for the foreground buildings.

**3 Placing art to use as templates.** You'll now need to create a few temporary layers for placing the artwork or scans you've collected to use as tracing templates. For each image you want to use as a template, make a new layer and use Place to select the scan or artwork to be placed into this layer. Then move the Template layer directly below the object layer upon which you will be tracing and lock it. Stahl created a layer, which she named "EPS Images," and then placed the buildings that she would be tracing for the skyline. Using the Layers palette, she then moved this new skyscraper template below her "buildings" layer, onto which she created the Illustrator buildings, and then locked the EPS Images layer.

**4 Drawing into your layers.** Now you can begin drawing and tracing elements into your compositional layers. Activate the layer in which you want to draw (click on the layer's name), unlock and view the layer (there should be an Eye in the Show box and an empty Edit box) and start to work. Use the Layers palette to lock, unlock or hide layers, as well as to toggle between Preview and Artwork modes (⌘-click the Eye icon), switch your active layer or add a new layer. By so maneuvering, Stahl could easily trace a group of skyscrapers, create type against a locked background or develop one figure at a time.

2

Setting up layers to isolate key elements

3

The temporary layer and choosing Place

Moving the layer and setting up the Edit and Show options for tracing

4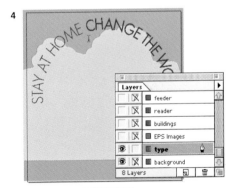

Isolating elements by viewing and unlocking only the essential layers

**5**

Clicking on a visible and unlocked layer to make it active for placing new art

**6**

Moving placed art within a layer to trace different objects

**7**

Clicking on the Trash icon, or choosing Delete from the Layers palette pop-up menu

---

**Changing placed art**

Select the EPS you wish to replace, and choose Place from the File menu. Choose your new art, in the dialog box which then appears, click to Replace the selected EPS with this new one. If you didn't intend to replace an EPS, click Don't Replace (which places the new EPS *in addition* to the one that was selected), or just Cancel.

---

**5 Adding new placed art to a lower layer.** If you need to import art into an existing layer, you must first make the layer visible and unlocked (in the Layers palette, the Eye icon should show and the Edit box should be empty) and then make it the active layer. For the subway poster, when Stahl needed additional building references, she viewed and unlocked EPS Images, clicked on it to make it the active layer and then used the Place command.

**6 Moving placed art within a layer.** Stahl's reference photos showed New York's buildings clustered differently from the way she wanted them for her illustration, so she devised a way to space the buildings as she worked. After tracing over one building, she unlocked EPS Images, moved the cluster of buildings slightly and relocked the layer. She then traced a different skyscraper in the new location and repeated the procedure for each building.

**7 Deleting layers when you finish using them.** Extra layers with placed art can take up quite a bit of disk space, so when you finish using a template, first save the file. Then, in the Layers palette, click on the layer you are ready to remove and click on the trash icon, or choose the Delete option from the Layers palette pop-up menu. Finally, use Save As to save this new version of the illustration with a meaningful new name and version number (such as "CVC without EPS-3.0"). Stahl eventually deleted all the layers she created as templates so she could save her final poster with all the illustration layers but none of the templates or placed pictures. ⬤

---

**Moving an object from one layer to another**

To move a selected object to another layer: open the Layers palette, grab the colored dot to the right of the object's layer and drag it to the desired layer. To move a copy of an object: hold down the Option key while you drag.

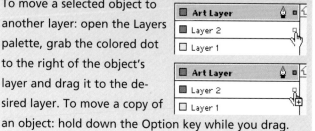

---

STAHL

## Gallery: Nancy Stahl

*Working with the computer, artists can now miraculously breathe new life into finished works. Nancy Stahl had created this image from one of her handpainted illustrations using Illustrator 3.2 (before there were layers). In order to simplify reworking this image, Stahl began by using Illustrator 5.5 to separate elements into distinct layers: the background, a layer for each of the figures, and a few layers to isolate the various foreground elements. She moved objects to the correct layers by dragging the colored dots representing them in the Layers palette. (See Tip at left, and reworked image on page 194.)*

# Viewing Details

*Using Layers and Views for Organization*

**Overview:** *Establish your working layers; use layers to organize distinct categories of elements; save zoom levels and viewpoints using the New View command.*

---

**WYSIWYG layers?**

In terms of printing, Illustrator isn't yet quite WYSIWYG (What You See Is What You Get). In order to ensure which objects and layers will (and won't) print in *all circumstances*, see step 3 on page 93 for detailed instructions.

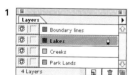

General organizational layers

Additional layers created to isolate categories of elements

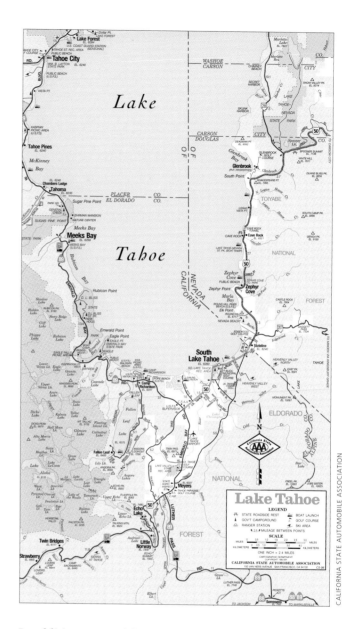

In addition to providing an ideal method for overlapping compositional elements, layers can help organize complex illustrations, even when many of the elements appear to exist on the same visual plane. When the California State Automobile Association (CSAA) creates road maps using Illustrator, the cartography department uses layers to delineate the different categories of labeling information. Even on the fastest computers, however, you can waste a lot of time zooming in and out, hiding and showing layers and toggling various layers between Preview and Artwork modes. That's why the CSAA saves frequently used views to navigate quickly and easily around its large format maps.

1 **Creating organizational layers.** In addition to layers you create for compositional elements (such as background or figures), try creating separate layers for each category of labeling information you're including. If you construct your image with layers organized by the category of element, it becomes very simple to view and change all similar text or objects at once. For its Lake Tahoe map, the CSAA created individual layers for park lands, creeks, lakes and boundary lines, as well as layers for roads, type, symbols and the legend.

2 **Saving frequently used views.** Instead of wasting precious time zooming in and out of your image and scrolling around to find a specific detail, you can preserve your current viewpoint for immediate return at another time. Along with "remembering" the specific section you zoomed to, saved views remember which of your layers were in Preview or Artwork modes. To save your current view, simply choose View: New View, name your current view and click OK. Your view will then be added to the bottom of the View menu. Each successive view you save will appear at the bottom of the menu. The CSAA saved separate views for each area of the map requiring repeated attention, which included each of the four corners, the legend box and three additional locations.

3 **Using views.** To recall a saved view, choose the desired view from the list at the bottom of the View menu. Using Edit Views, you can rename or delete views, although you cannot, unfortunately, change the viewpoints themselves. Another glitch is that Edit Views lists the most recently created or renamed view last, not alphabetically, so getting your layers to list in a specific order takes a bit of organization. 

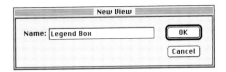

Saving and naming a viewpoint using New View

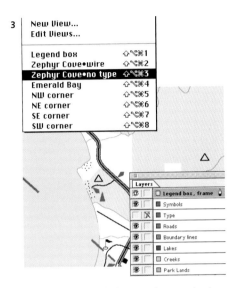

Recalling a view, which resets the zoom level, what portion of the image is visible, and which layers are visible or hidden, locked or unlocked

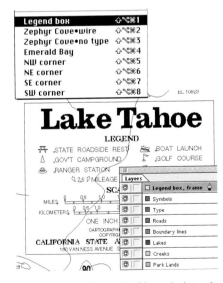

The Legend Box View, with all layers in Artwork

# Layer Registration
*Paste Remembers Layers' Magic Alignment*

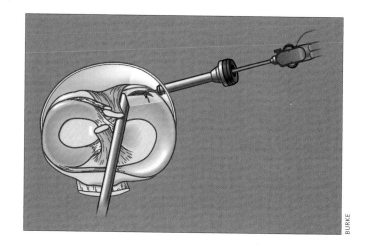

BURKE

**Overview:** *Create enough layers for all stages of your sequence; use New View to save settings for which layers are visible for each stage; control which layers print for proofing; set "Paste Remembers Layers" for separating stages for final printing.*

**1**

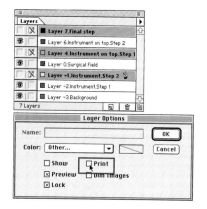

*The background layer (the filled rectangle only) and main surgical layer, "Layer 0"*

**2**

*Selecting saved views to recall various stages*

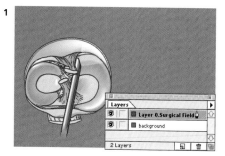

*⌘-selecting multiple layers and double-clicking to disable the Print option in Layer Options*

Organizing a series of interrelated illustrations in perfect registration with each other is simple using layers. This medical illustration shows three of the nine stages in a series that Christopher Burke created for Linvatec Corporation demonstrating the surgical procedure for repairing a knee injury once the fiber-optic light/camera is in place to illuminate the injury site.

**1 Creating layers to illustrate the unifying aspects of the series.** Create the necessary layers into which you'll construct basic elements common to the whole series of illustrations (for layers help, see pages 80–83). Burke's basic layers for this surgical technique illustration were the surgical layer illustrating the knee, and the background.

**2 Simplifying the creation, viewing and proofing of the various stages of your illustration.** Once the unifying aspects of your illustration are in place, use additional layers for creating variants. Use the Layers palette to hide and show various layers and thus isolate each of the different versions. Burke created all stages for the suturing technique in the same document. As he created a layer for a specific stage of the procedure, he would include that stage number in the layer name. For the numbering system, Burke named the main surgical layer "Layer 0"; this layer would appear in every stage. He numbered each progressive layer above it "1, 2, 3…" and then used "–1, –2, –3…" for each subsequent layer below.

When using layers to create a series of related illustrations, use the New View command to help you keep track of which layers need to be visible or hidden for each individual illustration. Once you've done this, choose New View from the View menu and save these settings. By selecting the proper view for each illustration from the bottom of the View menu, you'll easily be able to toggle between each stage in the series.

To avoid having to make unnecessary changes to multiple documents, keep the file together as long as you can. Therefore, the safest way to print proofs of your separate illustrations from this one large file is to use Layer Options to determine which layers won't (or will) print for each version. Hold down your ⌘-key to select the layers you're choosing *not* to print, double-click on one of these selected layers to open Layer Options and disable or enable the Print option to set which layers will print.

**3 Preparing final versions for printing.** In the Layers pop-up menu enable "Paste Remembers Layers." This option ensures that your objects will stay in the correct layers, and that layers will be automatically replicated (or unlocked) as you move them into other files.

To print the final illustrations, copy each completed stage into its own file. Select your saved views for the first stage, making sure all layers necessary to the illustration are visible and unlocked (all Eye icons should be visible and the Edit column should be empty). If you've hidden or locked any elements individually, choose from the Object menu: Unlock All and Show All (or *QK:* ⌘-Option-2, and *QK:* ⌘-Option-3). Then select and copy this version and, in a new document, use Paste In Front (⌘-F). When you use Paste In Front, all needed layers will miraculously appear in the Layers palette and the image will be in perfect registration so you can still move objects back and forth between files. Repeat this step for each stage of the illustration. If you're printing from another application, save these in EPS format (see page 25).

3

Setting "Paste Remembers Layers" in Layer Options and the warning you'll get if you try to paste copied objects to locked or hidden layers (see page 88 for moving objects to other layers)

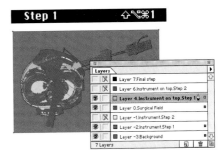

Choosing Step1 view, then selecting all needed layers for copying and pasting into a new file

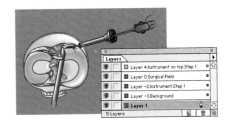

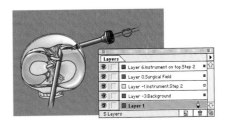

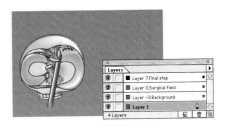

Each of the three stages pasted into its own document, with layers appearing automatically

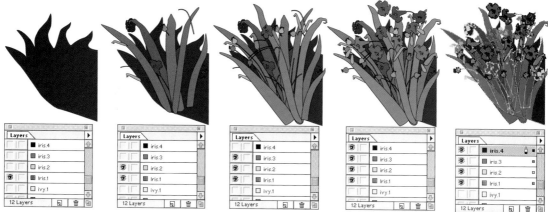

## Gallery: Jeffrey Barney / Barney McKay Design

*For this image, serving as part of a five-tier pop-up promotion for* The Secret Garden, *Jeffrey Barney used dozens of layers to isolate various elements. Barney began by creating seven separate documents which, from front to back, were Ivy, Poppies, Roses, Irises, Mary (the girl), Sunflowers and Tree/Sky—each of the files containing between four and twelve named layers. To arrange elements into the final five files for the pop-up properly, Barney kept the "Paste Remembers Layers" option enabled (see page 92). In this way, he could move objects between files while keeping them on the correct layers and in perfect registration. He needed other arrangements of different layers for other materials, including the close-ups of Irises and Sunflowers for a CD cover (shown with an "onionskin" overlay) and other print materials designed with Scott Franson.*

## Gallery: Dorothea Taylor-Palmer

*For this image, artist Dorothea Taylor-Palmer used the technique of placing one of her drawings on a top layer and painting the colored swatches in layers below (see page 84). She began with a traditional sketch and experimented with running it through a copier while moving it slightly until she captured the illusion of movement she had in mind. After scanning the sketch into Photoshop, Taylor-Palmer saved it as a transparent, 1-bit EPS file, which she then placed into Illustrator. After locking the layer with the EPS, she created another layer and moved it below the first. Into the lower layer, Taylor-Palmer painted swaths of color to show through the white portions of the placed sketch.*

TAYLOR-PALMER

PALMER

## Gallery: Charly Palmer

*Although a professional illustrator for many years, Charly Palmer has only recently begun using Illustrator, under the tutelage of his wife, Dorothea Taylor-Palmer. Even though his method of working is fairly similar to that which Taylor-Palmer used for the image above, his own vision and hand are strongly evident in this profile. After placing a scanned drawing that was saved as a transparent EPS onto an upper layer and locking it, Palmer used colors and blends to complete the composition.*

# Varied Perspective

*Analyzing Different Views of Perspective*

### Advanced Technique

**Overview:** *Draw and scan a sketch; establish working layers using your sketch as a template; in a "Guides" layer, draw a series of lines to establish perspective; make the perspective lines into guides; using layers to control what is visible, construct your image according to the applicable perspective guides.*

The template with a custom layer ready for placement of guides

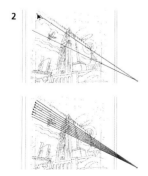

Dragging a perspective line to form a "V," then blending to create in-between perspective lines

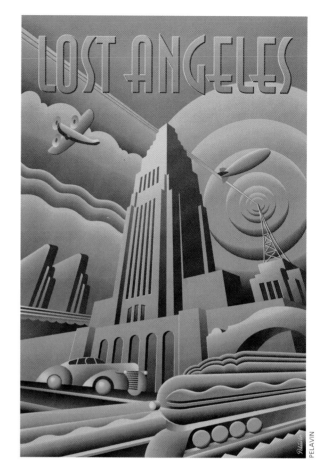

PELAVIN

Since the Italian Renaissance, the conventions of vanishing-point perspective have helped artists to organize their two-dimensional artwork. You can use Adobe Illustrator to establish vanishing points with the help of object guides. The following few pages include perspective approaches by two different artists. This section will not so much teach you how to construct an image using vanishing points as it will help you to translate your knowledge of perspective into techniques to use within Illustrator. The slightly distorted perspective in Danny Pelavin's "Lost Angeles" demonstrates how that knowledge can translate into results that are quite fantastic.

**1 With a scanned sketch as a template, setting up the necessary layers.** Draw a sketch of your composition establishing some basic perspective guidelines. Scan the sketch, save it in TIFF format and open it as a template in Illustrator (see pages 80–83). Once in Illustrator, create the essential number of layers to isolate the various compositional elements, plus one extra layer for your guides.

2 **Establishing the location of vanishing points.** Activate your "Guides" layer (by clicking on the layer name) and lock all other layers. Using your template as a reference, decide where to place the first vanishing point and use the Pen tool to draw a line along the horizon line through the vanishing point. (It is fine if your vanishing point extends beyond the picture border.) With the Direct-selection tool, select the anchor point from the end of the line that is opposite the vanishing point. Grab the point, then hold down your Option key and swing this copy of the line up so it encompasses the uppermost object that will be constructed along the vanishing point. You should now have a "V" that goes from your horizon line, through your vanishing point, then to an upper portion of your composition. To create in-between lines through the same vanishing point, select both of the original lines, use the Blend tool to click first on the outer anchor point of one of the lines, then on the outer anchor point of the other line, and next specify the number of in-between steps. For each different vanishing point, repeat the above procedure. While creating his perspective guides in Illustrator, Pelavin discovered that his previous technique of using a thumbtack and a piece of string was nowhere near as accurate.

3 **Making your perspective lines into guides.** Once you have completed your perspective lines, choose Select All (⌘-A, or Edit: Select All), then choose View: Make Guides (⌘-5). You have now transformed the lines into nonprinting dashed guides. In addition to being able to lock or hide your guides from within the Layers palette, you can take advantage of some unique properties. If you wish to select, align, or manipulate your guides, then disable the View: Lock Guides option (by selecting it).

3

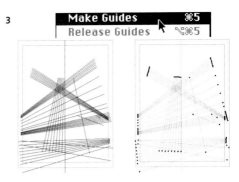

*Perspective lines before and after being made into guides*

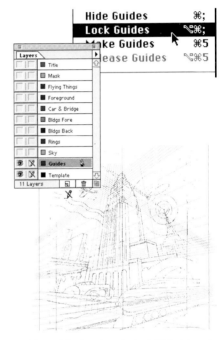

*Locking guides by using the Lock / Unlock toggle from the View menu and locking the layer*

### Grouping guides with objects

When guides are unlocked, you can select them freely as objects. This option applies to horizontal guides dragged from the ruler as well as custom guides. Try grouping guides with related objects so you can move, hide, scale and rotate them along with their associated objects.

**4**

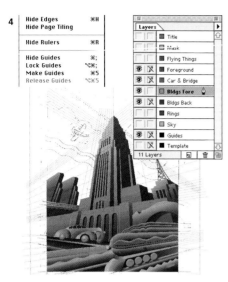

Tools for hiding and showing elements

**5**

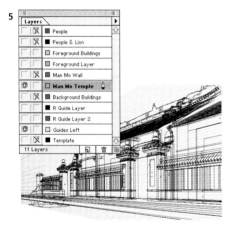

"Guides Left" layer shown with buildings drawn in Artwork mode on Man Mo Temple layer

TATE

Tate's final image

Note, however, that the Lock/Unlock Guides option will affect all open documents. If you wish to transform your guides back into objects, unlock them, select the guides you wish to convert, and choose Release Guides from the View menu.

**4 Creating your illustration using guides and templates as necessary.** As you actually create your illustration, control what you're viewing on the screen at any one time with the View and Object menus. Also, from the Layers palette, toggle to control which layers are visible, hidden, locked, unlocked, or in Preview or Artwork mode.

**5 Variations on a theme.** Pelavin's solution to perspective guides on the Mac is a reflection of his drawing style. Other artists use the same techniques differently. For his "Man Mo Temple," instead of reserving one layer for perspective guides, Clarke Tate used three separate layers. Because of the nature of the architectural detailing he was creating, Tate wanted more than just general perspective lines; he wanted to be able to actually create every building line from his perspective grid. Since having so many lines is visually distracting, Tate created two layers for his right-facing perspectives, each containing every other line, with a third layer reserved for the left-facing perspective. With this system, Tate could use the Layers palette to show only the specific perspective lines he required for the construction of each object. ◐

**Scanning true horizontals and verticals for tracing**

When preparing templates for detailed renderings that rely on true horizontal and vertical lines (such as the architectural images in this technique or the Andrea Kelley computer renderings on pages 114 and 158), you must scan your template image into the computer perfectly straight. Take an image (or copy of an image) and cut the edge of the paper perfectly square to the image so you can line up the paper edge to the edge of the scanner bed itself. — *Andrea Kelley*

# Blends & Gradients

# 5

This chapter illustrates many uses for blends and gradients, and will start with an explanation of how they differ.

## BLENDS

Think of blends as a way to "morph" one object or color, or shape and color, to another. After selecting two objects, click with the Blend tool *exactly* on corresponding anchor points on each object and specify the number of steps you want to place in between. Using fewer steps results in clearly distinguishable objects, while a larger number of steps results in an almost "airbrushed" effect.

When the blend first appears, it will be selected and grouped. If you Undo immediately (⌘-Z), the blend will be deleted, and your two source objects will be selected, ready for you to blend again. If you later wish to change your blend after completing it, you must select the blend only (by clicking twice with Group-selection tool), delete the blend, select your two source objects and blend again.

### Recoloring blends

Although Illustrator 7.0 doesn't yet include a "live blend" feature (as found in FreeHand or CorelDraw), you *can* use filters to recolor groups of blended objects. Direct-select and recolor the fill for the start and/or end objects in a blend (this doesn't affect strokes, nor compound paths). Then select the entire blend and choose Filter: Colors: Blend Front to Back. Your object fill colors will be reblended based on the new start and end colors. Also try Blend Horizontally/Vertically, Adjust and Saturate! 🐾

*"B" Blend  tool*
*"G" Gradient tool*

## Adding color to your gradient

To add a color to your gradient:

- Drag a swatch from the Color or Swatches palette to the gradient slider until you see a vertical line, indicating where the new color stop will be added.
- Drag the swatch from the fill icon at the bottom of the Toolbox, as long as it's a solid color.
- Hold down your Option key to drag a copy of a color stop.
- Option-drag one stop over another to *swap* their colors.
- Click on the lower edge of a gradient to add a new stop.
- To load a color from anywhere on your screen into the current, selected color stop, Shift-click with the Eyedropper tool.

## Don't lose that gradient!

Because gradients in Illustrator 7 are not automatically stored, you must take steps to ensure you don't inadvertently lose the gradient you are masterfully creating:

- To design a gradient for only one object, keep your object selected and see your gradient develop within the object itself.
- To design a gradient for later use, or for multiple objects, drag the initial gradient square from its palette to the Swatches palette to store it. Keep Option-dragging from your gradient square to that initial swatch to update the stored gradient.

## GRADIENTS

Gradients, now in their own palette, are purely color transitions that you can select from the Swatches or Gradient palette. To open the Gradient palette: double-click on the Gradient tool, click on the gradient icon at the bottom of the Swatches palette, or choose Window: Show Gradient. Gradients can be either radial (circular from the center) or linear (in straight lines). Make your own gradients by placing and spacing pointers (stops) representing colors along the lower edge of the color scale in the Gradient palette, and by adjusting the midpoint of the color transition by sliding the shapes along the top of the scale. You can adjust the length, direction and center-point location of selected gradients, as well as unify blends across multiple objects, by clicking and dragging with the Gradient tool (pages 108–111). To fill type with gradients, convert the type to an outline (see page 138). To create the illusion of a gradient within a stroke, convert the stroke to a filled object (see Tip on page 64).

### Gradients into Blends...

Choose Object: Expand Fill to convert any gradient into a blend. You'll be prompted to specify how many steps you want when the gradient is converted into a blend. Expand Fill doesn't group the objects once the expand function is completed; so make sure you group (⌘-G) immediately after Expand Fill so you don't end up having a large number of ungrouped objects to deal with! Another use for Expand Fill is if you're trying to include a gradient within a pattern (see page 75).

## Watch that swatch when you Option-drag...

Since stored gradients aren't "auto-updated" as you edit them, you must Option-drag a new swatch over an old one to manually update it (see Tip at left). But be careful—it's easy to accidentally "update" the wrong swatch if you're not paying attention! This caution applies to Option-drag updating or replacing any swatch.

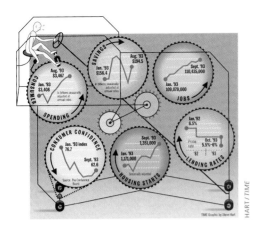

HART / TIME

**Gallery: Steve Hart / *Time***

*Gradients make shifts of color very simple; Steve Hart first designed a gradient for one gear, then only needed to duplicate the gradient and change the color for each of the other gears.*

HESS / AGNEW MOYER SMITH, INC.

**Gallery: Kurt Hess / Agnew Moyer Smith, Inc.**

*Blends are necessary for creating realistic, irregularly shaped reflections of light (see page 112 for help with realistic blends).*

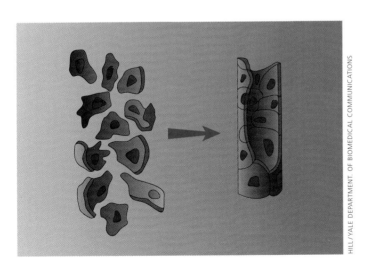

HILL / YALE DEPARTMENT. OF BIOMEDICAL COMMUNICATIONS

**Gallery: Wendolyn Hill / Yale Department of Biomedical Communications**

*Using the Gradient tool, Wendolyn Hill changed the direction of the gradient to create the illusion of inside versus outside in this medical illustration of "vasculogenesis," or vessel formation.*

# Examining Blends

*Learning When to Use Gradients or Blends*

**Overview:** *Examine your objects; for linear or circular fills, create basic gradients; for contouring fills into complex objects, create blends.*

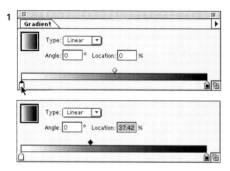

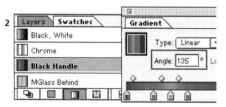

*Adjusting the placement of colors, and then rate of color transition in the Gradient palette*

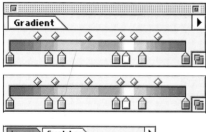

*Selecting a gradient from the Swatches palette and setting the gradient Angle*

*One gradient duplicated and altered for application to different related objects*

You need to take a number of factors into consideration when you're deciding whether to create color transitions with blends or gradients. Steve Hart's magnifying glass, created for *Time* magazine, is a clear-cut example demonstrating when to use gradients or blends.

**1 Designing gradients.** Select an object you'd like to fill with a linear gradient. Open the Gradient palette. Click on the gradient icon at the bottom of the Swatches palette. Choose Name from the Swatches pop-up menu and click on the "Black, White" gradient. This initially minimal gradient has two colors: white (at the left) and black (at the right). Click on the left pointer to display its position on the scale from 0–100% (in this case 0%). Slide the pointer to the right to increase the percentage displayed in the scale, and increase the black area of the gradient. Click on the bottom edge of the scale to add additional pointers. Click on a pointer to access its numeric position, or to change its color or tint. Between every two pointers is a diamond shape indicating the midpoint of the color transition (from 0–100% between each color pair). Grab and drag a diamond to adjust the color transition rate, or type a new position into the percent field.

**2 Storing and applying gradients and making adjustments.** To store a new gradient you've made within a selected object, Option-click the New Swatch icon and name your gradient. For help adding color to gradients, see Tip below and page 100. Hart filled his magnifying glass handle with a gradient set at a 135° angle (in the Gradient palette). He created slightly different variants for gradients representing the metal rings around the outside, along the inside, and inside behind the glass. To create variants of a current gradient, make color adjustments first, then Option-click the New Swatch icon to name your new gradient. Although you can experiment with changing the angle of a gradient, be forewarned that continued adjustments to a gradient in the Gradient palette, will not update the gradient stored in the Swatches palette! See Tips on bottom of page 100.

**3 Using blends for irregular or contoured transitions.**
For domed, kidney-shaped or contoured objects (such as shadows), only a blend will do. Make two objects with the same number of points (try scaling one to create the other). Set each to the desired color and click on a related anchor point on one, then the other, with the Blend tool. Try setting the number of steps that the Blend dialog box recommends; you can experiment with fewer, but there is rarely a need for more. The more similar the colors, the fewer steps you'll need. (See "blending" in the *User Guide* for hints on troubleshooting blends.) Hart used blends for only the glow in the glass (20 steps), the knob of the handle (22 steps) and the shadow (12 steps).

---

## Automatically updating colors

For Gradients:
- If you use spot colors (see *Chapter 3*) for your gradients, changes to your spot color will automatically update whatever gradients use that color.

For Blends:
- If you blend between two objects that are tints of the same spot color (Hint: Tints of 0% = White), then changes to the spot color will also update the blend!

—*Agnew Moyer Smith, Inc.*

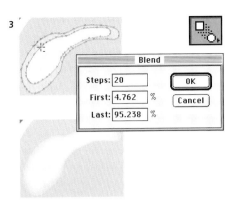

3

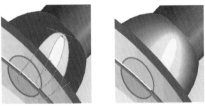

*Clicking first on a selected point of one path, then on a selected point of the other to open the dialog box to specify 20 steps; and the blended objects*

*Two selected paths, and after a 22-step blend*

*Before and after a 12-step blend to create a shadow*

*The final image as it appeared in* Time

# Shades of Blends

*Creating Architectural Linear Shading*

**Overview:** *Create an architectural form using rectangles; copy and paste one rectangle in front; delete the top and bottom paths and blend between the two sides.*

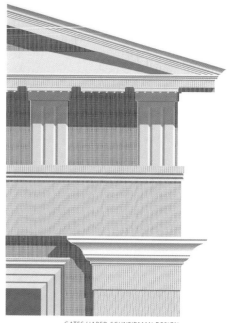

GATES / JARED SCHNEIDMAN DESIGN

**1**

*A selected rectangle copied and pasted in front in full view, and in close-up*

**2**

*The top and bottom deleted with the sides selected*

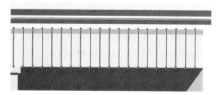

*The full blend and a close-up detail (⌘-H hides— or shows—selection edges; see page 19)*

Without much difficulty, Illustrator can help simulate the traditional artistic conventions for rendering architectural details. Jared Schneidman Design developed a simple but exacting method to apply vertical line shading.

**1 Creating an architectural structure.** After establishing the overall form, color and tonality of your illustration, select and copy one rectangle. Choose ⌘-F (Edit: Paste In Front) to place the copy on top, then set the fill to None and the stroke to .1-pt Black. Choose Window: Show Info to note the line's width in points (to change your ruler units, see Tip, "Changing measurement units," page 21). Calculate the width of the rectangle divided by the spacing you'd like between lines. Subtract 2 (for the sides you have) to find the proper number of steps for this blend.

**2 Deleting the top and bottom and blending the sides.** Deselect the copy, Shift-Direct-select the top and bottom paths and delete, leaving the sides selected. With the Blend tool, click on the top point of each side and specify the number of steps you determined above. 🖱️

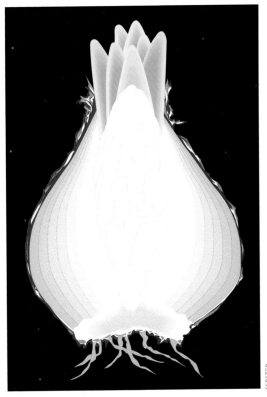

FERSTER

## Gallery: Gary Ferster

*For his client Langeveld Bulb, Gary Ferster used blends to create the in-between layers in this flower bulb. He began by styling the outer peel with a .5-pt stroke in a dark brown custom color and filled the object with a lighter brown custom color. He then created the inner layer, filled it white and gave it a .5-pt white stroke. Selecting both objects, Ferster specified a six-step blend that simultaneously "morphed" each progressive layer into the next while lightening the layers towards white. Blends were also used to create the leafy greens, yellow innards and all the other soft transitions between colors.*

## Popular San Francisco Buildings

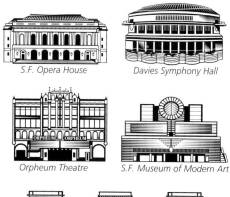

S.F. Opera House

Davies Symphony Hall

Orpheum Theatre

S.F. Museum of Modern Art

Palace of Legion of Honor

## Fish in the San Francisco Bay

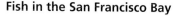

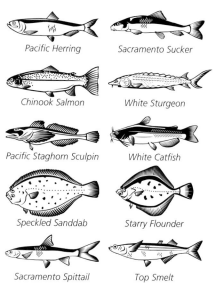

Pacific Herring

Sacramento Sucker

Chinook Salmon

White Sturgeon

Pacific Staghorn Sculpin

White Catfish

Speckled Sanddab

Starry Flounder

Sacramento Spittail

Top Smelt

SHOULAK / SAN FRANCISCO EXAMINER

**San Francisco Museum of Modern Art**

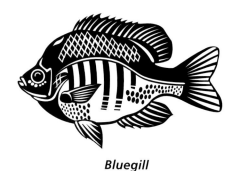

**Bluegill**

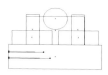 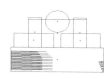

## Gallery: Joe Shoulak / *San Francisco Examiner*

*Joe Shoulak frequently uses blends to create in-between repetitive shapes. Given the deadlines at a busy newspaper, the Blend tool has proved an essential production tool for generating the horizontal and vertical lines in buildings (for an article on "Retrofitting the Arts") as well as the sequence of organic shapes (as in the fins of fish for the series "Bay in Peril"). Shoulak also relies heavily on filters—using the Offset Path filter to create white inset shapes that follow the contours of outlines, and the Outline Path filter to convert all stroked lines in final images to filled objects (so he doesn't accidentally resize without properly scaling the line weight). See Chapter 6 for more on filters.*

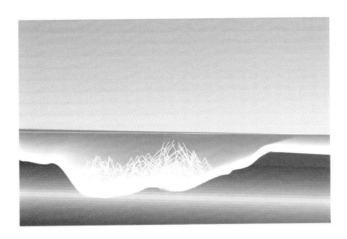

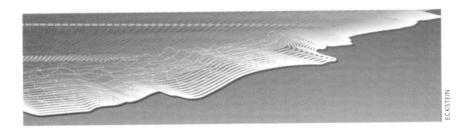

ECKSTEIN

## Gallery: Linda Eckstein

*Linda Eckstein created these beautiful seascapes in Illustrator using blends. Instead of merely control-ling the regularity of blends to depict the ocean, Eckstein needed to control the irregularity of the blends as well. On the back layer of her image are blends that establish both the general composition and the broad color schemes. On top of these tonal-filled, object blends are irregularly shaped linear blends that form the waves and surf. Using the Direct-selection tool, she isolated individual points and groups of points to stretch and distort the waves.*

# Unified Gradients

*Redirecting Fills with the Gradient Tool*

**Overview:** *Fill objects with gradients; use the Gradient tool to adjust fill length, direction, center location, and to unify fills across multiple objects.*

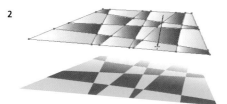

The Gradient palette, and the Gradient tool (This tool has the same name and icon as the one in Photoshop, but is completely different.)

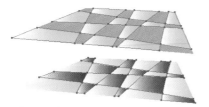

Filling the first group with the cyan gradient fill, then the other group with the purple gradient

2

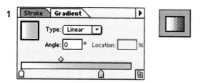

Clicking and dragging with the Gradient tool to unify the gradient fill across multiple objects, and to establish the gradient's rate and direction

### How long can a gradient be?

Click and drag with the Gradient tool anywhere in your image window; you don't need to stay within the objects themselves. Also, see the *Wow!* disk for Eve Elberg's "Comet" Gradient tool exercise.

The Gradient tool allows you to customize the length and direction of gradient fills, and to stretch gradients across multiple objects. For this *Medical Economics* magazine illustration, Dave Joly used the Gradient tool to customize each gradient and unify the checkerboard floor.

**1 Filling objects with the same gradient.** Select multiple objects and fill them with the same gradient by clicking on a gradient fill in the Swatches palette. Keep your objects selected.

**2 Unifying gradients with the Gradient tool.** Using the Gradient tool from the Toolbox, click and drag from the point you want the gradient to begin to where you want it to end. Hold down the Shift key if you want to constrain the angle of the gradient. To relocate a radial gradient's center, just click with the Gradient tool. Experiment until you get the desired effect. To create his checkerboard, Joly used the Knife tool to segment the floor, grouped every other tile together and filled these with a cyan-to-white gradient fill. He then duplicated the gradient, changed the start color to purple and applied this purple gradient to the remaining tiles. With all tiles selected, he again applied the Gradient tool. 🌀

GORSKA

## Gallery: Caryl Gorska

*Caryl Gorska created "Bountiful Harvest" as a package design for Nunes Farms' dried fruits, nuts and chocolates. She used the Gradient tool to customize her radial blends (made of process colors). Parchment paper, scanned in Photoshop and saved in EPS, is the background layer (see Chapter 4).*

### Resetting gradients to the default settings

After you make angle adjustments with the Gradient tool, other objects that you fill with the same or other gradients will still have the altered angle. To "re-zero" gradient angles, Deselect All (⌘-Shift-A) and fill with None by pressing the "/" key. When you next choose a gradient, angles will have the default setting. Or, for linear gradients, you can type a zero in the Angle field.

GAVIN

## Gallery: Kerry Gavin

*Kerry Gavin is the first to admit that without the Gradient tool, he couldn't have created the image "Golden Parachutes." The miniature version of "Parachutes" at the right shows the figure in the room without out the benefit of the Gradient tool. The sense of place and light that is so present in Gavin's final version is noticeably absent in the miniature, where the fills aren't customized.*

### Gallery: Hugh Whyte / Lehner & Whyte

*In this image designed for a spring calendar, Hugh Whyte used gradients and the Gradient tool to create a colorful, cut-out look that is both flat and volumetric. The Artwork view at the right reveals that Whyte constructed the image entirely of gradients, with no blends.*

# Unlocking Realism
*Creating Metallic Reflections with Blends*

**Overview:** *Form the basic shapes of objects; create tonal boundaries for future blends that follow the contours of the objects; copy, scale, recolor and adjust the anchor points of tonal boundaries; blend highlights and shadows.*

1

*Designing the basic objects and choosing a base tone (Note: Gray strokes added to distinguish objects)*

*Creating tonal boundaries for future blends by following the contours of the objects*

Achieving photorealism with Illustrator may appear pro-hibitively complex and intimidating, but with a few simple rules-of-thumb, some careful planning and the eye of an artist, it can be done. Brad Neal, of Thomas•Bradley Illustration & Design, demonstrates with this image that you don't need an airbrush to achieve metallic reflectivity, specular highlights or warm shadows.

**1 Preparing a detailed sketch that incorporates a strong light source, and setting up your palette.**
Before you actually start your illustration, create a sketch that establishes the direction of your light source. Then, in Illustrator, set up your color palette (see *Chapter 3*). Choose one color as a "base tone," the initial tint from which all blends will be built, and fill the entire object with that value. After you create the basic outlines of your illustration, work in Artwork mode to create separate paths—following the contours of your objects—for each of your major color transitions. After completing the initial line drawing of the lock set, Neal visually and then physically "mapped" out the areas that would contain the

shading. He added a few highlights and reflections in the later stages of the project, but the majority of blends were mapped out in advance.

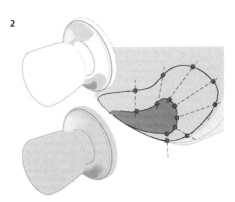

*Pasting In Front a scaled down and adjusted copy with the same number of aligned points*

**2 Using your color transition paths to create blends.**
Next, use the contouring paths you've created to map out your tonal boundaries. Choose one of the objects and fill it with the same color and tonal value as its underlying shape. In the Neal locks, this initial color is always the same color and value selected for the base color. Then, copy the object and use ⌘-F to Paste In Front. Next, fill this copy with a highlight or shadow value, scale it down and manipulate it into the correct position to form the highlight or shadow area. You can accomplish this step by one of two methods: by scaling the object using the Scale tool or by selecting and pulling in individual anchor points with the Direct-selection tool. In order to ensure smooth blends without ripples or irregular transitions, the anchor points of the inner and outer objects must be as closely aligned as possible and must contain the same number of points; *this is a critical stage of the process.*

Finally, to complete this highlight or shadow, select both objects and, with the Blend tool, click on a selected anchor point of one object, next on the corresponding anchor point of the other object, then specify the minimal size blend to achieve a smooth look. The blend in Figure 2 required eight in-between steps.

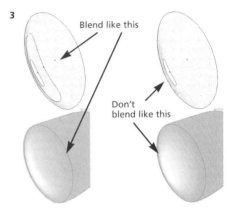

*Adding an in-between contour to help control the rate and shape of blends; blending with too few contours flattens the image*

**3 Blending in smaller increments.** Some blend situations may require more than two objects to achieve the desired look. For instance, to control the rate at which the tone changes or the way an object transforms throughout the blended area, you may wish to add an intermediate object and blend in two stages, instead of one.

**4 Using blends to soften hard transitions.** Always use blends when making tonal transitions, even when you need a stark contrast shadow or highlight. A close look at Neal's shadow reveals a very short but distinct blend. 🌀

*Long, close-up and Artwork close-up views of highlight and shadow transitions*

# Blending Realism

*Keeping Blends Clean and Accessible*

**Overview:** *Delete the side of a rectangle; offset the top and bottom open ends horizontally; blend this open object with another smaller, darker object; place caps on top and bottom; create contouring blends on the sides.*

The final illustration in Artwork mode

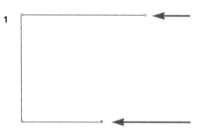

Two copies of a rectangle pasted on top with right side removed and points shifted left

Before and after blending offset objects

A quick look at an illustration in Artwork mode usually reveals a lot about how an image is constructed. However, when you look at Andrea Kelley's Apple Computer product illustrations in Artwork mode, you would probably mistakenly guess that she uses gradients to create her tonal changes. But since her renderings are used on-screen as well as printed, Kelley often uses blends for more exacting control over her tones (gradients can look banded on the screen even if they print well). Her techniques can help you create a monitor screen with a soft, ambient lighting effect.

1 **Creating an "offset" blend.** Make a rectangle and fill it with a 35% tint of black. Copy and Hide (Object menu, or *QK:* ⌘-3) the rectangle, then use Paste In Front (⌘-F) to place the copy on top. Direct-select and delete the right side of the path. Since open objects remain filled in Illustrator, the object looks identical in Preview mode. With the Direct-selection tool, grab the top right point and slide it to the left slightly (about .25"), using the Shift key to constrain movement horizontally. Then grab the lower right point and slide it over to the halfway point on the rectangle (again, use your Shift key). Now select and copy the adjusted object, use Paste In Front to move the

copy and change the tint of this new object to 65%. Use the same technique you did before, but this time slide the bottom right point all the way to the left and the top right point over towards the left corner. (This polygon should look almost like a triangle.) Next, select the top right points of the two objects you just made, click on each point with the Blend tool and use the recommended number of steps. In Artwork mode, instead of the expected sea of diagonally blended lines running across the screen, your monitor should appear "clean" and uncomplicated.

2 **Creating the rounded top and bottom.** Object: Show your hidden back rectangle (*QK:* ⌘-Option-3). With the Pen tool, draw a bow-shaped "cap" filled with a 35% tint of black that overlaps the top of your blend with a long, almost horizontal curve. Have the points meet beyond the blend on either side, arcing into a bow shape above. To add shadow detail, copy the bottom path of the bow (the long, almost horizontal line) and Paste In Front to place a copy of the path. Change the Fill style of this path to None, with a .25-pt stroke weight at a 40% tint of black. Lastly, copy and reflect the full filled cap along the horizontal axis, place it along the bottom of the blended monitor screen and set it to a 10% tint of black.

3 **Contouring the sides.** To create the illusion that the monitor is inset, create three long, overlapping rectangles on the left edge of your blended monitor screen, running from cap to cap. (Adjust the points as necessary so the objects run flush against the cap.) From left to right, make the rectangles 10%, 50% and 45% tints of black. Select the right two rectangles and blend between them, then lock the blend so you can easily blend the left two rectangles. Repeat from the right side of the monitor with rectangles of 5%, 10% and 25% (from left to right). You can make the monitor case the same way as the screen, but shade the case with 10% on the left, blending to 25% on the right. (See *Chapter 8*'s Advanced Techniques for blending and masking curved objects.) 🖱

2

*Rounded "caps" put on top and bottom of the blended screen*

3

*Placing three rectangles of different shades on the left side of the screen (deleting the sides to reduce clutter), then blending the middle object first to the dark, then to the light*

*Placing three rectangles of different shades on the right side of the screen (again, deleting the sides to reduce clutter), then blending the middle object first to the light, then to the dark*

*The final monitor screen in Preview*

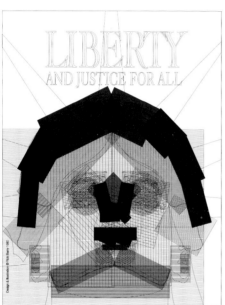 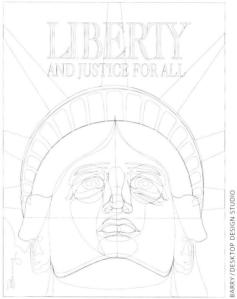

## Gallery: Rick Barry / DeskTop Design Studio

*To demonstrate the difference between blends and gradients, Rick Barry took an image he created with blends in Illustrator 3.2 (upper left Preview, lower left Artwork), selected the blends (by clicking twice with the Group-selection tool on one of the blend objects) and deleted them. The objects used to create the blends remained, and Barry filled these objects with custom gradients and then adjusted the rate and range of the gradients with the Gradient tool (upper right Preview, lower right Artwork).*

# Pathfinder & Other Filters

## 6

You'll save a lot of time constructing images in Illustrator if you learn to use the Pathfinder and other plug-in filters. However, filters can irrevocably change your objects, limiting their editability, so you should *always* work on *copies* of your objects in files that are backed up.

Instead of memorizing the filters, learn what effects and techniques are possible; then locate the filters most likely to result in the desired effect. If the filter doesn't work as expected, use Undo and try another. The plug-ins available to you will vary depending on your version of Illustrator, and which third-party plug-ins you use.

### PATHFINDER FILTERS

The charts on pages 120–121 demonstrate Pathfinder filters as applied to simple geometric objects, and to *Wow!* artists' work as further explanation. Also, see the Plug-ins folder on the *Wow!* disk for printable charts detailing the settings for the more complex filters.

Outside of making sure you apply filters to copies and not originals, here are a few more tips for working with Pathfinder filters:

### • Pathfinder Options

Illustrator 7 no longer requires you to reset Pathfinder Options each time you start your program, and the default settings are set more logically so that "Divide" and "Outline" leave fill styles intact. Choose Object: Pathfinder: Options to make any changes to this setup.

## Find filters (or plug-ins) fast!

Illustrator 7 reorganized the locations of some filters and plug-ins:

- **Objects** filters Outline Path, Offset Path, and Add Anchor Points are in the Object: Path menu (Mac users see top Tip on page 119). Align and Distribution are now **Align** palette functions.
- **Pathfinder** filters are in the Object menu (⌘-4 applies the last-used *Pathfinder* filter).
- **Select** filters are in the Edit menu (see pages 118–119).
- **Star, Polygon, Spiral, Twirl** and **Knife** are now in the toolbox (see Tip on page 8 for details).
- **Text filters** are built into the Type menu (see Chapter 7).
- **Transform Each** (Object: Transform menu) replaces Rotate, Scale and Move Each. **IMPORTANT:** *Using this filter will transform each object independently even if they're grouped!*
- To make an EPS Riders file (it used to be in the Filter menu) see the *User Guide*.

When you create a compound path of multiple objects (see "Make compound paths" at right), the back object will "drop out" as white where it overlaps other objects. To avoid this, temporarily add another object and choose Object: Arrange: Send To Back. After compounding all the objects, Direct-select and delete this extra object and proceed.

See the following for more info:

• For step-by-step and Galleries using **Ink Pen** and **Path Pattern** see pages 124–128 and the "Plug-ins Folder" on the *Wow!* disk (this includes the "Ink Pen Effects.pdf" demystifier by Victor von Salza, the "Cohen/ H-K Ink Pen" detailing the fish Gallery on page 128, and custom hatch Ink Pen patterns). Also see the top Tip, page 117.

• For **Text** filters, see *Chapter 7*.

• For Filter: Colors: **Overprint Black**, see Tip on page 55.

• For Object: Pathfinder: **Trap**, see page 64 and the *User Guide*.

Numerous third-party companies provide a wide range of plug-ins, tools and filters. See the *Wow!* disk for samples and demos.

• **With most Pathfinder filters, the top color will be maintained.** With the notable exception of the Minus Front filter, which subtracts the front object from the back (keeping the back object's color), most Pathfinder filters that combine objects will result in an object the color of the topmost object. Be aware that some filters (such as Merge and Trim) delete the path strokes of your objects (another reason to keep originals).

• **Make compound paths to run Pathfinder filters on multiple separate objects.** Some filters, such as Minus Front (or Minus Back), result in one single object, affected by all other objects. If, instead, you wish to maintain multiple separate objects that are affected by just one single object, copy the group of objects you want to have operate together and choose Object: Compound Paths: Make (⌘-8). All objects will now be styled as the backmost object (if your objects overlap, see the Tip at left) and will operate as a unit when you apply the filter. Then, use the Direct-selection tool to edit individual objects. ✎

### THE IMPROVED, THE MOVED, AND THE CHANGED...

Distort filters **Scribble and Tweak**, and **Punk and Bloat** combine previously separate filters (see RandyL's Special charts for these in the Plug-ins folder on the *Wow!* disk). The fairly new **Zig Zag** filter, amazingly enough, allows you to "zigzag" your objects in a variety of ways.

The Objects: **Mosaic** filter is improved; any linked or embedded bitmap can be used, and it automatically groups the completed mosaic. The **Adjust Colors** filter, now includes a Preview option and lets you color-convert color modes between CMYK, RGB and Grayscale. With the **Saturate** filter (integrating the previously separate Saturate, Saturate More, Desaturate and Desaturate More filters) lets you adjust the saturation of objects *and* image objects via sliders, or numerically. (For a Technique using Adjust Colors and Saturate, see pages 124–127.)

Having trouble selecting all but a few objects? Select the few you don't want, and choose Edit: **Select Inverse**.

A wonderful filter is Edit: **Select Stray Points**, which selects lone points so that you can delete them before they cause trouble. Illustrator's Object: Path **Cleanup** can also delete stray points. But beware: it could also delete unstroked, unfilled objects that you need (like masks). **Note:** *Selecting a lone point by accident can prevent you from Joining properly, or could even cause your objects to disappear if you choose to mask when a point is on top!*

And if you're one of those who don't like the 7.0 version of **Fill & Stroke** for Mask, see page 140. Aficionados of the **Ink Pen** much prefer the Illustrator 6 version, and moving **Add Anchor Points** to the Edit: Path menu means it can't be reapplied with a keystroke— but see Tip, top right, for a Mac workaround. (Ink Pen users also see Tip, "More info on these filters," at left.) 🔘

## PHOTOSHOP AND THIRD-PARTY RASTER FILTERS
### The fun, the fear

Web and multimedia designers will love being able to use Photoshop compatible filters from within Illustrator. If your files are going to be "Screen Resolution" (72–96 ppi), being able to use third-party filters in Illustrator is great (see *Chapter 10* for more on working in RGB and filtering). However, if you are working for print, there are some intrinsic problems with filtering raster images:

- **Most Photoshop filters work in RGB, not CMYK.**
  This is not a problem, per se, since you can now work in RGB in Illustrator, but if you apply your filters to an RGB image and forget to convert it to CMYK, then colors won't print as you expect. Also, simply converting colors to RGB and back to CMYK can generate muddy colors (see top Tip on page 24). Don't forget to always "save as" a version of your file before you convert color modes.

- **Running filters on a linked image embeds it.** This means that you can't auto-update the file as you can with linked images, and this will also increase your file size. (See *Chapter 9* for more on linking and embedding.) 🔘

**Ink Pen and Add Anchor Points**

Adobe won't sanction this: Mac users put the Illustrator 6 version of these into the 7 Plug-ins folder for Filter menu access; this also means you can use ⌘-E to repeat Add Anchor Points filter (you can't repeat if from Object: Path)! —*Victor von Salza*

**Reopening the previous filter**

To apply the last-used "Filter menu" choice, select it from the top of the Filter menu (⌘-E). The next menu item (⌘-Option-E) reopens the last filter. To apply the last-used *Pathfinder* filter: ⌘-4.

**Filtering image-object edges**

Many Photoshop filters will not affect the *edges* of "image-objects" when applied in Illustrator. To filter the entire image-object, including the edges, place a rectangle filled with white behind the object, then group and rasterize. *Now* apply the filter! —*Sandee Cohen*

**Use an alias for those filters!**

To gain access to Photoshop plug-ins from within Illustrator, make an alias of (Mac) or shortcut for (Windows) the Photoshop Plug-ins folder to put into the Illustrator Plug-ins folder. The next time you launch Illustrator, those filters will be available for *image objects* (see *Chapter 9* for more on this).

# Pathfinder Filters

*The default settings for 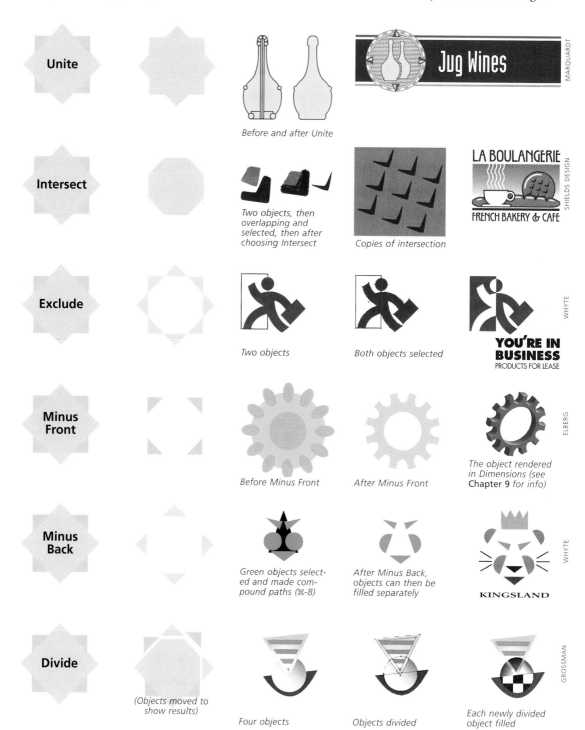 were used unless otherwise noted. Artists' work may use custom settings.*

**Unite**

*Before and after Unite*

MARQUARDT

**Intersect**

*Two objects, then overlapping and selected, then after choosing Intersect*

*Copies of intersection*

SHIELDS DESIGN

LA BOULANGERIE

FRENCH BAKERY & CAFE

**Exclude**

*Two objects*

*Both objects selected*

WHYTE

YOU'RE IN BUSINESS

PRODUCTS FOR LEASE

**Minus Front**

*Before Minus Front*

*After Minus Front*

*The object rendered in Dimensions (see Chapter 9 for info)*

ELBERG

**Minus Back**

*Green objects selected and made compound paths (⌘-8)*

*After Minus Back, objects can then be filled separately*

KINGSLAND

WHYTE

**Divide**

*(Objects moved to show results)*

*Four objects*

*Objects divided*

*Each newly divided object filled*

GROSSMAN

# Pathfinder Filters (continued)

*The default settings for*  *were used unless otherwise noted. Artists' work may use custom settings.*

## Outline

*(Objects moved and line weights **increased** to .5-pt to show results)*

*Before Outline*

*After Outline, and resetting line weight*

STEUER

## Trim

*(Objects moved to show results)*

*Before Trim; in Preview and Artwork*

*After Trim; overlaps are reduced, BUT strokes are lost*

SHIELDS DESIGN

## Merge

*(Objects moved to show results)*

*Before Merge in Artwork*

*After Merge; like fills are united, BUT strokes are lost*

STAHL

## Crop

*A copy of the fish in front to use for Crop*

*After Crop; objects are now separated*

DROBLAS GREENBERG

## Hard

*Same color objects don't mix, so overlapping objects were colored differently*

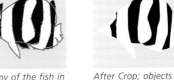

*After Hard filter; Each overlap is now a separate object*

*After using the Eyedropper to switch the colors in the front objects*

MARGOLIS PINEO (digitized by Steuer)

## Soft

*Before Soft filter; the blue wave overlaps the detail along the bottom of the rocks*

*After Soft filter (see "SandeeC's Mix Soft Chart" in the Plug-ins folder on the **Wow!** disk)*

FERSTER

# Practical Path-cuts

*Preparing for Blends with Pathfinder Filters*

**Overview:** *Use a bisecting path with Divide; combine drawn elements and copies using Unite; create see-through details using Exclude.*

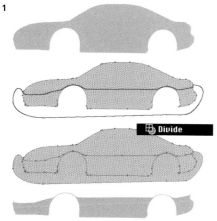

An object; drawing a bisecting path; selecting and dividing; extraneous objects deleted

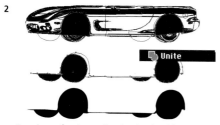

Drawing a fender-well; selecting it with copies of tires to unite; the final path united

The outer portion of the wiper and drawing the inner objects; selecting them both to exclude

Pathfinder filters can be astounding time-savers for creating realistic renderings. To form the basic shapes then used for photorealistic blends, Thomas Neal (of Thomas• Bradley Illustration & Design) used to painstakingly cut and join the paths using the Scissors tool with Average and Join (see page 52 for cutting and joining, and pages 112 and 162 to see the resulting blends). Pathfinder filters practically automate Neal's tasks for preparing basic objects to use for blending. (See *Chapter 4* for help with hiding, locking and reordering objects.)

1 **Using Divide to create a subsection of your car.** Copy your car-body object, Lock it (Object menu, or *QK:* ⌘-2) and use Paste In Front to paste a copy exactly on top. Using the Pen tool, draw a path bisecting the car, then loop the path around to create a closed path surrounding the car so that the car can only be divided along your bisecting path. Select both objects and choose Object: Pathfinder: Divide, then delete the extraneous objects.

2 **Using Unite to create the undercarriage.** Using the Pen tool, draw a path that defines the shadow in the fender-wells. Copy and Paste In Front (⌘-F) the four wheels, and use ⌘-G to group them. With the Shift key, select the fender-wells with the grouped wheels and choose Object: Pathfinder: Unite.

3 **Creating see-through details.** Create an object that forms the outline of your wiper. Using filled black objects, draw the areas you want to cut out of the outline. Select the outer and inner objects and choose Object: Pathfinder: Exclude.

## Gallery: Michael Kline / Acme Design

*When Michael Kline uses Pathfinder filters, he always uses a copy of the object in case he needs that object again for something else. With this illustration for* Kids Discover *magazine, Kline kept an earlier version of the house handy so that, if he needed to, he could quickly copy the original and use Paste In Front to place that into the working version.*

*For the lines in the roof, Kline used the Brush tool, set at 2.5 points, 130° calligraphic angle, and 60% black. Once all the lines were drawn, he used Pathfinder: Crop to "cookie-cut" the basic shape of the roof. He used the same treatment for most of the siding. (The bushes were given a random look with the calligraphic Brush tool in varying shades of green, then "ruffled" using Distort: Roughen.) Kline also used Pathfinder filters in the "cookie-cutting" of objects into other objects. He did almost all the detail in the shadows using Pathfinder: Soft at varying percentages—again, using a copy of all his objects to retain the integrity of originals in case he needed to reuse them.*

# Instant Variations

*Composing with Ink Pen and Path Patterns*

**Advanced Technique**

**Overview:** *Rasterize a pattern; create primary elements and layers; alter copies of objects; create Path Patterns; make color variations; apply Ink Pen textures; color-correct final elements.*

1

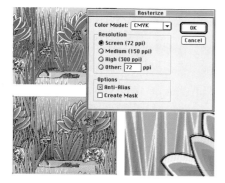

*Before rasterizing the pattern, and the rasterized object in detail and full view*

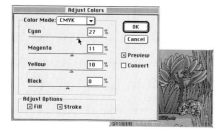

*Using Adjust Colors to tint the rasterized object*

## Taking control of layers...

Hold Option and choose New Layer Above from the Layers pop-up menu to place the next layer above the active layer (for details on layers, see *Chapter 4*). To visually crop objects across multiple layers use Layer Masks (see the Introduction to *Chapter 8*).

Sometimes the best way to become familiar with a new version of a program is to design a project using the new features; this project was focused on using Adobe Illustrator's Path Patterns, Ink Pen and Colors filters.

**1 Rasterizing a pattern to use as a template.** There are many ways to create Illustrator templates, but for this illustration I wanted to use my repeating jungle pattern (see "Intricate Patterns," *Chapter 3*, pages 72–75). Because patterns take so long to redraw to the screen, I rasterized the pattern. First, draw a rectangle the correct size for your template and fill it with a pattern. After adjusting the pattern so that it repeats as you wish within the rectangle (see the section "Transformations," *Chapter 1*, page 13, and Tip on page 74, *Chapter 3*), choose Object: Rasterize, and select options appropriate to your needs. I rasterized at 72 ppi, in RGB, and antialiased. For easier tracing, or as a guide to final colors, you can colorize your template using Filter: Colors: Saturate or Adjust Colors. I used Adjust Colors to apply a tint.

**2 Blocking basic compositional elements into separate layers.** Start by renaming as "Template" the layer containing your template (double-click on the layer name in the Layers palette) and locking that layer (click next to the eye icon). Then, using separate layers whenever appropriate (see *Chapter 4* for help working with layers), block in the basic elements of your composition starting with the background objects on the bottom layers (I began with the sky, sand, tree and water, each on separate layers). If the template becomes obscured by objects on subsequent layers, Hide layers (click on the Eye to toggle between visible and hidden) or change that layer to Art-work mode (⌘-click the Eye).

**3 Using previously drawn elements to create new objects.** Often new objects are made most easily by altering existing ones, rather than starting from scratch. Begin by selecting a source object and making a new layer. In the Layers palette, Option-drag the colored dot to the right of the layer name to the new layer (this places a copy of the selected object in exact registration on the new layer). So that I could apply different gradients to each of the branches and the trunk, I Option-dragged the tree to a new layer, locked all layers except the new one, then used the Knife tool to cut around first one branch and then the other—separating each branch.

**4 Creating Path Patterns to generate foliage.** While Path Patterns can be used to create seamless borders that miraculously fit any shape, Path Patterns can also generate complex illustrations. In a separate document, design your pattern tiles; for objects that will "grow" on both sides of your path (such as vines and leaves), design your pattern horizontally. For asymmetrical patterns that will run in one direction only (like grass and ferns), design the pattern vertically. Define each tile with an unstroked, unfilled rectangle behind the objects (on a layer below is easiest), select your pattern elements (including the bounding rectangle), and choose Edit: Define Pattern to name your pattern. Next, to copy each named pattern into your main document, deselect all objects, click on a named pattern swatch and Copy (⌘-C). Then in your main document click on the New Swatch icon! (To access multiple swatches see "Color Systems…" on page 24.)

**Reselecting Path Patterns**

Once applied, Path Patterns are sets of grouped editable objects. To select an applied tile, click twice with the Group-selection tool, click once more (total of three clicks) to select all tiles applied to the same path.

Blocking the basic elements into layers over the template layer

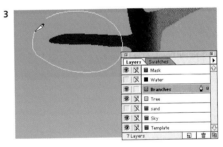

Using the Knife tool to separate branches

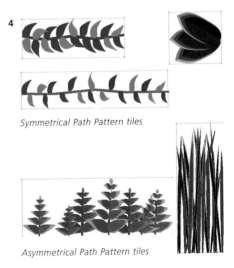

Symmetrical Path Pattern tiles

Asymmetrical Path Pattern tiles

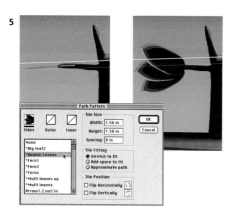

*A path before and after Path Patterns is applied to create the leaves*

*A path, the Path Patterns grass applied and selected, then deselected*

*Creating color variations on vine Path Patterns using Filter: Colors: Adjust Colors*

**5 Applying Path Patterns.** In your main document, lock all other layers, then create a new layer. With the Pen tool, draw a path (each at least one tile in length) onto which the path patterns will be created and, while it's selected, choose Filter: Stylize: Path Pattern. In the Path Pattern dialog box, click on the "Sides" icon, then choose the pattern, make certain that the "Stretch to fit" option is chosen and click OK. Path Patterns can be applied to multiple paths at one time, or can be reapplied to another path (choose Filter: Path Pattern, or ⌘-E). The applied Path Patterns are actually individual objects, sub-grouped in tile-length clusters, then grouped together with the other tiles along each path—the original path remains intact underneath the Path Pattern.

**6 Using Adjust Colors to create color variations in Path Patterns.** Instead of defining dozens of Path Patterns with different color variations, use Adjust Colors to vary the Path Pattern objects after they are created. Select a group of Path Pattern objects by clicking with the solid Selection tool. To see the color adjustments as you experiment, hide the selection edges (View: Hide Edges, or ⌘-H). Next, choose Filter: Colors: Adjust Colors. Experiment with color adjustments, then enable the Preview box to view your adjustments—the Preview will update after each slider adjustment. When you are satisfied, click OK. Don't forget to Show Edges (⌘-H).

**7 Using Gradients, the Ink Pen and Saturate to create texture.** Fill a background object with a Gradient and use the Gradient tool to adjust the length and range of the gradient within the object. With your background object selected, create a New Layer Above your current layer (see Tip on page 124), name it "Texture," then Option-drag a copy of the background object to the Texture layer. With the copied object still selected, lock the original background layer and choose Filter: Ink Pen: Effects. Play (endlessly!) with the various setting options. (For hints, see the Ink Pen folder on the *Wow!* disk.) For the "Atmosphere" texture I selected the "Grass" preset from the Settings pop-up, and chose "Match Object" from the "Hatch Color" pop-up. The result will be hundreds of objects replacing the selected gradient. To make Ink Pen objects visually separate from the original gradient (which should be locked on a layer below), while the objects are still selected, hide edges (⌘-H), then open Filter: Colors: Saturate and increase the saturation 15%.

8 **Using the Ink Pen to create a reflective surface.** This time, create an Ink Pen effect that *contrasts* with the original. As before, create an object on one layer and Option-drag a copy to a new layer immediately above. (To create the water in my jungle, I resized the copy so it was slightly inset from the original.) Next, fill the copy with a contrasting gradient and, while it's selected, reopen the Ink Pen dialog (choose Filter: Ink Pen: Effects, or if it's available, choose Filter: Effects). Select a hatch pattern and settings open enough that you can see the original object below, and set the "Hatch Color" to "Match Object." Although I experimented with creating my own Ink Pen "hatch" in waterlike shapes (by creating a path, then choosing Filter: Ink Pen: Hatches and clicking New), ultimately I ended up choosing the "Wood Grain Light" settings with the "Match Object" hatch color. **Note:** *Screenshot is of Illustrator 6 Ink Pen because, unlike version 7, you can see all the modifiers in one screen.*

9 **Final color and light adjustments.** For final color correction and adjustments, unlock appropriate layers so that you can make necessary changes to gradient fills (with the Gradient tool or by adjusting the gradient itself), or Path Pattern and Ink Pen objects (hide edges and apply Adjust Colors and Saturate filters).

7

A selected "texture" created with the Ink Pen (dialog is Illustrator 6), the texture after Hide Edges, then after Filter: Colors: Saturate

8

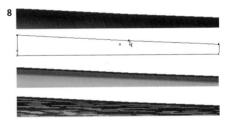

Making an inset copy, filling the copy with a gradient, and applying Ink Pen to the gradient

9

The final layers, and a detail shown before and after final color corrections

**Reversing an upside-down path pattern**

If your vertical Path Pattern is facing the wrong direction, adjust the top and bottom anchor points so that the bottom point is to the right of the top point.

## Gallery: Diane Hinze Kanzler & Sandee Cohen

*Starting with Diane Hinze Kanzler's "Goldfish" illustration (near right), Sandee Cohen used the Ink Pen filter to add texture. The coral was given a plain pink fill. The Ink Pen filter was then applied using the "Swash" hatch. The same Swash hatch was also used on the top fin. The body of the fish was created using the "Dots" hatch. The two wavy fins at the back were filled with the "Wood grain" swatch. The front fins were filled with the "Vertical lines" hatch, set for different angles. The middle wavy fins were filled with the "Worm" hatch. Finally, a hatch was defined for the bubble. Then a large rectangle was created over the entire illustration and filled with bubbles. See the "Cohen/H-K Ink Pen" file on the* Wow! *disk for specific steps and settings.*

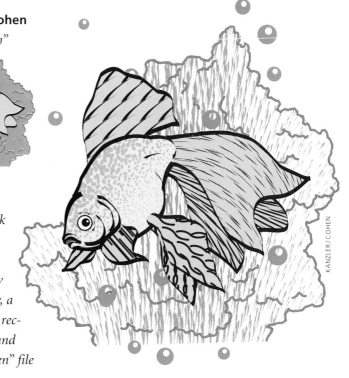

KANZLER / COHEN

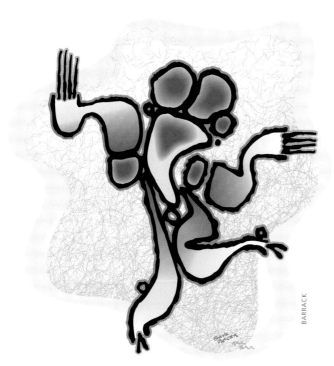

BARRACK

## Gallery: Kevin Barrack

*Kevin Barrack began "Batik Dancer" by applying Streamline (see* Chapter 9*) to one of his scanned drawings. In Illustrator he then filled the body shapes with gradients (see* Chapter 5*), and on a separate layer, he created "blobby" shapes for the background. In another layer, called "Ink Pen," he created a new blobby shape with a green fill. To this shape he applied Filter: Ink Pen: Effects, to set the fourth "color" indicator box, Hatch = Worm, Color to Match Object, Background = Hatch Only, Fade = None, Density = 75%, Dispersion = Constant 180, Thickness = Constant 70, Rotation = Random 10–180, Scale = Linear 56–610, 270°. Lastly, Barrack added thick strokes to the black solid-filled shapes outlining his figure.*

## Gallery: Wendy Grossman

*Wendy Grossman was inspired by the prospect of a* Wow! *filters chapter and spent a weekend playing with the filters to create this cubist image. She used the Pathfinder: Unite filter to frequently combine multiple objects. She used the Pathfinder: Divide filter to segment objects into smaller, discrete objects, and the Pathfinder: Soft filter for blending colors between objects (such as the 70% Soft filter used in the "color wheel"). The Star and Spiral tools (once filters) were used throughout.*

# Fanciful Filtering
*Creative Experimentation With Filters*

### Advanced Technique

**Overview:** *Create objects as the basis for filtering; use various filters on different groups of objects; make color and object adjustments as necessary.*

**1**

*The template with grid before and after the first ovals and lines are drawn and text is placed*

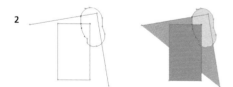

*Before and after circles are cut and joined*

**2**

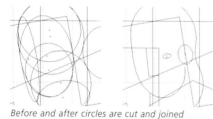

*Three objects selected in Artwork and Preview*

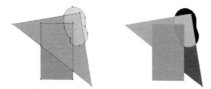

*The Soft filter applied, then objects recolored*

A wonderful way to learn new techniques is through creative experimentation. When Ron Chan was commissioned to create artwork for the University of Minnesota, he used the opportunity to experiment with filters. Don't forget that many different ways exist to achieve the same effect, and you might gravitate towards an entirely different set of filters.

**1 Preparing your basic objects from which to work.**
Create the objects that will form the basis for your filtering. Chan used methods discussed elsewhere in the book to prepare the initial objects, including scanning a sketch to use as a template (page 80), creating a custom drawing grid (see Tip on page 137) in its own layer (page 96) and making a masking layer (page 152). He also cut and joined circles to form the head (page 52). In final preparation for filtering, Chan drew bisecting lines with the Pen tool, which he later used as guides in applying filters.

**2 Selecting overlapping objects and applying the Pathfinder: Soft filter.** After creating a few overlapping objects, you might choose to see how those objects "cut into" each other. First, select the objects with any selection tool (you can even select part of an object using the Direct-selection tool). Although you can use Pathfinder: Divide to create separate objects for each point where the objects intersect, Chan prefers to use the Pathfinder: Soft filter, because the Soft filter creates new colors where objects overlap, making the intersections easy to see. He can then recolor like-colored objects as a unit by Direct-selecting one color and using the Edit: Select: Select Same Fill Color filter, which selects all objects of that color. Chan also uses Direct-select on particular divided objects for recoloring individually.

**3 Offsetting and outlining paths.** To create an offset of a path, choose Object: Path: Offset Path and specify how much larger or smaller the offset path should be. Chan offset the jaw path smaller at −6 points, used Direct-select on the original and offset paths' endpoints to join (⌘-J) them and then filled the new joined object. Since strokes can't contain gradients or patterns (see *Chapter 5* for gradients; *Chapter 3* for patterns), use Object: Path: Outline Path to convert stroked paths into filled objects that can be styled with more flexibility.

**4 Cropping copies for an overlay look.** To create a transparent overlay look in a section of your image, first select and copy all the objects that will be affected. Then deselect everything (Shift-⌘-A), and use Paste In Front (⌘-F) and Group (⌘-G) on the copy. Using any tools you wish, create a closed object to define your cropping area and, with your Shift key down, use the Selection tool to select the grouped copy and its cropping object; then choose Object: Pathfinder: Crop and group the cropped objects. Try experimenting with the Colors: Adjust Colors filter to see if you can achieve a color cast you like (see page 126). Or, just Direct-select objects to customize their styling. ✎

**Pathfinder: Soft filter options**

In addition to letting you choose the color mixing percentage, the Soft filter also lets you convert custom colors to process. If you disable this option, then overlapping custom colors won't mix at all; they'll merely divide.

3
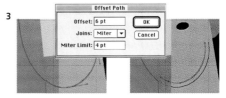

*Before and after offsetting the path −6 points*

*Joining the two paths and then changing style*

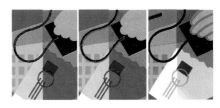

*Lines selected, then outlined, then customized*

4
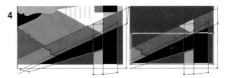

*Objects copied, then after Paste In Front and being selected with a defining rectangle*

*After Pathfinder: Crop, then recolored*

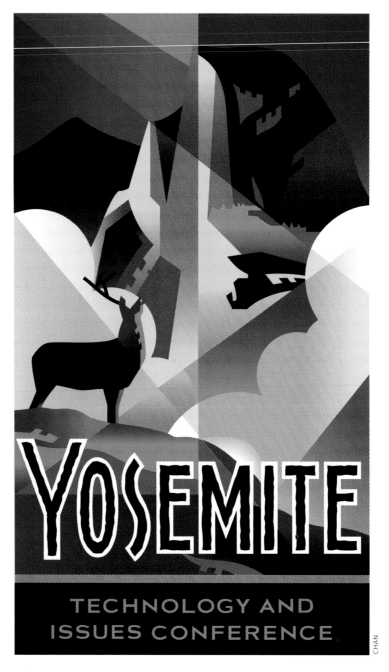

### Gallery: Ron Chan

*In very much the same way he made the image for the University of Minnesota discussed on the previous two pages, Ron Chan created this poster for a Yosemite conference. For the general composition, Chan used Soft, Outline Path, Offset Path and Crop filters. He used Type: Create Outlines to convert the "Yosemite" title to Bézier objects filled white, then used Offset Path, filled the inner offset objects with black and applied the Roughen filter.*

# Type & Layout

# 7

Illustrator is a powerful tool for graphically controlling type. Although you're likely to prefer a page-layout program (such as QuarkXPress or PageMaker) for multipage documents like catalogues and long magazine articles, and PageMill or BBEdit for web page layout, this chapter will show you many reasons to stay within Illustrator for single-page documents. The Type chapter of Adobe's *User Guide* covers the creation and manipulation of type in great detail, so this introduction will focus on essentials, "what's new" and production tips.

For creating and manipulating type, there are two palettes you can open from the Type menu: Character (⌘-T; for "Type") and Paragraph (⌘-M). When you first open these palettes, they may be in a collapsed view. To cycle through display options for either palette, double-click its name tab (or use the Palette pop-up menu).

There are three major type options in Illustrator accessible through the Type tool (press "T"): *Point Type*, *Area Type* and *Path Type*. The flexible Type tool lets you click to create a Point-Type object, click-drag to create an Area-Type object or click within any existing type object to enter or edit text. You can gain access to type created in other applications by using the File: Open or File: Place commands from the desktop menu.

Select letters, words or an entire block of text by dragging across the letters with the Type tool, or use a selection tool to select text as an *object* by clicking on or marqueeing the type's baseline (the baseline is the line that the type sits on, and is visible in Artwork mode).

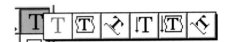

The Type tool, Area-Type tool, Path-Type tool, Vertical-Type tool, Vertical Area-Type Tool, Vertical Path-Type tool—striking "T" cycles through these type tools

## One option you may not want

Turn off the "Type Area Select" option by deselecting the checkbox in File: Preferences: Keyboard Increments: Type Area Select. This will keep you from accidentally selecting type when you're trying to select an object. You can still select type at its baseline.

## Typographic controls

Default keyboard-accessible typographic controls can be set in Preferences (most settings are found in "Keyboard Increments," while Type units of measurement for is set in "Units & Undos"). See the "Type" section in the Adobe *Quick Reference Card* for a listing of the keyboard shortcuts for adjusting your kerning / tracking, leading, point sizes, baseline shifts and justification.

Double-click a Tab name to cycle through the palette display options (or use the "Show Options" pop-up menu)

- **Point Type.** Click with the Horizontal-Type or Vertical-Type tool anywhere on the page to create Point Type. Once you click, a blinking text-insertion cursor called an "I-beam" indicates you can now type text using your keyboard. To add another line, press the Return key. When you're finished typing into one text object, click on the Type tool in the toolbox to simultaneously select the current text as an object (the I-beam will disappear) and be poised to begin another text object. To just select the text as an object, click on a selection tool.

- **Area Type.** If you click-*drag* with the Type tool, you'll create an Area-Type rectangle, into which you can type. Once your rectangle is defined, the I-beam awaits your typing, and the text automatically wraps to the next line when you type to the confines of the rectangle. If you've typed more text than can fit in your text rectangle, then, in Artwork mode, you'll notice a plus sign along the right side of the rectangle. To enlarge the rectangle to allow for more text, use the Direct-select tool to deselect the text block, then grab one side of the rectangle and drag it out, holding down the Shift key to constrain the direction of the drag. To add a new text object that will be linked to an existing text object in Artwork mode, use the Group-select tool to grab the rectangle only (not the text), hold down the Option key and drag a copy of the rectangle. Text will automatically flow to the new rectangle.

  The other way to create Area Type or Vertical Area Type is to construct a path (with any tools you wish) forming a shape within which to place type. Then choose the Area-Type or Vertical Area-Type tool (click and hold down on the Type tool to access it, or keep striking the "T" key to cycle to it) and click on the path itself to place text within the path. Distort the confining shape by grabbing an anchor point with the Direct-selection tool and dragging it to a new location, or reshape the path by adjusting direction lines. The text within will reflow. **Note:** *If you use the Vertical Area-Type tool, you'll see that your text will flow automatically, starting from the right* edge of the area flowing toward the left! For those of you who use non-CJK (Chinese, Japanese and Korean) fonts and typographic standards, you really won't have much use for this tool since non-CJK type flows from left to right . (For more on Multinational fonts see page 137.)

To set up tabs for Area Type, choose Type: Tab Ruler. To create paths for custom tab alignment, first create paths that align with the tab markers, then Direct-select your text object with your paths and choose Type: Wrap: Make. You can also use text-wrapping to flow text around objects. After paths are wrapped to text objects, reshaping the paths causes text to reflow. To add a new path, ungroup (⌘-Shift-G) the current text and path objects, then reselect the text with the old and new paths and choose Type: Wrap: Make. (For more information on tabs and wrapping text around objects, see the *User Guide*.) **Note:** *You'll have to use Type: Wrap: Release or Ungroup before you can apply some filters to wrapped text.*

- **Path Type.** The Path-Type tool allows you to click on a path to flow text along the perimeter of the path (the path will then become unstroked/unfilled). To reposition the beginning of the text, use a Selection tool to grab the special Path-Type I-beam *itself* and drag left or right. Drag the I-beam up or down (or double-click it) to *flip* the text so it wraps along the inside or outside of the path (also see the top Tip on page 136).

As with Area Type, use the Direct-selection tool to re-shape the confining path itself; the Path Type path will automatically readjust to the new path shape.

### ADDITIONAL TYPE FUNCTIONS (FORMER FILTERS)

- **Check Spelling**, **Find Font**, **Find** and **Smart Punctuation** all work whether or not anything is selected, although some of these filters give you the option to work within a selected text block if you have one selected.

**More about Find Font:** If you try to open a file and don't have the correct fonts loaded, Illustrator warns you, lists

---

### Linking multiple blocks of text

To link multiple text objects so text flows from one object to the next, select the desired text blocks, making sure the baselines are selected, and choose Type: Blocks: Link Type.

### The quick-changing Type tool

When using the regular Type tool, look at your cursor very carefully in these situations:

- If you move the regular Type tool over a closed path, the cursor should change to the Area-Type icon.
- If you move the Type tool over an open path, it will probably change to the Path-Type icon.

### Type-tool juggling

To toggle a Type tool between its vertical or horizontal mode, first make sure nothing is selected. Holding the Shift key will toggle the tool to the opposite mode.

### Grab your type by the bottom!

By default, "Type Area Select" is *on* in File: Preferences: Keyboard Increments. I suggest turning it *off*, because it's likely you'll select type when trying to select other objects. It's easier to maintain selection control by clicking on or marquee-selecting type by its baseline.

**Current Font List:** 3

Helvetica
Eurostile-Bold √
Futura-Book √

**Replacement Font List:** 288

Bodoni-Italic
Bodoni-Poster
Bookman-Bold

Font List: System

☐ Multiple Master  ☒ Type 1
☒ Standard  ☐ TrueType
☒ Roman  ☐ CID

Done
Find Next
Change
Change All
Skip
Save List...

the missing fonts and asks if you still want to open the file. You need the correct fonts to print properly; so if you can't load the missing fonts, choose Find Font to find and replace the missing fonts with fonts you do have.

When you open the filter, the top list displays the fonts used in the file; the missing fonts will be indicated by a "√". In order to access all fonts that you can use as replacements, deselect the options you don't want to use (e.g., TrueType); any different choices will force you to make your selections all over again. When you're ready to select font replacements, click on the fonts you'd like to replace from the top list; note that Illustrator shows you where the font occurs. After you choose a replacement font from the bottom list, you can individually replace each occurrence of the font by clicking Change and then clicking Find Next. Otherwise, simply click Change All to change all occurrences of the top fonts with the font selected from the bottom list.

## If you don't have the fonts...

If you're missing fonts, don't be afraid to open the file, make changes, save, copy, paste the missing type or resave the file, because Illustrator remembers which fonts you're *supposed* to be using. However, the file won't print correctly until you load or replace the missing fonts (see "More about Find Font" at right).

## Making a new text object

Reselect the Type tool to end one text object; the next click will start a new text object. Or, deselect the current text by holding down the ⌘ key (temporarily turning your cursor into a selection tool) and clicking outside the text block.

## Type along the top and bottom

To create the illusion that Path Type is falling along the top *and* bottom of a path, hold down the Option key as you flip the I-beam: this flips a *copy* of the type.

- **Change Type Orientation** lets you change orientation from horizontal to vertical or vertical to horizontal by choosing Type: Type Orientation: Horizontal or Vertical.

- **Change Case** requires you to select text with the Type tool before you use the filter.

- **Rows & Columns:** You can use Rows & Columns on any selected rectangle or Area Type. Use a Selection tool (not the Type tool) to select the entire text object and double click the palette tab. You can enter your text first, or simply begin setting up your columns by choosing Rows & Columns. In this filter, specify the number and sizes of the rows and columns and whether you wish to use Add Guides. This creates grouped lines that you can make into Illustrator guides with View: Make Guides (⌘-5); see also page 96 for more on guides. Keep Preview checked to see the results of your specifications while you work, and click one of the Text Flow options to choose whether text will flow horizontally or vertically from one block to another.

- **MM Design** stands for Multiple Master fonts. Adobe includes a couple of Multiple Master fonts in the Fonts folder on the *Adobe Illustrator 7 Application CD-ROM*. There's also a separate MM Design palette to aid in customizing your Multiple Master fonts on the fly (see the documentation that ships with your fonts for how to modify them). At this writing, Illustrator is the only vector drawing program with this capability.

## Multinational options and CJK font support

With Illustrator 7 there's new and wider support for Multinational fonts, including CJK (Chinese, Japanese and Korean). To access the Multinational portion of the Character palette, simply double-click on the palette tab to expand it until it opens to its fullest extent. To utilize some of the CJK font capabilities you must have the proper fonts and character sets loaded into your system, as well as special system software (see the *User Guide* for more on Multinational fonts). Some options do not work on non-CJK fonts, for example, U.S. and U.K. English.

- **Glyph Options** is a new feature and can only be accessed if you have the appropriate Japanese Kanjii font loaded. This option is only available for Macintosh users (see Multinational options above for more information). 🖱

## CONVERTING TYPE TO OUTLINES

As long as you've created your type with fonts you have and can print, and provided you've finished experimenting with text as type elements (e.g., adjusting your line spacing or kerning/tracking, or wrapping text around a path), you have the option to convert your text objects to Illustrator Bézier curves with compound paths. Compound paths form the "holes" in objects, such as the transparent center of an **O** or **P**. You can use the Direct-selection tool to select and manipulate parts of the compound paths separately. To convert a font to outlines, select the type with a Selection tool and choose Type: Create Outlines (⌘-Shift-O), and, while the type is still

## Glorious grids

One of Illustrator's hottest new features is customizable grids.

- In a new document, set the division and subdivision for your grid (in Preferences: Guides & Grid) and choose either dotted divisions or lines and the color of those lines.
- You can toggle the grid between in the front or back of your artwork by selecting or deselecting the "Grids in back" checkbox.
- Quickly access grids with ⌘-' (apostrophe), or from the context sensitive menu with no objects selected.
- Toggle "Snap to Grid" on and off by pressing ⌘-Shift-".
- To tilt the grid on an angle, choose File: Preferences: General, and in "Tool Behavior" change the Constrain angle. **Note:** *Changing the Constrain angle also affects the angle at which your objects are drawn and moved—see pages 56–59 where Constrain angle is adjusted for creating isometrics.*

## What's white? What's not?

One of the coolest benefits of grids is that you can see whether objects are unfilled, filled with white, or are see-through compounds (like doughnuts; see pages 118, 155 for more on compounds).
— *Sandee Cohen*

*Graphically transforming Bézier curves (artwork by Javier Romero Design Group)*

*Filling with patterns or gradients*

*Masking with type (see page 140) (artwork by Min Wang / Adobe Systems)*

*Transporting foreign or unusual fonts (artwork by Kathleen Tinkel)*

*Using pre-Illustrator 7 vertically scaled type (artwork by Pamela Drury Wattenmaker)*

selected, choose Object: Group (⌘-G) to group the individual elements for easy reselection.

### Why convert type to outlines?

- **So you can graphically transform or distort the individual curves and anchor points of letters or words.** Everything from the minor stretching of a word to extreme distortion is possible.

- **So you can fill type with patterns or gradients.**

- **So you can make type into a masking object.** See page 140 for an example of this technique.

- **So you don't have to supply the font to your client or service bureau.** Converting type can be especially useful when you're using foreign language fonts, or when your image will be printed when you're not around.

- **So you can work with vertically scaled type created in earlier versions of Illustrator.** Type is calculated differently in the various versions of Illustrator, so opening an earlier document with a later version of Illustrator may cause type to reflow. In lieu of re-editing, if possible, re-open the original version and output directly, save as EPS or convert type to outlines.

- **But...if you *don't* want to convert to outlines: Embed it and forget it.** Illustrator 7 gives you the option to embed the fonts if you save the file as EPS. Though this text can't be edited, you may not *have* to transport the fonts with the artwork. ◉

**Gallery: James Young / Adobe Systems, Inc.**

*This alphabet (which would have been a nightmare to create in QuarkXPress or PageMaker) was simple to construct in Illustrator. James Young arranged individual Point-Type letters using the Selection tool and resized each visually using the Scale tool with the Shift-key down (to constrain scaling to proportionate only; see page 38 for scaling help). Because Young created this graphic using the Nueva Multiple Master (MM) font, he was able to select letters to change their width and weight (see page 142 for more on MM fonts).*

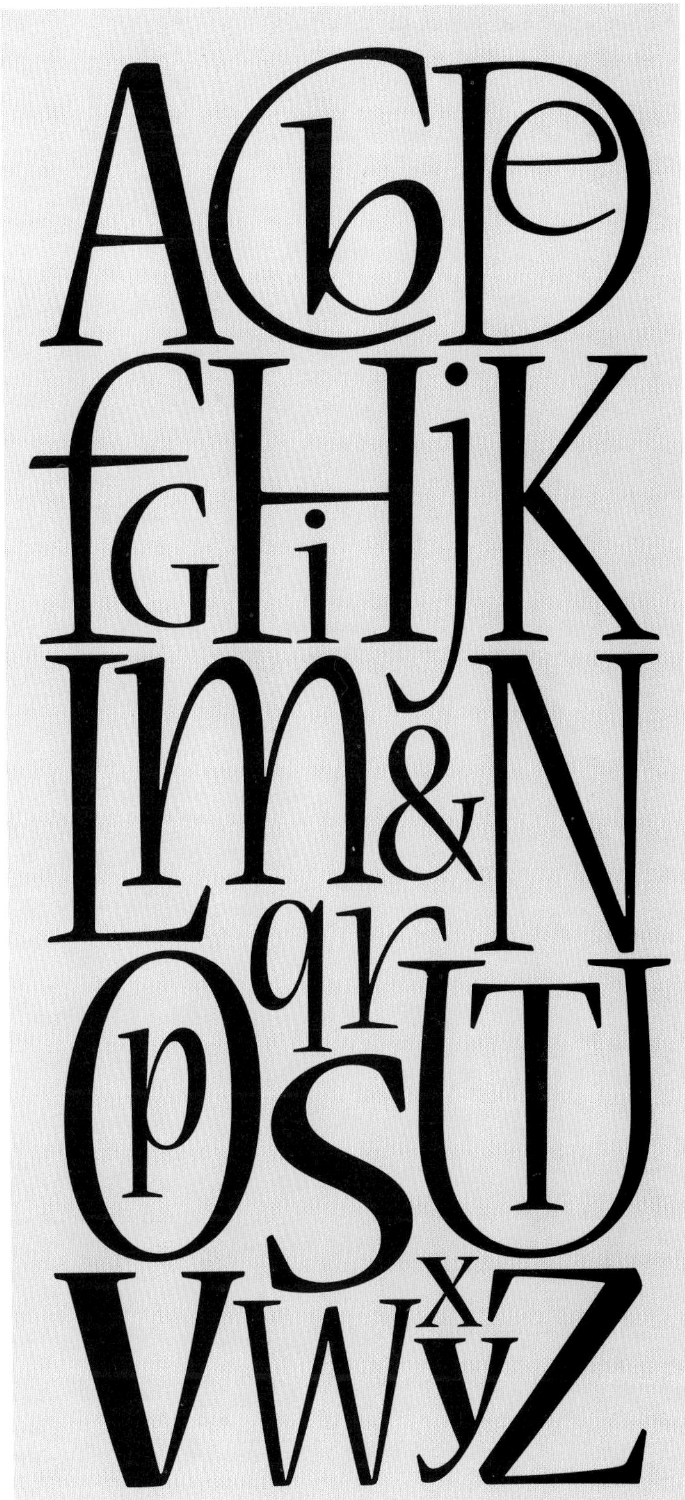

YOUNG / ADOBE SYSTEMS, INC.

# Masking Type

*Placing Type Within Type Using Masks*

**Overview:** *Create a large letter and arrange other objects in relation to it, then convert the letter to outlines; use Paste In Front to paste a copy of the letter in front to give llusion that the mask is stroked, Paste In Back a copy of the letter to create the fill illusion.*

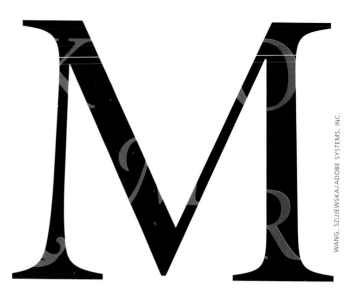

**1**

*Arranged type objects and the "M" outlined*

**2**

*"M" brought to front and all objects selected*

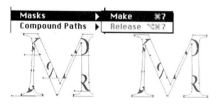

*"M" masked, then copy Pasted in Front ready for styling as fill or stroke*

### Why not use the filter?

While the Fill & Stroke for Mask filter in version 7.0 creates its own preset objects, unless you want a 1-pt black stroke *and* a 25% black fill, you'll find it easier to make your fills and strokes by hand. Updates may fix this filter.

This "M" was created by Min Wang (Laurie Szujewska, art director) for the Adobe Minion type specimen book. Unlike ancient versions of Illustrator, masks are now the topmost object (see *Chapter 8* for more on masks).

**1 Positioning type elements and converting the large letter to outlines.** Using the Type tool, click to create a Point-Type object and type one letter. Choose a typeface of a heavy enough weight and in a large enough size for other elements to show through the letter form itself. Then arrange other type elements (or other objects) in relation to the large letter (you'll be able to move them later). Wang arranged separate Minion type characters in relation to a 297-pt "M." Select the large letter with a Selection tool and choose Type: Create Outlines (⌘-O).

**2 Creating the mask and "filling" it.** Select the letter outline and Cut (⌘-X), then Paste In Front (⌘-F) so it's the top object. Then select all objects and apply Object: Mask: Make (⌘-7). Since masks can't really be stroked or filled, extra objects will create the illusion. To create a fill (with your copy still on the clipboard): Paste In Back (⌘-B), and then style it. To create a stroke: Paste In Front (⌘-F) and style. Then group the objects (⌘-G). Finally, Direct-select individual objects to adjust their placement.

### Gallery: Laurie Szujewska / Adobe Systems, Inc.

For Adobe's Poetica type specimen book, Laurie Szujewska was inspired by a "love knot" poem from the book Pattern Poetry by Dick Higgins, and created a similar spiral path with the Pen tool. She used the Path-Type tool to place the text on the path. She then meticulously kerned and placed spaces along the type path to prevent text overlaps, and to get things just right.

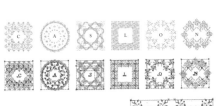

### Gallery: Laurie Szujewska / Adobe Systems, Inc.

For Adobe's Caslon type specimen book, Szujewska created these decorative ornaments by placing, rotating and reflecting groups of separate Point-Type objects filled with a gray color.

# The Shape of Time

*Trickling Type with Variations of Type Style*

**Overview:** *Create the outside border and path baselines for your type; import text into the first line; cut and paste text into appropriate path lines, changing the typestyle each time; use Point Type for "trickling type" and baseline shifts for lines at the bottom.*

1

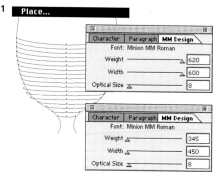

2

### Weight

| (Bold | - | Light) | ÷(# of steps -1) | ▼ |
|---|---|---|---|---|
| (620 | - | 345) | ÷ (17) = | 16 |
| Line 1 | | | | 620 |
| Line 2 | 620 | - | 16 = | 604 |
| Line 3 | 604 | - | 16 = | 588 |
| ... | | | | |

### Width

| (Extended | - Condensed) | ÷(# of steps -1) | ▼ |
|---|---|---|---|
| (600 | - 450) | ÷ (17) = | 8.8 |
| Line 1 | | | 600 |
| Line 2 | 600 | - 8.8 = | 591.2 |
| Line 3 | 591.2 | - 8.8 = | 582.4 |
| ... | | | |

### Size

| (12-point | - 6-point) | ÷ (17) = | ▼ .35 |
|---|---|---|---|
| Line 1 | | | 12 |
| Line 2 | 12 | - .35 = | 11.65 |
| Line 3 | 11.65 | - .35 = | 11.30 |
| ... | | | |

To illustrate the effects of varying the weight and width of a Multiple Master (MM) typeface, James Young (with Laurie Szujewska) created this interpretation of George Kubler's *The Shape of Time*. This lesson shows how to calculate exact instances for MM fonts using the MM Design palette (Type menu). To do this by eye (after entered your MM text), click on the Direct-selection tool, then use the sliders in the MM Design palette. You'll find a couple of MM fonts in the "Fonts" folder on the Illustrator 7.0 CD.

**1 Creating your baselines.** Draw an hourglass-shaped path with the Pen tool (see page 4 for help), and decide on a starting type size and style. Set your leading between lines one point larger than your type. Just move copies of your path *up* a distance equal to your leading; select the path, double-click the Selection tool, specify a Move equal to the desired leading, and click Copy. Then ⌘-D to make copies for each line of type. Young started with Minion MM Bold Extended at 7.88 points , with 8.88-pt leading, and 18 lines of type. To cut the paths to fit the hourglass, copy the hourglass, select the paths and Paste In Front (⌘-F) a copy. Shift-select the paths with this hourglass copy and choose Object: Pathfinder: Outline, then select and delete the paths outside the hourglass.

**2 Preparing your type.** In a word processor, thoroughly proofread and spell-check your text, as making changes later will be difficult. Next, calculate and write down the variations in style to be placed on each path line, using the chart at left for help. Each MM typestyle has a numeric value that you'll be using for calculations. For the top line of type, Young used Bold Extended with a weight value of 620 and a width value of 600, and for the bottom, a Light Condensed with a weight of 345 and a width of 450. To

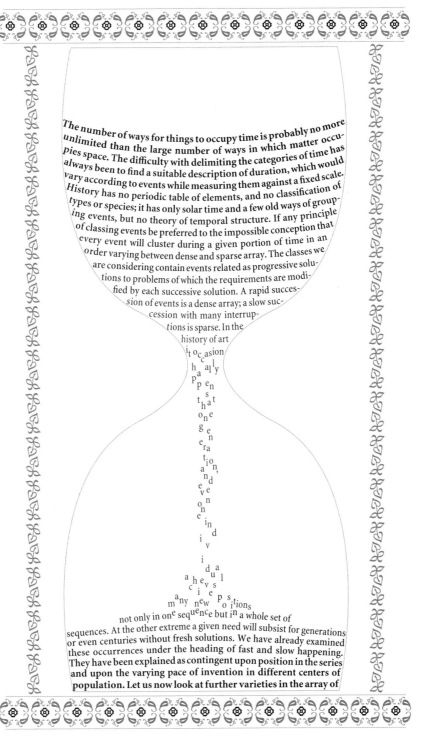

The number of ways for things to occupy time is probably no more unlimited than the large number of ways in which matter occupies space. The difficulty with delimiting the categories of time has always been to find a suitable description of duration, which would vary according to events while measuring them against a fixed scale. History has no periodic table of elements, and no classification of types or species; it has only solar time and a few old ways of grouping events, but no theory of temporal structure. If any principle of classing events be preferred to the impossible conception that every event will cluster during a given portion of time in an order varying between dense and sparse array. The classes we are considering contain events related as progressive solutions to problems of which the requirements are modified by each successive solution. A rapid succession of events is a dense array; a slow succession with many interruptions is sparse. In the history of art it occasionally happens that one generation, and even one individual achieves many new positions not only in one sequence but in a whole set of sequences. At the other extreme a given need will subsist for generations or even centuries without fresh solutions. We have already examined these occurrences under the heading of fast and slow happening. They have been explained as contingent upon position in the series and upon the varying pace of invention in different centers of population. Let us now look at further varieties in the array of

YOUNG/SZUJEWSKA/ADOBE SYSTEMS, INC. with text from George Kubler's *The Shape of Time*

3

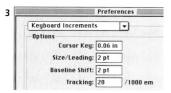

Changing the Cursor-key increments for typographic controls in General Preferences

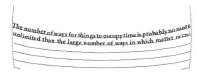

Cutting and pasting type into paths with the Path-Type tool

4

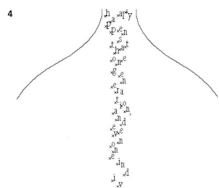

Trickling type using separate Point-Type objects

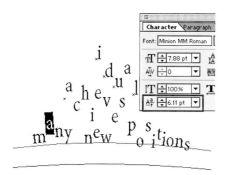

Graphically adjusting baseline shifts and viewing the shifts in an expanded Character palette

calculate the weight and width values for each of the in-between steps, he subtracted the lowest value from the highest and divided it by the number of steps (18) minus 1. The resulting value (16 for weight and 8.8 for width) represented the size of the steps from one line of text to the next. Starting with Bold Extended at 620/600, Young subtracted 16 from 620 to get the weight of the second step (604), and 8.8 from 600 to get the width of the second step (591.2). He subtracted the same values from the second step to calculate the third, and so on.

3 **Placing type into baselines.** With your Path-Type tool, click on the top path and choose File: Place to place your text onto the path. Direct-select the text-insertion I-beam and drag it until the text begins just inside the hourglass. Then click with your Type cursor at the end of the word closest to the right side of the hourglass (add a hyphen if you must), press ⌘-Shift-↓ to select all text beyond the line and cut the selected text. If necessary, place the Text cursor between words and kern slightly using Option-←/→ (set the units for Cursor-key distance in General Preferences). After adjusting the first line, click with the Path-Type tool on the second line and paste the cut text. Set the typestyle based on your "line 2" calculation, and repeat the above procedure until text is placed on all existing lines. Then click-drag to create an Area-Type object in which to paste the remaining text temporarily.

4 **Creating the trickling type.** Select and cut one letter at a time, then click within the hourglass to paste each letter as Point Type. Create the paths for the bottom of the hourglass, and calculate the values for increasing the weight/width (or size) of the styles. Click inside the temporary Area-Type object, press ⌘-A (Select All) and cut the text. With the Path-Type tool, place the text into the remaining paths at the bottom, placing fewer words just before the type hits the bottom. On these shorter lines, drag across individual letters with the Type tool and use Option-Shift-↑/↓ to create a baseline shift graphically. ◉

## Gallery: Laurie Szujewska / Adobe Systems, Inc.

For the Adobe Caslon type specimen book, Laurie Szujewska created this reinterpretation of Lewis Carroll's handwritten, shaped poem from Alice's Adventures Underground. Szujewska created the curved Bézier paths as described in "The Shape of Time" (page 142), but this time with a 14-pt distance for the leading and 28 duplications (⌘-D). After placing the appropriate text individually onto each line in 12-pt Adobe Caslon Italic (by clicking with the Path-Type cursor), Szujewska used the Direct-selection tool to adjust the angles of the curves. She then adjusted the starting point of each line of text by grabbing the I-beam and dragging it along the path. Finally, she individually selected each of the words in the last phrase (from "as he sat…") and progressively reduced them in size from "as he" at 11-pt to "Think of that!" at 6-pt.

We lived beneath the mat warm and snug and fat but one, & that was the cat! To our joys a clog, in our eyes a fog, on our hearts a log, was the dog! When the cat's away, then the mice will play. But, alas! one day, (so they say) came the dog and cat, hunting for a rat, crushed the mice all flat, each one as he sat underneath the mat, warm, & snug and fat …Think of that!

# Bookcover Design

*Illustrator as a Stand-alone Layout Tool*

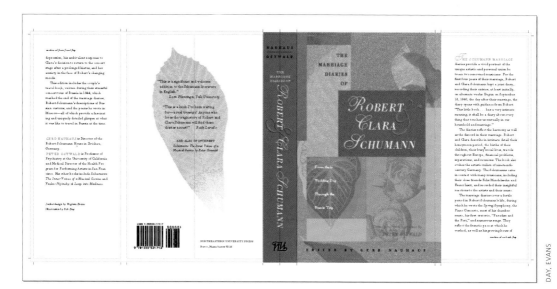

DAY, EVANS

**Overview:** *Set your document size; place guides and cropmarks; place EPS files and make Area Type for columns and Point Type for graphic type; visually track type to fit.*

Page layout programs such as QuarkXPress and Page-Maker are essential for producing multipage, complex documents. However, Rob Day and Virginia Evans use Illustrator exclusively for their single-page design projects; for example, their book jacket designs.

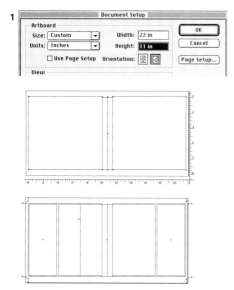

*Setting up the Artboard and layout specs*

**1 Setting up your page.** Choose File: Document Setup (⌘-Shift-P) to set up the Artboard for your design. Click on landscape or portrait page orientation and enter your Artboard size, making sure it's large enough for crop and/or registration marks (the "Size" parameter will automatically switch to "Custom"). Disable "Show Placed EPS Artwork" to keep your Artwork view uncluttered (placed images will always show in Preview). Choose View: Show Rulers and "re-zero" your ruler origin to the upper left corner of where your page will begin (see page 21). Although you can generate uniform grids with Preferences: Guides & Grid, for columns of varying sizes, Day and Evans numerically created two sets of rectangles, one for bleeds, and one for the trims. With the Rectangle tool (see page 8), click to make boxes sized for each trim area; Day and Evans made boxes for the front, side, flaps and spine. For bleeds, Option-click on the center of each trim area to numerically specify a box .125" larger in each dimension. To place an overall trim mark, select the boxes representing the entire trim area and choose Filter: Create: Trim Marks. If desired, make additional trim marks.

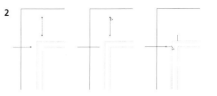

2 **Customizing your guides.** Select your trim and bleed boxes or columns (not the trim marks) and make them into guides (⌘-5), or View: Make Guides (see page 96 for more on guides). To shorten the trim marks, move the outside points inward until they touch the bleed guides (Direct-select an anchor point or Direct-select marquee multiple points and drag inward holding the Shift key).

*Shortening the trim marks; for folds, style with a dashed line (see page 54)*

3 **Placing the elements.** Choose File: Place to select EPS images to import into your layout. Use Area Type to place columns of text into your layout grid; use Point Type to place lines of type and individual type elements. To track type visually to fit a space, select a text object and use Option-←/→. (See the intro to this chapter for tips on how to change text and typestyles using filters.) 🖱

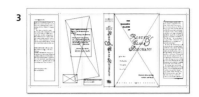

*All of the elements placed into the layout*

*Close-ups of an Area-Type object*

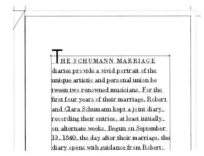

THE SCHUMANN MARRIAGE diaries provide a vivid portrait of the unique artistic and personal union between two renowned musicians. For the first four years of their marriage, Robert and Clara Schumann kept a joint diary, recording their entries, at least initially, on alternate weeks. Begun on September 13, 1840, the day after their marriage, the diary opens with guidance from Robert:

*Close-ups of Point-Type objects*

*Tracking a line of Point Type with cursor-keys*

---

### Creating "cropmarks," then "trim marks"

Create a rectangle that defines a cropping area, and choose Object: Cropmarks: Make. Cropmarks are visible in Illustrator but become invisible when placed into another program (such as QuarkXPress or PageMaker), except that they will reappear if you position objects beyond the cropmarks. To remove cropmarks, either choose Object: Cropmarks: Release, or make a new rectangle and choose again Object: Cropmarks: Make. More useful are the always-visible Trim Marks; select any objects (you don't need a rectangle) and choose Filter: Create: Trim Marks. Files can contain multiple trim marks, which you can customize (see Step 2 above), or make into dashed strokes for folds. To crop for export, create a "layer-mask" (see *Chapter 8*).

## Gallery: Pattie Belle Hastings, Bjørn Akselsen/Ice House Press & Design

*When Ice House Press & Design (IHP&D) began to design labels for three different lines of oils and vinegars for an Italian client, they chose Illustrator as the production tool. Each line had to have a distinct identity, yet fit within the prescribed arched label shape. IHP&D found Illustrator ideal for designing such packaging labels, which combine graphics with highly modified type. IHP&D treated every block of type as a logo, manually kerning between each letter and word by clicking with the Type tool between letters and using the ← and → cursor-keys. (See the "Typographic Controls" tip on page 135.) IHP&D then manually selected and moved each graphic element and block of type until the spacing between the elements was just right. The ® mark, for instance, was individually created and placed as a separate element for each of the labels. Through this sort of meticulous manipulation, the type actually became graphical elements in a way not easily accomplished in a page layout program. For the Veritas line of organic olive oils, IHP&D chose to print in two PMS colors with gold foil for elegance (see* Chapter 3 *for more on PMS colors). The Candoni line was designed for four PMS colors, while the third line (not pictured) was designed as a four-color process piece.*

## Gallery: Javier Romero Design Group

*Javier Romero Design Group converted the title in this illustration to outlines (Type: Create Outlines) and then manually distorted it. The resulting glowing effect, which the Design Group then applied to the type, can be used on any object—even regular, editable text objects. To replicate this effect, fill the top letter in a solid color, copy it and use Paste In Back (⌘-B) to place a copy of the letter behind the original. Set the Fill for this copy to None, with a 5.5-pt, medium-colored stroke (see page 54 for detailed instructions). Copy and Paste In Back this version and change the stroke weight to 7 points with a brighter color. Use Paste In Back again for an 11-pt, medium-colored stroke, and again for a dark, 16-pt stroke. (See Chapter 4 for help making layers to isolate the versions.)*

JAVIER ROMERO DESIGN GROUP

GORSKA (design), BALDWIN (illustration) / MAX SEABAUGH ASSOCIATES

## Gallery: Caryl Gorska / Max Seabaugh Associates

*After commissioning Scott Baldwin to create a nutcracker illustration (he used Macromedia FreeHand to re-create his linoleum cut), Caryl Gorska scanned a traditional, copyright-free Dover Publications typeface into the computer. She saved the scanned typeface to use as a template (see page 80) and used the Pen tool to carefully trace the letters she needed. She then created the frame into which the type would be placed and, using the Selection tool, she "hand-set" the type by copying and pasting letter forms. Lastly, she fine-tuned the letter spacing, checking herself by printing myriad proofs—both actual size and greatly enlarged (increasing the percentage in Page Setup). Although her typeface, Newport Condensed, was available as a PostScript commercial font, instead of spending time and money tracking down and purchasing the font, Gorska preferred to spend the time typesetting the letters herself. "It keeps me in touch with the real letter forms and how they fit together, in a way that we often miss, just doing typesetting on the computer."*

JAVIER ROMERO DESIGN GROUP

## Gallery: Javier Romero Design Group

*With a client as necessarily particular as Disney, Javier Romero needed the flexibility to create many design variations for children's clothing tags. And because the type needed to be fully integrated with the illustrations, Illustrator proved the most practical design tool. Of the dozens of designs that Romero presented, Disney selected as finals the designs shown in the photo above and to its right. Shown directly above are three of the comps, which include compositional elements contributing to the final design.*

# Masks & Special Effects
### Advanced Techniques Chapter

This Advanced Techniques chapter builds upon techniques and exercises covered in earlier chapters and combines techniques found in different chapters. With the masking effects in particular, the techniques will be easier to follow if you feel comfortable with layers (*Chapter 4*) as well as blends and gradients (*Chapter 5*), and are willing to tinker with the Pathfinder filters. Whenever necessary, I'll refer you to the proper chapter for more information on previously mentioned techniques.

Most techniques in this chapter make use of Illustrator's masks. Masks operate as stencils, or "clipping paths" that allow you to control which portions of objects will be visible. The simplest use of a mask is as a cropping tool. This defines the printable area of your page, cropping off from view or print any objects that extend beyond the boundary of the mask. Instead of using masks to define the printing boundary, many artists prefer simply to cover undesirable areas of an image with filled, white rectangles. But, the white rectangles end up being exported along with your image and creating false boundaries extending beyond the image. And, if you export an image with a masked boundary, the masks will actually trim off parts of the image beyond the mask's border.

A better way to crop boundaries is to create a "layer-mask." Working with a file that already has an image, choose Show Layers from the Window menu, make a new layer titled "Mask" and create your masking object in that layer (again, see *Chapter 4* for more info on layers). Then select the mask along with the backmost object in the

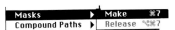

## Styling a masking object.

Through Illustrator 4, a mask needed to be *behind* the objects it masked. Now, when you choose Object: Masks: Make (⌘-7), the *topmost* object automatically becomes the mask, and is restyled permanently with no fill and no stroke. You therefore have to create the illusion that your mask is filled or stroked. Illustrator 5/6 introduced Filter: Create: Fill & Stroke for Mask, which allowed you to auto-generate fills and/or strokes to *your* specifications. As of now, the 7.0 version of this filter automatically generates *both* a new 25% black-filled object behind the masked objects, *and* a new 1-pt black-stroked object on top. Although updates to Illustrator may improve this filter, for the time being you'll probably prefer the manual technique (see page 140 for step-by-step help).

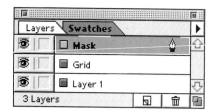

Ron Chan's Layers palette with a top Mask layer set to mask all lower layers

## Grouping masks

Group an object-mask with its objects (⌘-G) for easy reselecting. However, if you group a layer-mask (see previous page) with its objects, it converts to an object-mask, with all objects moving to the mask's layer.

## Inserting objects into a mask

To insert additional objects into a mask, make sure that Paste Remembers Layers is off (in the Layers pop-up menu), then cut (⌘-X) or copy (⌘-C) the objects you wish to insert into the mask. Next, select an object within the mask and use Paste In Front or Back (⌘-F or ⌘-B) to place the copied object into the mask (see page 78 for more on Paste In Front/Back).

## Selecting within masks

Use the Direct-selection tool to edit individual masked objects. Use the Group-selection tool to select one object, and click again on the same object to select the rest of the objects in the mask set.

stacking order that you wish to mask and choose Object: Masks: Make. Note that Illustrator masks any objects or layers between the mask and the backmost object you selected. Move objects or layers above or below the mask to prevent them from being masked.

But masks can do much more than simply create boundaries for printing and exporting. Masks can also directly affect objects or groups of objects. In an object-mask, the mask and the objects are all in the same layer with the masking object on top. To *create* an object-mask, select all the objects, including the top object, which will become the mask, and choose Object: Masks: Make (⌘-7). If you accidentally select objects on layers other than the one you want to mask, then all other objects in between the mask and the chosen object will also be masked. To correct this problem, use Shift-Direct-select on any objects that were inadvertently masked to deselect them, then group (⌘-G) the mask with the desired objects. Grouping places all masked objects (including the mask) on the same layer and restricts the masking effect to those objects within the grouping.

Illustrator's masking feature provides extraordinary control over what portions of objects, blends or images are visible. Masks let you easily adjust both the contour of the masking object and the contents of objects being masked, through use of the Direct-select tool to edit paths and the Group-selection tool to isolate objects.

### MASK PROBLEM-SOLVING STRATEGIES

As you work with masks, there are bound to be times when a mask doesn't work right, or Illustrator won't let you make an object into a mask. Here are some of the most common problems you may find when working with masks.

• **A type character isn't turning into a mask.** To use a type character as a mask, you must first apply Type: Create Outlines (⌘-Shift-O, as in "outline"). For step-by-step help with this technique, see page 140.

- **Text made into a mask only has one letter of the word act as the mask.** This occurs once you've converted text into outlines (see above), and tried to mask using multiple letters. Because only the topmost object can be the mask, the last letter of the text is the only one that acts as the mask. The solution is to select the text and make it a compound path before the mask command is invoked (see Technique following for compound help).

- **You're trying to make a mask, but a dialog box says "selection cannot contain objects within different groups unless the entire group is selected."** This means that the objects being selected as a mask are only part of a group. Cut (⌘-X) and Paste In Front (with the Paste Remembers Layers toggle *on*), then make the mask.

- **Moving a mask from one layer to another stops the masking effect.** Moving a layer-mask (see earlier in this chapter) will release the masking effect. You'll need to reselect and reapply the masking command.

- **You're having trouble getting a masked object to print.** If you have tested to see if the mask is indeed the culprit (see Tip, "Memory-hogging masks," below), on a copy of your image, as long as your masked objects don't contain strokes, select the mask and its objects. Then apply the Object: Pathfinder: Trim command (Trim deletes stroke styles!) to automatically trim hidden areas of the image. This makes it easier for the file to print (see pages 194 and 173 for Gallery examples). 🍪

### Memory-hogging masks

Too many masks, or complex masking paths, may demand too much memory and prevent you from printing. To test if a specific mask is a problem: select it with its masked objects, and temporarily hide them (Object: Hide, or *QK:* ⌘-3), and see if printing is easier. **IMPORTANT:** *Hiding only the mask will not affect the masked objects.*

### Figuring out if it's a mask

If you're not sure whether a current selection contains a mask, or is being masked, choose File: Selection Info: Objects. Or, see if the Release option is enabled in Object: Masks—indicating that a mask is affecting your selection.

### Finding masks

Deselecting all objects first and choosing filter Select: Select Masks should help you find most masks; layer-masks though (see text at left), aren't always detectable.

### When a mask isn't a mask

Masks were once the only way to achieve certain effects that you can now accomplish in other ways. For example, you can now use gradients to make transitions within complex objects both linearly and radially (see *Chapter 5* for more on blends and gradients). Even so, you'll see throughout this chapter many shaped blends that can't yet be created with gradients. Also, Pathfinder filters can now actually crop off unwanted parts of objects that at one time required masking (see *Chapter 6* and page 173). However, applying these filters irrevocably alters the shapes of objects, sometimes creating distortions (such as deleting strokes), and will greatly limit your ability to make changes at a later time.

# Colorful Masking

*Fitting Blends into Custom Shapes*

**Advanced Technique**

**Overview:** *Create a complex blend; mask it with a custom masking object; create a second mask-and-blend combination; make a two-object mask using compound paths.*

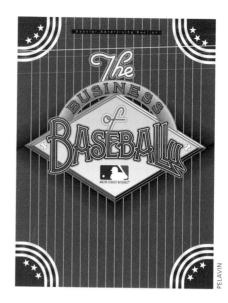

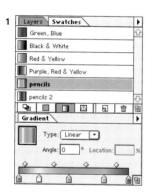

1

Layers / Swatches

| | |
|---|---|
| ■ | Green, Blue |
| ■ | Black & White |
| ■ | Red & Yellow |
| ■ | Purple, Red & Yellow |
| ■ | **pencils** |
| ■ | pencils 2 |

Gradient

Type: Linear
Angle: 0 °  Location: %

*The gradient for a pencil body*

2

*Creating objects and blending them in pairs, then creating an object to use as a mask*

| Masks | ▶ | Make | ⌘7 |
|---|---|---|---|
| Compound Paths | ▶ | Release | ⌥⌘7 |

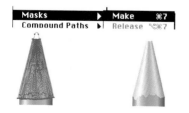

*Selecting the blends with an overlying object designed as a mask; the objects masked*

The best way to learn how to mask is to make some masked blends. With Laurie Grace's pencils, you'll learn how to mask complex blends to fit into custom shapes. And with the patriotic corners of Danny Pelavin's baseball illustration, you'll learn how to mask one blend into two different objects by using compound paths.

**1 Creating the basic elements not requiring masking.** Create your basic objects. For her pencils, Grace created the long barrel of the pencil with a gradient fill.

**2 Creating the first mask-and-blend combination.** To prepare a mask for the pencils, create a closed object outlining the shaved wood and pencil tip, and choose Object: Lock (*QK*: ⌘-2). To ensure that your blend will completely fill the mask, make sure that each created object extends beyond the mask. Then select and blend each pair of adjacent objects (see *Chapter 5*). Grace created the slanted outside objects first and the center object last so the blends would build from back to front towards the center. Object: Unlock (*QK*: ⌘-Opt-2) your pencil-tip object, choose Arrange: Bring to Front (Shift-⌘-]), select the blends with the mask and ⌘-7 (or Object: Masks: Make). Finally, group (⌘-G) the mask and blend together.

**3 Preparing the next masking objects and mask.** Select and copy your mask, then select and lock the mask with the masked objects to keep from accidentally selecting any of them as you continue to work. Next, use Paste In Front (⌘-F) to paste a copy of your previous mask on top, and make any adjustments necessary to prepare this object as the next mask. Grace cut and reshaped a copy of the full pencil-tip mask until it correctly fit the colored lead at the top. Finally, Object: Hide (*QK*: ⌘-3) this new mask-to-be until you've completed a new set of blends.

**4 Creating a new mask that overlies the first.** Create and blend new pairs of objects as you did for the previous mask. When your blends are complete, Object: Show (*QK*: ⌘-Opt-3) your hidden masking object and Bring to Front to place the mask on top of these latest blends. Then select the colored-tip blends with this top object, ⌘-7 to make the mask and, as before, group them (⌘-G) together for easy reselection. Finally, Object: Unlock the first blends (*QK*: ⌘-Opt-2), select the entire piece and group (⌘-G) it all together.

**5 Making a mask from a compound path.** Create a blend to be masked by two objects. As Pelavin did for his patriotic corners, start with a circle as a template. In Artwork mode, use the Pen tool with the Shift key to draw a straight line from the circle's center point to its bottom edge. With the Rotate tool, Option-click on the circle center to specify an 11.25° rotation and click Copy. Then press ⌘-D seven times to repeat the rotated copy a full quarter of a circle. Recolor every other line and blend from one to the next as above. Next, create two paths for a mask (Pelavin cut and joined quarters of concentric circles) and choose Object: Compound Paths: Make. Place the compound paths on top of the blends, select them all and choose Object: Masks: Make to see your blend show through both compound paths. Pelavin recolored a copy of the red blend with a range of whites, masked the white blend with a larger arc and placed it behind the reds. 🌀

*Completed objects selected and locked, then a copy of the last mask made into a new mask*

*New objects before and after blending, and after being masked*

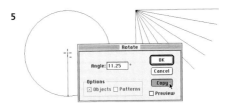

*Rotating a copy of a line about a circle's center 11.25°, then using ⌘-D to transform 7 times*

*Coloring every other line and blending in pairs*

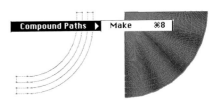

*Compounding paths and getting ready to mask*

*Blends masked by compounds and a final corner (shown here also with a masked white blend)*

# Offsetting Colors

*Using Masks to Create Relief & Shadows*

LERTOLA / TIME

Advanced Technique

**Overview:** *Create a basic object stroked in white; offset a copy in a medium tone; copy and Paste In Front light and dark copies and mask them; Paste In Front the final color.*

*Creating the basic three positions and colors*

*Making highlight, shadow and masking-object*

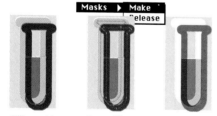

*Filling with no stroke or fill and creating the mask*

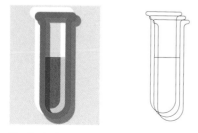

*The final tube in Preview and Artwork modes*

Creating the illusion of relief is a result of both finding the right colors and placing the objects in the correct relationship to each other. For a *Time* magazine article, "The Chemistry of Love," Joe Lertola relied solely on a limited palette, objects offset in three positions and Illustrator's masking feature to create this license plate.

**1 Creating a simple object stroked in white, then offsetting copies.** Set the ruler units to points (see Tip on page 20). Select any object and set it to have a 2.5-pt white stroke and no fill (for help setting styles, see page 54). Hold down the Option key and drag a copy down and to the right 2.5 points, or Option-click on the Selection tool to open the Move dialog box, specify a 2.5 Horizontal and −2.5 Vertical move and click Copy. Style this copy in a medium blue-gray. Using the same technique, make another copy halfway between the objects (−1.25-pt horizontal and 1.25 vertical), remove the stroke and give it a fill of red. For the tubes, Lertola cut this red, topmost object so it appears half-filled (see page 52 and *Chapter 6* for different approaches to cutting an object).

**2 Making the inner shadow and highlight.** Copy the white object, deselect, choose Edit: Paste In Front (⌘-F) and change the stroke to a light tint of the red. Then copy the blue-gray object, deselect, Paste In Front and style it with a dark burgundy stroke. Copy the red-filled object, deselect, and Paste In Front, styling this copy with no stroke or fill. Select this last copy, the original red object, the light tint and the dark shadow, and choose Object: Masks: Make. Offset a final copy of the full object's outline on top, in the halfway position, and set a blue, 1.8-pt stroke. ✐

## Gallery: Jean Tuttle

*In this Santa Barbara Film Festival image, Jean Tuttle created the wavy film sprockets by first setting the Constrain-angle to 45° (which rotates anchor points 45° off-center) and making a circle. From the center of this circle, she made a smaller, concentric circle by Option-Shift-dragging with the Oval tool. Selecting both circles, Tuttle used the Blend tool to create a third circle between them. Next, selecting the smallest circle, Tuttle Option-clicked with the Rotate tool on the lower right anchor point to rotate 180° and clicked Copy. From the center point of this copied circle, she made two smaller, concentric circles, dragging until they "snapped" to the next arc of the larger circle. She Direct-select marqueed the points on the circles above and below the wave shape and deleted, then selected and joined (⌘-J) each pair of overlapping anchor points. Tuttle next Option-Shift-dragged sideways a copy of the wave until it snapped into position so she could join it to the first. She dragged copies of the long wave downward and joined them to form both a wide black ribbon and a thinner, white path. After making two white rectangles and blending them to form regular strips across, Tuttle masked them with the thin wave path. She also recolored copies of the blended rectangles and used them elsewhere, such as the water (bottom of image) in which turquoise bars overlap a gradient rectangle made from tints of the same turquoise color.*

# Contouring Masks

*Using Masks to Control Realistic Tonality*

### Advanced Technique

**Overview:** *Create the full outline for your image; copy an object representing a surface; create a blend and mask it with a copy of the surface outline pasted in front.*

**1**

*Initial printer in Artwork mode (notice that objects don't overlap)*

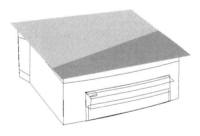

*The top objects before blending*

*The top blended and selected with top object before masking*

*The top masked*

There are a number of reasons why you should learn how to replicate the gradient effect (see *Chapter 5*) using blends and masks. First, blends which are made up of a limited number of steps print more quickly than gradients. Second, gradients that print smoothly won't necessarily look good for on-screen presentations. Finally, by learning this technique, you'll understand how to edit complex images saved in formats prior to Illustrator 5.

Since Andrea Kelley knows that her renderings for Apple Computer are often both printed in miniature (less than 1" tall) or viewed on computer monitors, she controls how the images will be displayed on the monitor, while reducing the printing time. Kelley uses blends and masked blends instead of gradients. For blends within straight-sided objects, she removes unnecessary paths to keep the blends clean in Artwork mode (see page 114). For rounded shapes, Kelley uses copies of an object's contour to mask her blends.

**1 After creation of a full image outline, creating and masking blends.** Create an outline version of your image, constructing each surface you'd like to mask out of one closed object (see page 122 for one way to create separate enclosed objects). Decide which surface you'd like to mask first, select the corresponding object and copy it, then choose Edit: Select All (⌘-A). Now Lock (Object menu, or *QK*: ⌘-2) all the selected objects. Create a blend that extends beyond the surface parameters, then use Paste In Front to paste the copy of your surface (your new mask) on top. Select the blend along with the top object and choose Object: Masks: Make (⌘-7). Then group (⌘-G) the mask with its blend. To access the other objects in your illustration, choose Object: Unlock (*QK*: ⌘-Option-2). Then continue to follow the above steps for each surface requiring a different tonality or color. As you work, make sure to lock objects you don't want to select accidentally, and to group masks with their objects as soon as they're made. You may wish to group related objects further for easy reselection—for example, all of the objects forming the top of the printer.

Simplify your tasks by making and using custom layers to isolate objects as you work (see *Chapter 4* for details on layers). Try, for instance, pasting the next object you intend to use as a mask into a new, upper layer labeled "red." After you create the mask, grouping it with the masked objects will automatically move the masked objects into the upper red layer. By having this red layer, you'll be able to identify instantly and lock or hide all previously masked objects as you select the next surface to prepare it for masking. And there's no need to stop at one extra layer. Whenever you find it difficult to isolate particular elements, create a new layer (assigning it a new selection color) and move the appropriate objects to the layer by dragging the colored dots at the right of the current layer to the new layer (see layer Tip on page 88).

2 **Creating details through careful observation.** Kelley uses 100% blacks and whites with occasional small, thin lines as highlights or shadows. Use copied parts of paths as accents (see pages 50 and 114 for suggestions). ◗

### Magically transform gradients into masked blends

To transform gradients into masked blends, save a copy of the file in Illustrator 3 format; upon reopening, gradients will be replaced by masked blends! — *A. Kelley*

2

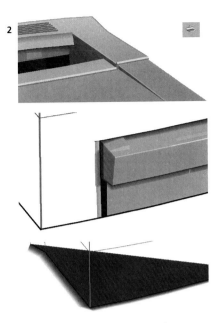

Details of the masked printer blends

The final printer in Artwork mode

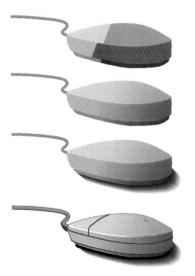

The mouse's mask-and-blend progression

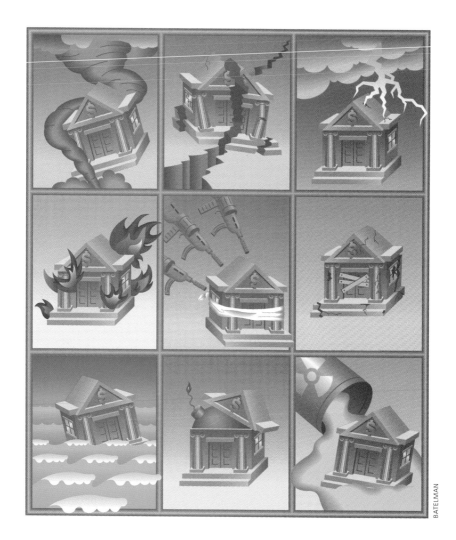

## Gallery: Kenneth Batelman

*Kenneth Batelman used masks to fit blends into contoured shapes all through-out this "Banking Disaster" illustration. Shown directly above are the stages of creating the flames, from making pure blends, to masking with a flame shape, to layering flames upon flames. Batelman used a similar technique to fit blends within a poured shape for the glowing, radioactive slime, and to shape the tornado funnel. He also used masks to create splits in the earthquake image (each split contains an entire bank, masked to show only the desired portion), and in the clouds and waves.*

MORRIS / SAN FRANCISCO EXAMINER

## Gallery: Christopher Morris / *San Francisco Examiner*

*Christopher Morris created "Mafia Chef" for a* San Francisco Examiner *story about a Mafia member who, after entering the Federal Witness Protection Program, wrote a cookbook and then went out on tour promoting it, only giving interviews in clandestine hotel rooms. To create this darkly satirical illustration, Morris constructed blends that fit roughly into compositional outlines that he had drawn with the Pen tool. He then used his compositional outlines as masks to fit the rough blends snugly into these contours. Shown directly above, from left to right is the chef, constructed only of blends (notice that the blends stick out in various places), next with the contouring masks in place, and then, after being masked. Also shown is the corner with the steaming pot before and after masks were applied.*

# Reflective Masks

*Super-Realistic Reflection*

**Advanced Technique**

**Overview:** *Move a copy of a blend area; if you're using type, convert it to outlines; skew and adjust it to the right shape; use filters to make an offset; recolor and remask blends; move blend back into position.*

*A blended area selected and a copy moved off the image area (by holding Option when entering "+1.5" in the Transform palette); and type converted to outlines*

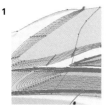

*Skewing outlined type, then adjusting and coloring it to fit the blend contour*

*Creating reflections for an "outline" by copying the type, then stroking and filtering it using Object: Path: Outline Path and Pathfinder: Unite*

Two techniques in earlier chapters demonstrated how Thomas•Bradley Illustration & Design (T•BI&D) used Pathfinder filters to generate its basic objects for blending (page 122), and how the blends themselves are formed (page 112). This technique focuses on replicating contouring blends to create reflectivity and surface variation.

**1 Replicating an area of your image for placing new details.** This process can be used to create color or surface variations, but we'll use the application of type detailing as a demonstration. After you've outlined your image and filled it with contouring blends, choose an area for detailing. With the Shift key down, use Selection and Group-selection tools to select all blends and originating objects for the blends that exist in that area. Open the Transform palette and click at the end of the current X value (the first text field). Type "+1.5" and then hold Option while pressing Return (this moves a copy 1.5" to the right). Set the Cursor-key distance to 1.5" (in Preferences) so you can now use the → key to continue to move the selected blends until they're in a blank area of your image. Next, use the Type tool to place a letter, word or number on top of the moved blend (see *Chapter 7* for more on type). Click a Selection tool to select the type as an *object* and choose Type: Create Outlines (⌘-Shift-O).

**2 Reshaping type to fit your blended contours and creating an offset.** Working from templates, references, or just your artistic eye, use the Rotate, Scale and Skew tools with Direct-selection to adjust various anchor points until the type fits the contour. For the type on the racecar,

T·BI&D skewed the letters (by clicking first in the center of a baseline, grabbing above right, and Shift-dragging to the right). Then they Direct-selected individual points and groups of points, moving them into the visually correct positions.

To create the outlining effect, first copy a solid-filled version, then set the stroke in the desired weight and color. While this object is still selected, choose Object: Path: Outline Path, then Object: Pathfinder: Unite.

3

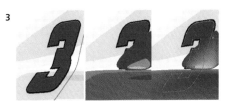

Re-creating blends in new colors and preparing to mask them with a copy of the "3" on top

With the red, reflective blends masked, creating a darker, offset "3"

**3 Pasting the original back on top, designing new colors for copies of the older blends and masking the new versions.** First, Paste In Front (⌘-F) the original, unstroked type element. Next, select and Lock blends or objects that won't fall within the detail (Object: Lock, or *QK*: ⌘-2), but that you want to keep for reference. Copy and Paste In Front (⌘-F) each of the source objects for new blends and recolor them for your detailing. To recolor a blend: Direct-select and recolor the two source objects, then select these recolored objects with the blend between them and choose Filter: Colors: Blend Front To Back. Reblend each pair of source objects using the same procedure, grouping these objects with their blends as you go. T·BI&D recolored the car blends for the red **3**, then added a tear-shaped blend for more detail. Select and copy (in Artwork mode if necessary) the original **3**, use Paste In Front (⌘-F), press the Shift key and click to add the new grouped blends to the selection, then choose Object: Masks: Make (⌘-7). Group (⌘-G) Object: Hide (*QK*: ⌘-3) these finished masked objects and repeat the recoloring of copied blends, masked by a top object for any additional highlights and shadows. Choose Object: Show All (*QK*: ⌘-Opt-3) when these masks are complete, group all the masks together and use the cursor-keys to snap this group of reflective details into position. T·BI&D created one more version of the **3** for a dark offset. For areas requiring more reflections, they constructed even more masks upon masks, as well as occasionally applying compound-masks (see page 155). ◌

The dark "3" and the entire group of objects complete, before and after being moved back into position with cursor-keys

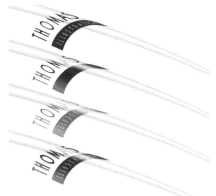

Other elements require more stages of blending (see page 155 for compounding multiple objects, like type elements, to apply as a single mask)

# Glowing Starshine

*Blending Custom Colors to Form a Glow*

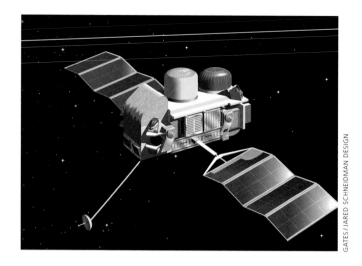

GATES / JARED SCHNEIDMAN DESIGN

**Advanced Technique**

**Overview:** *Create a custom color for the background and the basic object; scale a copy of the object; make object adjustments and blend a glow.*

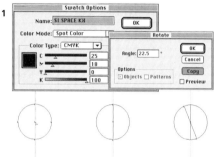

The background custom color; dragging a guide to the center of a circle, drawing a center line and rotating a copy of the line

After pressing ⌘-D six times, making guides and adding anchor points at guide intersections

After Shift-Option scaling the circle smaller and changing the center to 0% tint; Direct-selecting and moving top, bottom and side points outward

Before and after a 12-step blend

Illumination is the key to creating a realistic nighttime sky. This variation on a technique by Guilbert Gates and Jared Schneidman Design (JSD) will help you create glowing lights, not just stars, simply and directly.

**1 Creating a custom color and the basic object.** Create a background rectangle filled with a dark, custom color (see *Chapter 3*). JSD's background was 25% cyan, 18% magenta and 100% black. In Artwork mode, make a circle, then drag a guideline from the ruler until it "snaps" to the circle's center (see Tip on page 7). With the Pen tool, click on an edge of the circle where the guide intersects, hold down Shift and click on the other edge. Select this line, double-click the Rotate tool, specify 22.5° and click Copy. Type ⌘-D to repeat the rotate/copy six times, then select only the lines and type ⌘-5 to make them guides. Use the Add-anchor-point tool to add eight points, one on each side of the circle's original points at guide intersections.

**2 Creating the glow.** With the circle selected, use the Scale tool to make a smaller copy of the circle (hold the Shift and Option keys) and specify a 0% tint fill in the Color palette. Direct-select the top point and Shift-drag it outward. Repeat with the bottom and two side points. With the Blend tool, click on corresponding selected points from each circle and specify 12 steps. 〰

SNEBOLD

## Gallery: Bill Snebold

*To create this juggling clown, Bill Snebold first traced a scanned sketch (see Chapter 4) of the left side of the clown with the Pen tool, then made a flipped copy for the right side using the Reflect tool. Snebold traced the apple from a Polaroid photo and carefully created blends throughout (see Chapter 5). For the glowing apples, he made a full red apple using blends, then drew subsections of the apple to use as masks. For each color on the apple, he reconfigured the blend colors of the entire apple (see page 162), placed the appropriate subsection path on top and chose Object: Masks: Make. The glows result specifically from blending sections of the apple contour filled with white to the overlapping background color. Where the apple overlapped the face, Snebold had to create approximately 20 blends, many of them masked individually.*

## Gallery: John Kanzler

*In this illustration for* Soccer Jr. *magazine, John Kanzler wanted to create the appearance that his bold characters were outlined by variable-weight black strokes. Beginning with colorfully filled, unstroked objects, he added facial features and dividing lines with unfilled 3-pt black strokes. Kanzler then selected each set of objects that made up a figure to: Group (⌘-G), Copy (⌘-C), Paste In Front (⌘-F) and then Object: Lock (QK: ⌘-2). Next he selected the group of objects in back and set the fill to Black and Stroke to None. After deselecting the group, Kanzler then used the Direct-selection tool to select individual anchor points and move them outward to create the black "outlines." When necessary he added points with the Add-anchor-point tool. For some of the props, such as the chain links and locks, Kanzler customized unfilled stroked objects by varying the stroke Cap style (see page 49). For the locks he used a 3-pt colored stroke set to the Round-cap, then used Paste In Back to paste a copy behind, which he then set to 8-pt Black. For the chain links, Kanzler drew a few different individual color links with the Butt-cap and then grouped each link with a thicker black stroke pasted behind. To assemble the chains, he then "mixed and matched" the various outlined links.*

## Gallery: Andrea Kelley

*For a series of promotional baseball cards produced for Symantec Corporation, Andrea Kelley developed a system to distort the dozens of logos and pictures needing to be placed onto boxes in an identical turned-angle perspective. Kelley first drew a box using the Pen tool, then grouped (⌘-G) and scaled her first logo to a rectangle the size of the angled placeholder on the box (see* Chapter 2 *and the Tip "Scaling images to an exact size" on page 13 for scaling help). Because the turned face was thinner than a box front, she double-clicked on the Scale tool to specify 85% horizontal (100% vertical) scaling. She dragged the logo from the upper left corner until it snapped to the upper left corner of the turned face. With the Rotate tool, Kelley then clicked on the upper left point again, grabbed the upper right corner and swung it up until it aligned with the top of the box. Next, with the Skew tool, she clicked once more on the upper left corner of the face, grabbed the lower right corner and, holding the Shift key, swung it down until that line aligned with the spine of the box. After moving the logo into alignment with the left corner of the spine and top of the box, she aligned the lower right corner to the box by first clicking Reset and moving the lower right corner up the minimum amount, applying Filter: Free Distort twice. Finally, she held the Option key and chose Filter: Distort: Free Distort again to reset, then slid the right corner to the left a minimal amount.*

# Painterly Effects
*From Gradient Lighting to Painterly Trees*

**Advanced Technique**

**Overview:** *Create an illustration in full outline; use filters and manual cut and join tools to separate sections and soften edges containing gradients.*

1

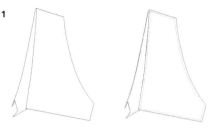

Artwork view of original roof outline and after the Offset Path and Unite filters

2

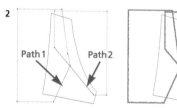

Path 1 and Path 2 objects before and after applying the Roughen filter

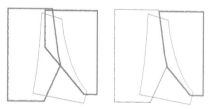

A copy of Path 1 selected with Path 2, then after the Minus Front filter

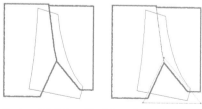

Copies of Path 1 and Path 2, and after the paths have been united, with a third path added

Some circumstances require more than just filling each object with a gradient fill (see *Chapter 5*). Clarke Tate's night rendering of Mann's Chinese Theater for *USA Today* contains many examples of layering gradients upon gradients and of using filters to transform Illustrator's normally hard-edged look into a more painterly effect.

**1 Making inset subsections of architectural objects and filling them with different gradients.** With the Pen tool, create detailed outlines of your image, using enlarged templates if necessary (Tate starts with 400% enlarged templates, *Chapter 4*). Since you'll be filling with gradients, make your outlines completely closed paths. Select a simple object, such as a roof, and create an inset copy of it. Choose Object: Path: Offset Path, and specify "−6 pt.

(if you are working on a smaller scale, you might prefer a smaller inset). With this path still selected, choose Object: Pathfinder: Unite, deselect the inner part of the inset (hold Shift and click it with the Group-selection tool), and then Delete the extraneous objects left by the filter.

**2 Creating roughened divisions to diminish contrast between gradients.** Start by selecting the roof inset and hiding everything else (hold Option while choosing Object: Hide, or *QK:* ⌘-Shift-Option-3). You're going to split the roof into four pie-shaped sections so you can vary the gradients within the roof. With the Pen tool, draw closed Path 1, which will surround the entire left side of the roof, bisecting two-thirds of the roof vertically and angling back toward the left so that it forms the left side of a "peace-sign." For closed Path 2, surround the entire right side of the roof, creating the right side of the peace-sign and overlapping Path 1.

　　Select both paths, choose Filter: Distort: Roughen and specify a 15% size and 30 segments with the Corner option. Make a new layer (see *Chapter 4*) and place a copy of Path 1 on that layer by selecting Path 1 and Option-dragging its dot in the Layers palette into the new layer. Shift-select Path 2 as well and choose Object: Pathfinder: Minus Front to cut the copy of Path 1 from Path 2.

**3 Creating the bottom of the roof sections.** Make a new layer, select Paths 1 and 2 and place copies of these paths in the new layer. With the paths still selected, choose Object: Pathfinder: Unite. Next, on a lower layer, create a triangle that extends beyond the bottom of the roof and overlaps Path 1 and Path 2. Then Shift-select the united path on top, and again, choose the Minus Front Pathfinder filter to cut the united path from the triangle.

　　Draw a last triangle surrounding the right half of the bottom section, choose Filter: Distort: Roughen and use the same settings as before. Now drag a copy of the bottom section to another layer, Shift-select the newest triangle and choose the Pathfinder: Intersect filter.

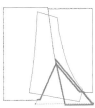
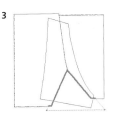

*After the Minus Front filter, and before using Intersect on the last roughened shape*

*Before and after the Crop filter*

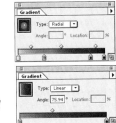

*The roof after being cut into sections and filled with custom gradients, and customized with the Gradient tool*

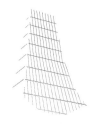

*Outlining paths to fill them with gradients*

*The final roof in Artwork and Preview*

5

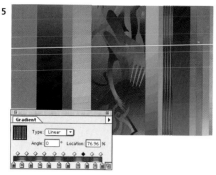

*A detail of the tower and a gradient, shown in both the Gradient and Swatches palettes*

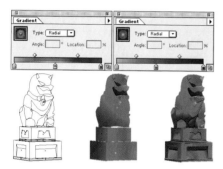

*The main and "recessed" gradients for the lion, shown in Artwork mode, then progressively filled with gradients*

*Progressive stages of theater detail and the taxi-cab gradient*

To fit all these objects within the original roof inset, drag a copy of the roof inset to the top layer. Shift-select all four sections of this copy, set a temporary fill style and choose Object: Pathfinder: Crop.

**4 Designing the roof lighting effects.** To represent different lighting conditions that affect a roof surface, design some custom gradients (see *Chapter 5*). Tate used two basic color ranges for the roof: a bright, wide-ranging, yellow-to-red radial, and a dark, linear gradient in a range of red-browns. Apply darker gradient to the back objects, with brighter gradients for the front objects. Use the Gradient tool to customize the fill direction in each section (page 108), then group (⌘-G) the roof elements.

Next, with the Pen tool, create stroked lines following the vertical slope of the roof and group them. Using a thicker stroke, create tiling lines that follow the horizontal slope of the roof and group them. Finally, select both the horizontal and vertical lines (with the Selection tool) and choose Object: Path: Outline Path to convert these strokes to filled paths. Now fill each group of "lines" with gradients, unifying them with the Gradient tool.

**5 Filling and customizing overlapping objects with multicolored gradients.** The more detail you'd like in your image, the more overlapping objects you'll need to create. Again, because you'll be filling these details with gradients, make sure to create closed objects. As you work, group (⌘-G) related objects together for easy reselection.

Design new gradients for different ranges of light and surface in other parts of the theater. Since you've grouped related objects together, Direct-select individual objects to fill each with a gradient. As with the roof, use the Gradient tool to customize each fill (again, see page 108). For his tower wall, Tate created elaborate multicolored gradients. For the lion, he used two radial gradients: the primary gradient covered a wide color and value range, while the shadow gradient remained dark in tone.

**6 Creating the front canopy for a painterly tree.** Make the basic object for your tree canopy, copy it, and lock it (Object menu, or *QK*: ⌘-2). Paste In Front (⌘-F) the copied canopy and apply these filters, one after the other: Add Anchor Points, twice (see top Tip, page 119); Distort: Roughen (specifying a 5% size, a detail of 10 segments, Corner option); and the default Stylize: Round Corners.

*The original canopy and after Add-anchor-points, Roughen and Round Corners filters*

**7 Creating the back canopy and "holes" for branches.** Object: Unlock (*QK*: ⌘-Option-2) the original, undistorted canopy and, while it's selected, apply the Add Anchor Points filter three times (see top Tip, page 119), then Distort: Roughen (specifying 5%, 10 segments and Rounded). Fill each shape with different solid colors so you can distinguish them in Preview. Make a new, irregularly shaped object to use as a hole in the front canopy. Select this new object with the front canopy and choose Pathfinder: Minus Front. Then create another object to use as a hole in the back canopy, of roughly the same size and location, but shaped differently enough so you can see parts of the back object while still seeing through to your background. Select this object with the back canopy and apply Minus Front (the last Pathfinder filter, ⌘-4).

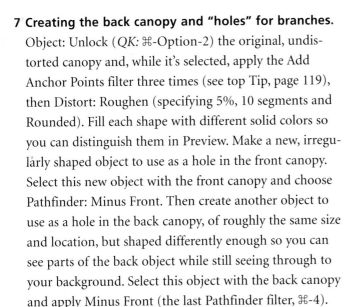

*Roughening the back and cutting holes*

**8 Creating the trunk and branches.** Set your palette defaults to a 4-pt stroke weight and no fill (see page 54), and draw a basic trunk with the Pen tool. For branches, create paths of progressively smaller line weights as you move up the tree, then group the branches with the trunk and transform these lines into filled objects with Object: Path: Outline Path. Now taper the objects of the trunk and branches, and fill each portion of the tree with custom radial gradients by using the Gradient tool.

*Adjusting outlined paths for trunk and branches*

**9 Creating the leaves.** For the finishing foliage, Lock the tree and create random-sized, light-colored circles with the Oval tool. Select all the circles, group them and apply Filter: Distort: Roughen (specifying 60%, 10 segments, Rounded). Direct-select to refill individual leaves. ◠

*Making leaves from filtered circles*

New side walls above stage and terrace consisting of 88 panels constructed of molded fiberglass and steel tubes filled with 66 tons of sand for acoustical density

New stage lighting above terrace level

Side and center terrace seating raised and angled

Side doors have been replaced by four wider doors on Orchestra level

New box seating on the sides and back orchestra level with private vestibules and new box-level bar

Increase of disabled seating from 34 to 64 seats (mostly in front 3 rows)

59-panel adjustable plexiglass canopy above the stage

Quadratic resonating diffusers around stage area and along back walls of orchestra section

New cherrywood grill-work stage walls raised and backed with sound diffusers and reflectors

Other improvements

▶ New sound and color video systems
▶ Orchestra and chorus risers
▶ Replacement of 'bulinose' projections in stage area with solid cherrywood lips and caps surrounding the stage
▶ Upgrade of ventilation systems
▶ Modification of pit elevator to create new piano lift
▶ Refurbishment of orchestra lobby
▶ New burgundy-colored carpeting throughout the hall

Stage

Orchestra seating

SOURCE: San Francisco Symphony

EXAMINER/JOE SHOULAK

SHOULAK / San Francisco Examiner

Addition of two aisles on Orchestra level reconfigured for better access and the elimination of 320 seats, reducing capacity from 3,063 to 2,743

New parquet floor on Orchestra level with new wood subfloor for acoustical purposes

## Gallery: Joe Shoulak / *San Francisco Examiner*

*For this illustration detailing the renovation of Davies Symphony Hall, Joe Shoulak drew the first row of seats, then duplicated, moved, darkened, rotated and skewed it. He then blended the two rows using 18 steps. Shoulak next selected and grouped the left seats and, with the Reflect tool, he Option-clicked to the right of the seats to specify a reflection along the vertical axis, and clicked Copy. For the Plexiglass canopy, he skewed, scaled, and reflected rounded rectangles. Shoulak united a copy of the rectangles into one object (by placing an overlapping solid object with the rectangles, and choosing Pathfinder: Unite). He copied the objects that he wished to have appear through the canopy, moved them into a new document (in perfect registration) using Paste In Front, and desaturated the colors (Filter: Colors: Desaturate). Shoulak pasted the united canopy on top of the desaturated panels and masked with it. He stroked the rectangles white (no fill) and pasted them on top of the masked panels. Then he grouped and copied the entire Plexiglass section and used Paste In Front to bring it back on top of the main image.*

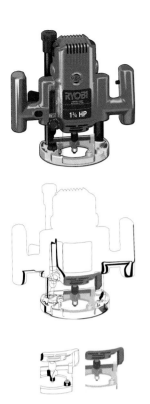

CROUSE

## Gallery: Scott Crouse

*Scott Crouse finds masked objects cumbersome to work with, so he uses Pathfinder filters to eliminate his masks. After completing the illustration of the router itself, he used the Pen tool to draw an object defining the Plexiglass shield. Then, with the Group selection tool, he selected the lower third of the illustration (encompassing the base and the shield), created a new layer and placed a copy of this selection into the new layer by Option-dragging the colored dot (at the right of the current layer) to the new layer (see page 88). Crouse then locked the original layer, selected and copied the path drawn for the plastic shield, and then applied Paste In Front (⌘-F) and Hide (Object menu, or QK: ⌘-3) to this pasted copy. Next he selected all (⌘-A) and chose Object: Mask: Make to turn the shield object (the topmost object) into the mask for the rest of the selected art. Crouse then grouped the entire selection, hid the selection edges (⌘-H), chose Filter: Colors: Saturate and desaturated the colors. With the objects still selected, he then chose the filter Pathfinder: Crop to use the top object (in this case the mask) to cut away and delete everything outside the mask. Whereas the Pathfinder filter reduces the number of objects in your illustration (which means smaller file size, easier selections, and faster printing), you won't be able to reshape the mask—so make sure the shape of the mask is final and correct. (Also Crop will delete strokes, so you can only perform this action on unstroked objects.) To finish this illustration, Crouse chose Show All (Object menu, or QK: ⌘-4) to reveal the hidden copy of the shield. This object was then cut in two places—the top part was stroked with white, and the bottom part was stroked with a dark gray to depict the lighting along the edges of the Plexiglass shield.*

 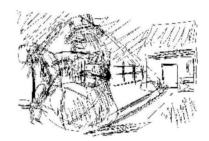 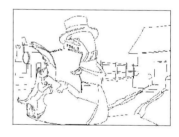

## Gallery: Lester Yocum

*Lester Yocum created "The Morning Paper" as his first card in his* Sno'folks *line of greeting cards. In preparation for the composition, Yocum first assembled a poseable model snowman out of foam balls, pushpins, twigs and props for testing expressions, perspective and lighting. Drawing directly from the model, Yocum used the Pencil tool with the Wacom drawing tablet to develop a rough sketch that he then locked on a layer named "Template" (see pages 80–83). In a series of layers on top of this template sketch, he used the Pen tool to draw enclosed objects (white fill, 1-pt black stroke). Once he had blocked out the composition, to ensure predictable color for printing, Yocum used process color reference books to select a palette of colors that reflected the restrained distortions of misty, early morning light. Blended objects were used for the snowman's arms and the dog's back, but the light and shadow in the rest of the image were created with radial and linear gradients that were then customized with the Gradient tool (see* Chapter 5 *for more on blends, gradients and the Gradient tool).*

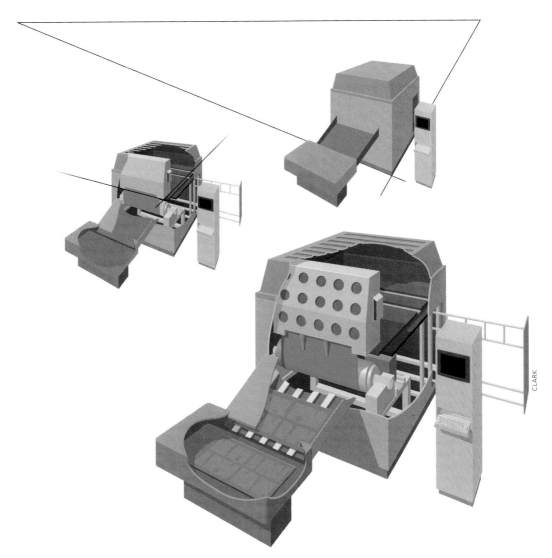

## Gallery: K. Daniel Clark

*To create this "plate maker" for* Publish! *magazine, K. Daniel Clark began with a variation of the perspective guides covered on page 96. With the Pen tool Clark drew three lines: one horizontal line and two vanishing lines (one facing right, one facing left). Instead of converting these lines to guides, Clark kept the lines as paths so he could direct-select a free anchor point (not the vanishing point on the horizon line), and swing that line to a new location. Using these lines as guides, Clark constructed the exterior on an upper layer, and the internal components on the layer below. To create the cut-away illusion, he set the upper "exterior" layer to Artwork mode and locked it (see "Previewing" tip, page 81), then cut away the exterior objects with the Scissors tool in order to expose the objects below. For finishing touches, Clark connected the cut objects with the Pen tool, gave the walls "some thickness," created shadows and highlights, and placed additional details within the plate maker and processing tray. He deleted the perspective lines in the versions of the image that he sent to the client.*

### Gallery: Alan James Weimer

*Alan James Weimer achieved the detailed symmetry in this design by using features of Illustrator's Rotate tool. He began by making a circle divided into sections, with guides (see page 164). Then he created individual elements of the design, such as the leaf, by drawing half of the leaf with the Pen tool and reflecting a copy for the other side with the Reflect tool (see Exercise 9, page 35). Next, with the leaf selected, Weimer selected the Rotate tool and Option-clicked the cursor once on the exact center of the circle. In the dialog box he entered 45° and clicked Copy. To calculate the number of degrees, he simply divided the number of objects needed into 360°. Then Weimer pressed ⌘-D six times to rotate more copies of the leaf around the circle. He repeated these steps to add more elements to his design.*

## Gallery: Alan James Weimer

*To create the diamond-shaped "tile" in the center of this design, Alan Weimer used the techniques shown on the opposite page. He then grouped the primary tile objects and Option-dragged copies of the tile onto a grid of guidelines to ensure proper alignment (shown at right). To complete the design, he used a rectangular layer-mask to "crop" the design (see pages 151–152) on one layer, and on a layer above the mask he added a border of blended, stroked rectangles.*

# Illustrator & Other Programs

# 9

## Supported file formats

Illustrator 7 supports many file formats, including PDF (Acrobat) and PS or EPS files (see Tip below). See Adobe's website for the latest plug-in formats, and the *Wow!* disk for "Ulrik's Format Help."
**Illustrator Opens and Places:** CMX, WMF, PSD, IFF, BMG, JPG, PCD, PICT, MPT, PX1, PCX, TIFF, PNG, PXR, PX1, TGA, GIF89a, Macromedia FreeHand 4/5 (Mac).
**Illustrator Exports:** EPS, PDF, WMF, PSD, IFF, BMP, GIF89a, JPG, PCX, PNG, PXR, TGA, TIFF, and PICT.

## Open sesame

You can open files created in any program that allows you to save in "raw" PostScript: From the host application, print the file to disk, which saves it as raw PostScript. Then, from within Illustrator, choose File: Open and select the PostScript file, which you can now edit in Illustrator. Be careful; text can get chopped into small text blocks, making editing messy.

A full exploration of the interrelationship between Illustrator and other programs would require, at the very least, a full chapter per program. Therefore, this chapter is presented instead as an overview, introducing you to a range of work in Gallery format, demonstrating Illustrator in concert with other frequently used programs. With luck, this will whet your appetite for delving into the world of software juggling (and mastery!), as well as broaden your vision of how to use Adobe Illustrator.

One of the most compelling reasons to use Illustrator's vector-based images (instead of bitmaps, made of pixels), is that they can be resized without sacrificing detail or affecting file size. This makes Illustrator ideal for artwork needing to be scaled to extremes, from billboards (page 197) to miniatures (page 158). Bear this in mind when you are determining how your Illustrator image will be integrated with other programs. ✐

## ILLUSTRATOR, PHOTOSHOP & RASTERIZATION
Until recently, you had to use Photoshop to rasterize Illustrator images (turn them into bitmaps). Now, at least for low-resolution images, you can easily rasterize from within Illustrator 7 (see *Chapter 10*).

However, Photoshop still represents the best way to rasterize complicated artwork in high-resolution. Once an image is properly sized, you can rasterize it "anti-aliased" (smooth, non-jaggy) in Photoshop to preserve an incredible amount of detail (see pages 182–184). Because Adobe Systems develops both Illustrator and Photoshop, the interrelationship is, well, almost symbiotic, especially with the "suite" approach to its programs, which include Illustrator and Photoshop. Each interface is being refined and all keyboard shortcuts reassigned, so that there will be greater cross-application similarities in "look and feel." And since so many people use Photoshop, this chapter includes a step-by-step technique for bringing Illustrator images into Photoshop, as demonstrated by renowned artist and author Bert Monroy.

### About the Illustrator Rasterize command

To rasterize selected Illustrator objects, choose Object: Rasterize. You'll then be able to specify the color model (grayscale, RGB or CMYK), and resolution (pixels per inch). Since bitmaps are always contained within a rectangular bounding box, you'll also have the option to create a mask outlining the object being rasterized (you'll need plenty of RAM for this). Once you've rasterized it becomes an embedded "image object" (see Tips at right for details). **Hint:** Photoshop rasterizes complicated artwork at high resolution *much* faster. 🌀

### ILLUSTRATOR, DIMENSIONS & STREAMLINE

Two other Adobe programs popular with Illustrator users are Dimensions and Streamline. Dimension allows you to create 3D-looking files that you can edit in Illustrator, or distort Illustrator files in 3D space (see pages 198–199). Streamline is a program for converting bitmapped images (painted or scanned) into Illustrator files. Streamline is a much more sophisticated auto-tracing tool than Illustrator's Autotrace tool (see the *User Guide* for more on this tool), and can also be used to create line art quickly for comp purposes. However, beyond its use as a tracing aid, a number of artists are using Streamline creatively to translate scanned drawings or photos into Illustrator images that look completely different from what you usually think of as Illustrator images (see pages 190–192). 🌀

**You should embed when...**
- The image is low in resolution or small in file size.
- You want to apply Photoshop-compatible filters from within Illustrator. Remember that, unlike Photoshop, Illustrator has multiple Undos, meaning you can apply several filters and then undo them all.
- You want to view the bitmap in full detail.
- You want to colorize a 1-bit image (TIFF only).

**You should *not* embed when...**
- You need the image to have a clipping path attached.
- You want to filter only a selected a portion of the image.
- The image is of high resolution or large in file size.
- The file you are working on needs to be used in a version of Illustrator prior to 7.0.
- The alignment of the image being placed is critical. David Nelson discovered that there were some times wher the alignment of an EPS image was calculated more accurately—this was only a problem when he needed to integrate bitmapped images into detailed Illustrator-drawn maps.

For more details on the hazards of embedded bitmaps, see Paul Rauschelbach's "Images in Illustrator" file on the *Wow!* disk.

## Painter drag and drop

Drag and drop from Illustrator to Painter 5 to rasterize *and* bring in path outlines as "shapes"!
— *The Painter 5 Wow! Book*

## Illustrator for "clipping paths"

Just as you can use masks in Illustrator to define irregularly shaped boundaries for your objects, or for the entire image (see *Chapter 8*), a number of programs allow you to save in formats that use Illustrator paths to create a "clipping path." Clipping paths define the boundary of an image when it's placed in other programs. Shown below is Photoshop's method.

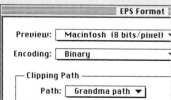

*Creating and defining a clipping path in Photoshop, then applying the clipping path to the image when saving in EPS format.*

## Colorizing 1-bit TIFF images

For details on colorizing 1-bit TIFF images, see Tip on page 82.

## ILLUSTRATOR PATHS & OTHER PROGRAMS

In addition to being able to bring Illustrator *objects* into other programs, you can import and export Illustrator *paths* (as they appear in Artwork mode). Painter lets you import Illustrator paths as "friskets," or stencils, which allow you to isolate regions of your image to apply painting and other effects selectively (page 194). Photoshop allows you to copy and paste paths, export paths to Illustrator, or create Illustrator-like paths within Photoshop itself. In Photoshop, paths can define selection areas for isolating areas of your image, or can be used to define "clipping paths" (pages 181–187, and Tip at left).

Lastly, you can import Illustrator paths as outlines and extrusion paths into 3D programs, so you can transform these paths into 3D objects. Unlike Dimensions, which creates Illustrator objects that only look as if they are 3D, true 3D programs maintain their three-dimensional characteristics until you decide to "render" an image as an antialiased bitmap. Strata's StudioPro (page 195), and RayDream Designer (pages 193–194) are two 3D programs you can use in combination with Illustrator. Be aware that each 3D program sports a unique interface, and you're likely to feel more comfortable in some than others. Try to see demos of each 3D program, and plan to get at least some training in the program you choose. 🖱

## COPY & PASTE OR DRAG & DROP

You can now copy and paste or drag and drop selected objects between Illustrator 7 and Photoshop 4.0 (and any other program that supports PostScript drag and drop). Depending on what application you are dragging or copying Illustrator objects into, you will be either bringing in paths or rasterizing the objects (see earlier sections on rasterizing and paths for more details). With Photoshop, for example, you'll be given the choice (pages 184–185), and you can even drag paths from Photoshop to Illustrator. If you are trying to rasterize in the drag and drop process, be mindful that your Illustrator art will automatically be rasterized at the same physical size, at whatever ppi ratio you have specified in the other program. You can also drag a selection to the desktop, which creates a "picture clipping" file for Mac (in PICT format), or a Scrap file for Windows. These can now be dragged into another document. **IMPORTANT:** *Print designers, be aware that dragging and dropping bitmaps from Photoshop to Illustrator results in only 72 ppi RGB files. Instead, save your Photoshop file as a TIFF or EPS and Place it into Illustrator to preserve the desired resolution and color mode.*

## BITMAPPED IMAGES IN ILLUSTRATOR

Illustrator 6 introduced the concept of "image objects": bitmapped images embedded in an Illustrator file. Image objects can be created either by rasterizing Illustrator objects, or by placing bitmapped images such as TIFF, PICT, JPEG, etc. (see also "Other image formats" section in *Chapter 1*). In contrast to *linked* bitmapped images, image objects can be filtered and permanently altered. But there are a number of issues to watch for, concerning embedded image objects.

First, because embedded images become part of your Illustrator file, your file increases in size with each image you embed. Bitmapped images themselves require a lot of disk space, and when Illustrator embeds the file, it uses almost double the space required for the image alone.

But more serious problems exist with transporting or color-separating files containing placed images in anything other than linked EPS format (Grayscale, CMYK, or 1-bit). In order for your service bureau or client to be able to open your image in a previous version of Illustrator and keep your images linked, the image must be EPS format. Why do you want your images to remain linked? So you can make changes to a placed file and resend only that to the service bureau or client for auto-replacement into the file, without further editing the Illustrator image. Therefore, most experts agree that, for final printing, you should replace embedded image objects with linked EPS files (see Tip, "Swapping placed files," at right for explicit directions).

## When is CMYK not CMYK?

If you use the Eyedropper to pick up a color from a linked CMYK EPS image, it won't pick up a CMYK value! It reads the "screen preview" colors in RGB or HSB. Refer to the Color palette, and change the mode as necessary.

## Swapping placed files

Selecting a placed file In Illustrator and then choosing File: Place will allow you to select another image, to *theoretically* replace the first selected one. Although updates may increase swapping flexibility, Illustrator 7.0 only allows swapping of images of the *same file format*. For now, to replace an existing *untransformed* image with an image of a different format:

- Select the first image
- Re-zero the ruler to the upper left corner of the selected image
- In the Transform palette, click the upper left proxy (page 14)
- Place the new image, relocate it with the Transform palette and delete the original.

## So you think it's linked, eh?

If you apply a filter to a *linked image*, Illustrator will *embed* it, meaning your file will increase in size, and you can't update the link any longer. Instead, apply filters to the image in Photoshop *first*, then place it into Illustrator.

—*Robin AF Olson*

## CMYK-to-RGB in Illustrator

Many Photoshop-compatible plug-in filters only work on RGB images. If need be, you can use Illustrator's Rasterize command to change your existing image object to RGB. Then apply the desired filter and use the Rasterize command again to convert your image back to CMYK. But be aware changing color spaces can result in muddy colors (see top Tip on page 24 for cautions on this conversion).

## Resizing and line weight

In Illustrator, if you double-click the Scale tool, you can resize your selection with or without altering line weights (see page 13):

- To scale a selection while also scaling line weights, make sure to enable "Scale line weight."
- To scale a selection while maintaining your line weights, disable "Scale line weight."
- To decrease only line weights (let's say, 50%) without scaling objects, first scale the selection (200%) with "Scale line weight" disabled. Then scale (50%) with "Scale line weight" enabled. Reverse to increase line weights.

STEUER

## EXPORTING ILLUSTRATOR TO OTHER PROGRAMS

Illustrator 7.0 has improved the options for saving (or exporting) in other formats (see Adobe's *Read Me* file on the Illustrator CD, and Tips, page 178, for more details).

Unlike continuous-tone, bitmapped images, which tend to get very large in size, many Illustrator-format images remain small—and even fit on a floppy disk. However, to place your Illustrator image into a program such as QuarkXPress (see page 193), you must save a copy of your image in EPS format, making certain it is a CMYK color mode, which increases the file size dramatically (PageMaker can place raw Illustrator formats).

In Illustrator 7.0, exporting an image in raster formats often downsamples the resolution to 72 dpi, and in most cases, will not antialias your objects. With these limitations bitmaps will look crude and Illustrator objects will appear jaggy, for now. Check the Adobe website (www.adobe.com) for possible updates to plug-ins supporting high-resolution, antialiased exporting. Meanwhile, when creating high resolution bitmaps for print, rasterize your images in Photoshop (see pages 184–185).

Bitmapped TIFF images do look better on-screen in Illustrator than their EPS counterparts. However, at the time of printing, most experts agree: all bitmaps should be replaced with linked EPS. Yet there is one circumstance in which TIFF format images *are* preferable for output: when the final image needs to be rasterized. As of version 7.0, linked EPS files can't be part of an image being rasterized. Instead, swap these EPSs for linked or embedded TIFFs (see Tip, "Swapping placed files," previous page), or embed them by printing your Illustrator file to disk (as in Tip, "Open sesame" page 178). 

## CAD designers should keep on checking

Some file formats used for exporting and importing artwork into CAD and Engineering programs were not included in the shipping version of Illustrator 7! Check the Adobe website for updates and announcements: www.adobe.com

## Gallery (with Photoshop): Sharon Steuer

*For* The Traveling Radio Show Goes to New Orleans *cassette/CD cover illustration, I wanted to combine soft painterly images with crisp Illustrator forms. After scanning a pencil sketch and painting into it in Photoshop, I saved two versions of the file: one TIFF (so the preview looked good on the screen while I was working in Illustrator), and one in EPS for final printing. Placing the TIFF image on a locked layer below (see pages 80–81), I used the Pen and Brush tools to create the main objects on layers above. In order for the cloak objects to fall behind the dog, I needed to place another version of the Photoshop dog on a layer above the cloak. Back in Photoshop, on a copy of the background painting, I created a selection that outlined the dog with the Pen tool. From the Paths palette, I converted the selection to a path, and named the path "Dog." So that the shape of the dog would be "clipped" by the "Dog" path (once it was placed in Illustrator), I saved this version of the file as an EPS, choosing "Dog" as the clipping path. The dog details were added in Illustrator on layers above the placed EPS Dog. Finally, the Ink Pen filter was used to transform a gradient on a layer directly above the background painting into the "confetti" effect, and Path Patterns were used (without the "distortion" option) to apply the "beads" along various paths (see pages 124–128 for more on Path Patterns and Ink Pen).*

# Sketching Tools

*Illustrator as a Primary Drawing Tool*

**Illustrator with Photoshop**

**Overview:** *Create your details in Illustrator; place Illustrator images into Photoshop at the right size; render and finish in Photoshop.*

1

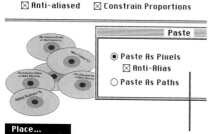

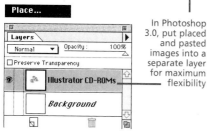

In Photoshop 3.0, put placed and pasted images into a separate layer for maximum flexibility

*Three ways Illustrator images can be brought into Photoshop: opening, pasting and placing*

With a Powerbook portable Macintosh, Bert Monroy meets with his clients to sketch ideas directly in Adobe Illustrator. Back in his studio, Monroy transforms these sketches into intricately detailed illustrations, which he then scales to the desired size, without sacrificing any of the detail. Monroy constructs his Illustrator images in flat colors and then brings them into Photoshop, where he can rework them into scenes rich in texture, light, shadow and volume.

**1 Bringing detailed Illustrator images into Photoshop.** There are a number of ways for you to bring Illustrator images into Photoshop. First, from within Photoshop, choose File: Open and select an Illustrator file. Specify the size and resolution at which you plan to rasterize (turn into a bitmap) the image. Experiment with the results of changing the options. Second, copy the image in

Illustrator, and paste directly into Photoshop, choosing to paste "as pixels." Pasting "as paths" (introduced in Photoshop 3) imports paths to use in defining selections, or to serve as "clipping paths" for saving Photoshop files with nonrectangular boundaries. Third, if you have an open image, you can choose the File: Place command. With the Place command, you can visually resize your Illustrator image before it's rendered. If you have Photoshop 3 or newer, place or paste Illustrator files into separate layers so you can easily alter and move them in relation to the rest of the image.

**2 Measuring in Photoshop and resizing in Illustrator.**

One of the greatest strengths of bringing Illustrator images into Photoshop is that you can render the maximum amount of detail at any resolution. If you resize (smaller or larger) a rendered Illustrator file, you'll sacrifice detail, so the key is to bring Illustrator files into Photoshop at exactly the right size. If simply using the Show Rulers command isn't exacting enough, in Photoshop, first measure the space into which you'll place an Illustrator file. First open the Info Palette, then choose your Line tool, set the minimum opacity (1%) and, with the Shift key down, click and drag from the one side of the space to the other. While doing this, note the value in the Info palette representing the horizontal (ΔX) distance you just measured. In Illustrator, first make certain that "Scale line weight" is enabled in General Preferences (⌘-K). Then, select the object you want to move into Photoshop and resize it to fit the space you just measured. In the Transform palette, enter the X value as the new width (W), making sure to hold ⌘ as you press Return to maintain proportions (alternatively, you could note the ΔY to enter as the height).

Monroy's preferred method is to prescale and copy his Illustrator file, and from within Photoshop, select the area into which he wants to paste and then choose Edit: Paste Into. He can move the Illustrator image around within that selected area, then deselect it to make it part of the main image or put it into its own layer. 🖎

2

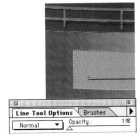

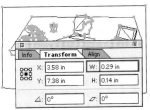

*An Illustrator image; next measuring the space for pasting from within Photoshop; then scaling the image to the right size in Illustrator*

*After selecting an area, using Paste Into to place the copied Illustrator image within the selection*

*In addition to using Illustrator (to create details) and Photoshop (for retouching), sometimes Monroy brings 3D elements (he doesn't use photos) rendered in RayDream Designer (see pages 195–196) to help him visualize large objects, such as buildings, from different angles*

© Bert Monroy 1994

MONROY

### Gallery (with Photoshop): Bert Monroy

*Bert Monroy constructed this image by placing and retouching Illustrator objects in Photoshop (see pages 184–185). Illustrator enabled Monroy to work with perspective lines (page 96), create microfine lines (such as the bicycle spokes), maintain letter-form details, and make quick, local-color changes.*

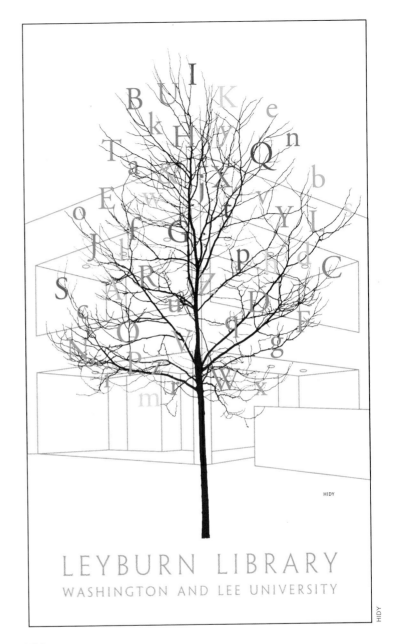

HIDY

## Gallery (with Photoshop): Lance Hidy

*Lance Hidy began this illustration by scanning a photo of the Leyburn Library into Photoshop. After days of painstakingly isolating the tree from the background, Hidy used Levels to establish a "threshold" determining which pixels would be black and which would be white. He then converted this tree (still technically grayscale) to bitmap and saved it as an EPS using the "Transparent whites" option (page 84). In Illustrator, Hidy traced the building (using a scanned pencil tracing as a template; see page 80 for more on templates) and then placed the EPS tree. Hidy added Point-Type elements (which he distributed randomly,) for the alphabet and used Area Type for the title (see* Chapter 7*).*

## Gallery (with Photoshop):
## Pamela Drury Wattenmaker

*Pamela Drury Wattenmaker initially created the microscope in Illustrator. In Photoshop, she then rasterized a version of the microscope without the type and saved it in EPS format. Drury Wattenmaker then placed the EPS back into Illustrator where she masked it with a rectangle placed on top of it (see* Chapter 8 *for more on masks). She then cut this masked EPS, selected the type and "frame" and Pasted In Back (⌘-B) the masked EPS to go behind the frame and type, yet in front of everything else.*

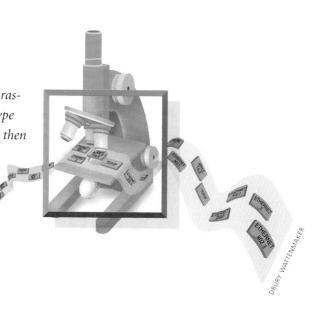

DRURY WATTENMAKER

## Gallery (with Photoshop):
## Michael Kline / Acme Design

*Michael Kline began this image in two separate Illustrator files: one for the background, and another for the "rays." He opened each in Photoshop at the exact same size and resolution so he could use Calculate: Duplicate to load the "rays" as a selection in the background. He then "feathered" the selection 3 pixels and used Brightness/Contrast to "ghost it back." Lastly, Kline saved the composite background as an EPS and placed it back into Illustrator, where he added the airplanes and type.*

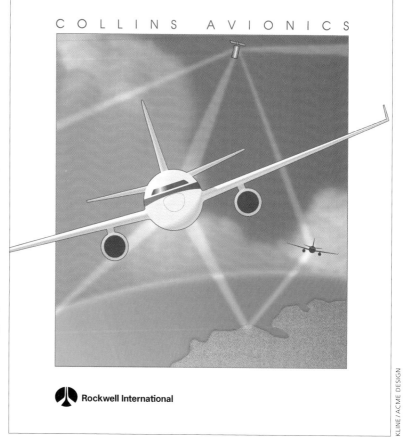

KLINE / ACME DESIGN

MORRIS (illustration), STOREY (photography) / SAN FRANCISCO EXAMINER

## Gallery (with Photoshop): Chris Morris / *San Francisco Examiner*

*For an article discussing issues of copyright protection with the advent of digital imaging, Chris Morris created an illustration using black, enclosed, flat-colored objects in Illustrator. Where he wanted eventually to place photographs, Morris created black-stroked, white objects as placeholders. Morris opened the Illustrator image in Photoshop, then from another file, he selected and copied a scanned photo of Peter Gabriel, shot by* Examiner *photographer John Storey. In the main rasterized image, he used the Magic-wand tool to select the first placeholder for the photo and chose Edit: Paste Into. While the selection was still active, Morris used Image: Effects (Scale, Skew, Perspective and Distort) to fit the photo properly within the selected space before he "stamped it down." Morris repeated this procedure for each image he wished to place. (**Hint:** In Illustrator, try using colors not used anywhere in your image as placeholders, making it simple to pick up these colors with the Magic-wand within Photoshop.)*

JACKSON/SAN FRANCISCO EXAMINER

### Gallery (with Streamline): Lance Jackson/*San Francisco Examiner*

*To achieve the hard-edged, yet warm, painterly Illustrator look in this image, Lance Jackson sketched with traditional drawing media, then scanned the drawings into the computer at both high and low resolutions. In Streamline, Jackson translated both resolutions into Illustrator format. Opening the two translated files in Illustrator, Jackson combined them, using primarily the lower-resolution version while copying and pasting details from the higher-resolution version (the face and hands, for example). Finally, Jackson selected and recolored individual objects until he achieved the final effect in this illustration entitled "Doper."*

SPOLLEN

## Gallery (with Streamline): Christopher Spollen

*Although his illustrations have the feel of bitmapped images, Chris Spollen creates them with Illustrator and Streamline. Spollen has developed a way of working with the computer that borrows from his traditional printmaking background. Beginning with scans of old magazines, and sketches of his own, Spollen runs these images through Streamline. Opening the files in Illustrator, he prints them out, and then physically cuts and pastes the printouts, rescans the resulting collages, and reruns the new scans through Streamline. Sometimes Spollen's files go through many "states" before he finally incorporates color into the image; often he reworks a piece using original drawings in Illustrator.*

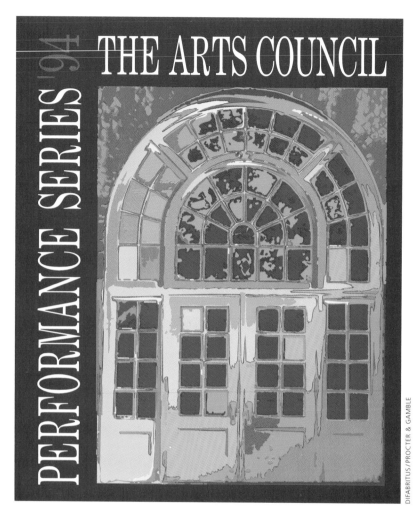

PERFORMANCE SERIES '94

THE ARTS COUNCIL

DIFABRITUS / PROCTER & GAMBLE

### Gallery (with Streamline): Vince DiFabritus / Procter & Gamble

*For this poster, Vince DiFabritus scanned the photo at the right, and opened it in Streamline where he set the Color/Grayscale Setup option to a Posterization of 26 colors. DiFabritus then opened the posterized file in Illustrator, and, because Streamline created custom spot colors (instead of process colors), he was able to double-click on a color name in the Swatches palette, and make adjustments to the colors Streamline had generated. As he adjusted the color recipes of some colors slightly, while redefining others completely with TruMatch colors, Illustrator automatically updated the image (see* Chapter 3 *for more about custom colors).*

**Gallery (with modems / QuarkXPress): Dan Cosgrove** *(illustration)*, **David Fridberg** *(design)*

*For a poster announcing the Smithsonian Institution's 1994 Jazz Orchestra Series, David Fridberg commissioned Dan Cosgrove to create the original illustration. The only problem was this: Fridberg lives in Washington, DC, and Cosgrove lives in Chicago, and the schedule was too tight to allow for even overnight mail deliveries. Illustrator's small file size (compared to Photoshop, for instance) made sending the working versions of the files via modem quick and easy. Cosgrove created rough sketches directly in Illustrator, then "modemed" them to Fridberg to comment on. With immediate*

*feedback, Cosgrove was able to complete the illustration for the poster in record time. Since he knew that Fridberg would be pulling out individual musicians from the full composition, Cosgrove created each musician in his own layer, making it simple for Fridberg to select and copy any of them by hiding and showing the appropriate layers (see* Chapter 4 *for more on layers). With the final illustration received in DC, Fridberg used a combination of Illustrator and QuarkXPress to complete the design for this two-sided, fold-out poster. He created all graphic text (titles and the text on a curve) in Illustrator, although he decided to assemble the full poster from within QuarkXPress. (**Hint:** Since this Wow! book is produced in QuarkXPress, in order to fit the large (14"x20") poster onto this page, I used the File: Save Page as EPS option, then resized the placed page in QuarkXPress.)*

## Gallery (with Painter / Photoshop): Nancy Stahl

*When Nancy Stahl decided to rework the portrait of the woman from her "Couple in the Field" (page 89), she rasterized and cropped the portrait in Photoshop. Next, Stahl both opened the rasterized image in Painter and imported Illustrator paths as friskets. Using the friskets allowed her to isolate distinct areas of the image for local painting and retouching, and for applying specific effects, such as lighting and texture. (**Hint:** Before importing paths as friskets, Stahl now uses the Pathfinder: Merge filter on a copy of the image to eliminate path overlaps; for more on filters, see Chapter 6.)*

GROSSMAN

## Gallery (with RayDream Designer / Photoshop):
## Wendy Grossman

*Wendy Grossman began her illustration "The Bicycle Race" by draw-
ing a tight pencil sketch, which she scanned and saved as a PICT so
she could open it as a template in Illustrator (see page 80 for more
on templates). Using the template, Grossman created the main composition in Illustrator. She constructed and rendered the flowers and
the shrubs in RayDream Designer, giving them the look of a pop-up
collage. Then she rasterized the Illustrator file in Photoshop, where
she assembled all of the RayDream Designer vegetation and
reworked the entire image using the painting and retouching tools.*

### Gallery (with RayDream Designer / Photoshop): Sharon Steuer

*Illustrator was the starting point for this cassette-tape liner (called a "J-card"). The first task I performed in Illustrator was to create separate outlines for each portion of the radio logo (with the Pen tool). Saving each radio outline in Illustrator 3 format, I imported them into RayDream Designer, where I gave each depth and texture, assembled all the radio objects, and rendered them as a PICT file with a mask. Back in Illustrator, relying on source photos for rough visual references, I used the Pen tool to draw the Seattle skyline and the "Space Needle" directly in Illustrator. To establish the overall color scheme, I created gradients and used the Gradient tool to specify their length and direction (see Chapter 5 for more on gradients). I created trim marks by placing an unfilled, unstroked rectangle the size of the final trim and choosing Filter: Create: Trim Marks. I then made the different type objects, rotated the "Goes to Seattle!" line and saved each type object into a separate Illustrator file. In Photoshop, I rasterized, retouched and color-corrected the skyline (see page 184 for more on rasterizing). I then brought each line of type into its own channel, loaded it as a selection and filled it, or, in the case of the drop shadow, offset and darkened it using Levels. Finally, I copied the masked radio and pasted it into place to complete the illustration. (**Hint:** Try pasting type as paths into Photoshop.)*

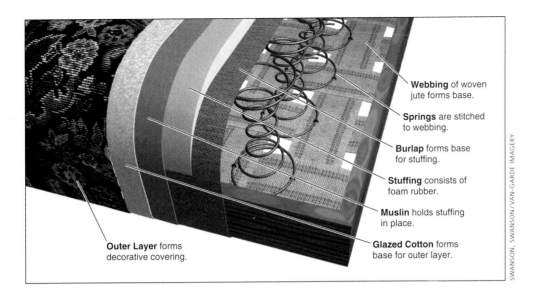

**Webbing** of woven
jute forms base.

**Springs** are stitched
to webbing.

**Burlap** forms base
for stuffing.

**Stuffing** consists of
foam rubber.

**Muslin** holds stuffing
in place.

**Outer Layer** forms
decorative covering.

**Glazed Cotton** forms
base for outer layer.

SWANSON, SWANSON/VAN-GARDE IMAGERY

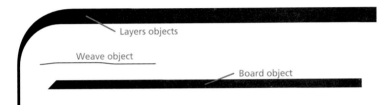

Layers objects

Weave object

Board object

## Gallery (with StudioPro / Photoshop): Dan and Darlene Swanson

*For Dan and Darlene Swanson, the first step in constructing realistic 3D renderings is to create accurate profiles of cross-sections in Illustrator. For the upholstery illustration above, the profiles for the various layers of fabric and foam were drawn in exactly the correct positions and sizes in relation to each other. The Swansons imported these profiles into Studio-Pro where they extruded them into the appropriate thicknesses and rotated them into the correct positions. They constructed the interwoven straps by creating a single modular "weave"*  *object, which they replicated and moved to form the "woofs" and "warps." They turned and duplicated the "board" object so the mitered corners would fit together. Texture maps, previously created in Photoshop, were then assigned to each layer, lights were directed into the assembled scene, and the full image was rendered in PICT format. The Swansons lightly retouched the final rendered upholstery image in Photoshop, saved it in EPS format and placed it back into Illustrator, where they added the labels and border. The glass award (above right) required a bit more retouching in Photoshop, namely a few extra highlights painted on the edges, and some reworking of the type.*

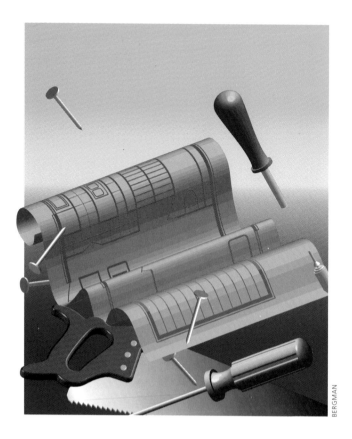

BERGMAN

Screwdriver

Nail

Blueprint profile

## Gallery (with Dimensions): Eliot Bergman

*Eliot Bergman used a combination of Illustrator and Dimensions to create this "Blueprint for Savings." Bergman began in Illustrator where he drew the flat views of each object, using many filters to help him along; for the handle of the saw, for instance, he chose Object: Pathfinder: Unite to combine basic objects, followed by the Stylize: Round Corners filter. Sometimes Bergman drew only one view of the object; at other times he needed to draw multiple views. For objects such as the saw, Bergman drew one side view only. In Dimensions he extruded the handle using the "Tall-Round" bevel, while giving the blade no bevel (the extrusion for the blade was much thinner than the handle). For the screwdriver, he drew half of the side view (revolving it around its profile) and the top rounded cap. The nails were also drawn in half-side view and revolved around their profiles. Bergman drew the blueprint full-front and converted the lines to filled objects using Object: Path: Outline Path. (See Chapter 6 for more on filters.) He drew another separate path with the Pen tool to define the profile view of the rolling blueprint. Although he formed and angled all objects independently in Dimensions, in order to avoid the excess objects that Dimensions generates when computing lighting, Bergman designed most of the lighting effects by using gradients as he assembled the separate objects in Illustrator.*

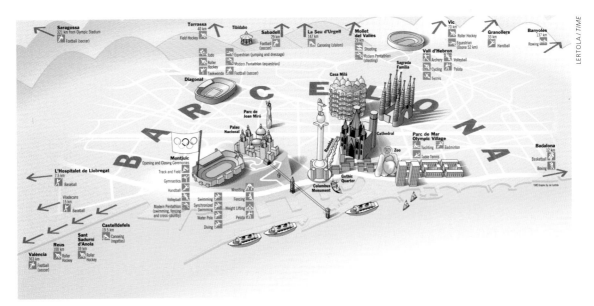

## Gallery (with Dimensions): Joseph Lertola / *Time*

*Joseph Lertola designed this map of the venues at the Barcelona Olympics using Illustrator. He drew an aerial view of only the roads and shoreline, converted the lines to filled objects using Object: Path Outline Path (see Chapter 6 for more on filters), and then brought this aerial view into Dimensions where he angled it back, gave it a small thickness and curved it slightly. Once he achieved this receding perspective, Lertola brought the aerial view back into Illustrator and recombined it with the detailed buildings and assorted icons representing the various events.*

## Gallery (with traditional airbrush): Paul Magliari / World Wrestling Federation

*Large billboards present unique challenges. Since Illustrator files don't decrease in resolution as they are enlarged, Illustrator could be considered the ideal design environment for the variable size reproduction needs of billboard creation. Paul Magliari began the illustration above by tracing over detailed skyline templates (see Chapter 4 for more on templates) and used custom blends to create subtle changes in color. The World Wrestling Federation then composited the skyline with a traditional airbrush illustration to form the billboard shown above right.*

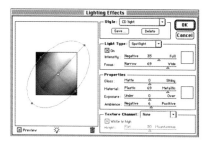

## Gallery: (with QuarkXPress and Photoshop)

**Barbara Sudick** *(design)*/ **Sharon Steuer** *(illustration)*

*Barbara Sudick began her typographic design of the cover in QuarkXPress, which we then saved in EPS and opened in Illustrator. All the placed images (or the sky background, the inner sky and the award) began as TIFFs, and were then swapped for linked EPS versions for printing (so I could re-modem individual elements if necessary, see Tip, "Swapping placed files" on page 181). The inner sky was masked by a palette drawn with the Pen tool (the hole was cut out using Compound Path—see page 155). The CD illustration was created by adapting a technique discovered by Bill Snebold: blends can be applied around a circle using Path Patterns! I created a multi-object blend, selected the blend and chose Object: Pattern to create it as a New Pattern. Selecting the circle, I chose Filter: Stylize: Path Pattern, loaded the new pattern into "Sides" and clicked OK. After adding more details, I chose Object: Rasterize in RGB with the Mask option (since rasterized objects have rectangular boundaries), then applied Filter: Blur: Radial Blur with a Spin of 5. To tint the CD gold for this edition of the book, I copied and pasted it into Photoshop, where I shifted the hue using Hue/Saturation, then applied Filter: Render: Lighting Effects. This CD was converted to CMYK and placed into Illustrator as EPS. The "Wow!" type began as Path Type on a curve. It was then converted to outlines and transformed using a Letraset Envelope and a KPT Vector Effects: 3D Transform filter. The extra anchor points generated by the 3D filter were eliminated using BeInfinite's Smart Remove Points. (The "Plug-ins folder" on the Wow! disk contains many goodies, including a free Mac-only version of BeInfinite's Smart Remove Points.) Finally, I copied and pasted a new center for the "o" (from another "o"), removed the original compound path, applied a new compound path, then scaled and remasked the shading.*

BEST COMPUTER BOOK 1997

The

Illustrator 7

Wow!

Book

*Adobe Illustrator 7 Tryout!*
**MACINTOSH**
**CD**
**WINDOWS**
*Wow! Mac QuicKeys, clip-art, more!*

*Sharon Steuer*

Tips, Tricks & Techniques from 100 Leading Illustrator Artists

**Step-by-Step!**

SUDICK (design)/STEUER (illustration)

# Web, Multimedia & Animation

# 10

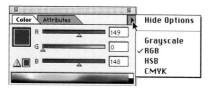

Choosing color modes from the pop-up menu;
you can also cycle through color modes by Shift-
clicking on the Color Spectrum

## Warning: RGB and CMYK

Because Illustrator 7.0 allows you
to make colors in CMYK and RGB
(and HSB) color modes, be cau-
tious: your artwork can now contain objects created in a *combination* of color modes! If you work
in print, this could cause all sorts
of unpredictable color results. If
you're doing print work, *always*
work in CMYK (see pages 22–25,
and *Chapter 3*). Work in RGB exclusively if you're *only* producing
for on-screen display. If you intend artwork to be used for both
print and on-screen, then create
the print art first and use "Save
As" to make a copy. You can then
change the copy's color mode and
export the appropriate file type
for your needs.

This chapter focuses on some of the ways you can use
Illustrator to prepare artwork for on-screen display.
Although everything in this chapter was begun in Illus-
trator, some of the techniques involve working with
Photoshop and rasterization. If you need more help
with either, see *Chapter 9: Illustrator & Other Programs*.

The actual assembly of animations and web graphics in this chapter were often produced using a number
of other programs, including: Macromedia's Director
and Flash2, Adobe's Premier, After Effects and PageMill,
Yves Piguet's GIF Builder, Thorsten Lemke's Graphic-
Converter, Bare Bones Software's BBEdit and Allegiant's
SuperCard. Although not all of these are cross-platform, you'll find demos or lite versions of many of
these programs on the *Wow!* disk. Also check out the
*Wow!* website for samples of animations and links to
related sites (www.peachpit.com/wow.html).

There are a number of other programs, including
Photoshop and AfterEffects, which can open "raw"
Illustrator files. Artists working with multimedia software, such as Macromedia's Director, can access Illustrator files saved as PICT or BMP. Web designers will
find that Illustrator 7 supports a wealth of file formats
that simplify the creation of web artwork.

### A NEW WORLD: WORKING IN RGB IN ILLUSTRATOR
Historically, Illustrator art was produced exclusively in
CMYK and output to print. Now, Illustrator 7 provides

you with the tools to create and output appropriate file types for on-screen images (viewed on a monitor or television), once done only in a raster-based program such as Adobe Photoshop. One of the most important new features is the ability to create artwork in RGB. While Illustrator 7 provides a great deal of support for creating on-screen artwork, along with that power comes a few cautions, especially if you're creating artwork for both CMYK and RGB. If you plan to design print *and* on-screen illustrations, please read this chapter thoroughly, starting with the warning Tip on page 202.

To create artwork in RGB, select RGB from the Colors palette pop-up menu (see top of previous page); this sets RGB as the color mode for the next colors you create. Or open an RGB "web-safe" palette of colors (explained later in this section) from Window: Library: Web. You can find a custom Illustrator Startup file that will automatically and exclusively load this web palette, in the "Custom Prefs" folder on the *Wow!* disk.

**A few thoughts on RGB and CMYK color...**

- **Don't keep converting the same artwork back and forth from RGB to CMYK if you intend to print in CMYK.** Converting RGB to CMYK tends to create muddy colors. If you need both CMYK and RGB versions of your artwork, just maintain two versions of your art—one in RGB and one in CMYK.

- **You can work in any color space (mode) if you're doing *screen* resolution graphics.** Remember though, CMYK files are larger than RGB, and if you're designing for the web, it's particularly important to keep file sizes to a minimum. (Also see "The Web Palette," following.)

- **Create your artwork in CMYK first** if you're going to use it for print, and then convert it to RGB. If you create your art in RGB first, you might use "Out of Gamut" colors (see warning Tip on page 24), which can't be printed with the same brilliance that you see on the screen. So,

**Converting CMYK to RGB**

If you already have artwork prepared in CMYK and you need to change color mode for on-screen RGB viewing, make sure you first "Save As" a copy of your file, then select all (⌘-A) then choose Filter: Colors: Convert CMYK to RGB. Be aware that converting from CMYK to RGB will cause you to lose any association to stored swatches. This means that editing swatches will no longer globally update objects filled with those colors.

**Rasterizing artwork for screen**

The process of turning vector art into bitmap is called *rasterizing*. Anyone creating artwork for the web or for multimedia applications will at some point need to rasterize vector art, and there are many ways to rasterize your artwork (see pages 178–187, and the remainder of this chapter for more on rasterizing). Before you do so, be aware that in Illustrator, rasterizing a *linked* file automatically embeds the file, and if it is an EPS file, you'll need to replace it with a TIFF (see middle Tip, page 181, for help).

## Auto-opening select palettes

You can set the swatch palettes accessible from Windows: Swatch Libraries to automatically open when you launch Illustrator. With the selected palette open, choose "Persistent" from that palette's pop-up. Choose it again to reset the palette to close by default.

## GIF or JPEG? Vector or raster

Export as GIF89a if your art has large solids and/or is made up of *vector* graphics (i.e. Illustrator objects). Export as a JPEG if your image includes *raster* images (i.e., photos) with a good balance of colors (or grays), or if your art contains gradients. If your image includes a high-contrast photo, or has large areas of solid color, export versions saved in GIF89a *and* in JPEG to see which looks best at the smallest file size.

## Adapting to GIF palettes

With GIF format, the goal is to use as few colors as possible while minimizing file size. Use the Adaptive palette option and export your file in different bit depths. Viewing each file in your browser, pick the best looking one with the lowest bit-depth.

## JPEGs in Illustrator 7.0

Exporting in JPEG always saves at 72 ppi. To make higher-res JPEGs, see the Gallery on page 211.

watch your color space! For *screen*-displayed art, RGB will give you more brilliant colors. But more important, for reliable results for *print* art, work *only* in CMYK.

## The Web Palette

Illustrator 7 includes a non-editable web-safe color palette. Its 216 RGB colors are common to both Mac and Windows platforms and are the most reliable colors for creating web artwork. To access this palette, choose Window: Swatch Libraries: Web, or open it directly (see the excerpt from *Coloring Web Graphics.2* on pages 216–217). To create a smaller custom palette from the web-safe palette, simply drag the desired color swatches to the Swatches palette for storage and save the file. (Remember to clear out your palette before you build your custom palette—see "Setting up your palettes" in page xi, *How to use this book,* and pages 216–217.) IMPORTANT: *Know your target audience. How your art will ultimately be viewed should direct how you create your artwork. For example, don't choose a Mac System palette when you export if you are going to a Windows browser. Your art doesn't have to look perfect on every browser, provided you've satisfied the needs of your target audience.*

## Welcome JPEGs

An important feature, especially for web designers, is the ability to export files as JPEG (File: Export: JPEG). JPEG (Joint Photographic Experts Group) provides a variable level of compression, but the more compression, the more detail is lost—thus, JPEG is considered "lossy." This is a very useful tool for web designers, who strive to keep their file size as small as possible while keeping quality as high as possible. It's also very helpful to any designer who needs to transfer a layout to a client for approval via the internet; smaller files transfer more easily (and sometimes more reliably) and JPEG compression can work very well, often without great sacrifice to detail.

Web designers who want to export Progressive (or interlaced) JPEGs (JPEGs that appear all at once in very rough form, then build up in increasing level of clarity until the image is finally appears in full on the web page) will not be able to do so as of version 7.0, even though it's documented as a feature in the *User Guide*. Please refer to the Adobe website for updates on this feature.

### Why GIF89a?

Adobe released a GIF89a plug-in filter for Illustrator 6 through its website (see, there's a good reason to check Adobe's site!). This plug-in allowed users to open or place GIF (Graphics Interchange Format) files for use on the web, but at a price: in order to save the file as GIF89a this release of the plug-in altered your original (never a good idea!). Now, with Illustrator 7, GIF89a is built in as an Export module that leaves your original file untouched.

GIF is the most widely used image format on the web. GIF compression works well with vector-based or files which have large areas of solid color (see Tip on page 204, "*GIF89a or JPEG...*"). GIF files also support transparency and interlacing. To export your artwork as a GIF file, choose File: Export, and select GIF89a from the pop-up on Mac, or from the Save as Type menu on Windows. You'll get a dialog box that will let you select Dither, Palette and other Options. Refer to the Tip at right and the *User Guide* for a more complete description of all the options for exporting GIF89a, and see pages 212–213. 🌏

### THE ATTRIBUTES PALETTE & URLS

Illustrator 7 also has a new Attributes Palette that can assign a URL (Uniform Resource Locator) to any object in your artwork. This is another essential tool for web designers—it allows designers to create an imagemap, to enable users to link to other web pages by simply clicking on different parts of the image. Illustrator creates a separate text file containing the URL information, which you can then import into your HTML(HyperText Markup Language) editor, such as Adobe PageMill or BareBones Software's BBEdit. To assign a URL to a selection, open the Attributes palette, select an object (Window: Show

## Which palettes are for you?

The GIF89a export module provides many palette options:

- **Exact palette:** Lets you have a minimal number of colors in your image when you don't need to dither (dithering optically mixes pixels, so a few colors can appear as many).
- **System palette:** (Macintosh or Windows) Creates a palette of either 256 (Mac) or 216 colors (Windows). The downside of this filter: results may not translate across platforms.
- **Web palette:** Works cross-platform and is most effective when you're using many images and want them to share the same color space. They will display much faster and present a more cohesive look.
- **Adaptive palette:** Can produce varying results. It relies on the web browser to select the most appropriate color palette based on available colors. This may shift the colors in your artwork when viewed using different browsers.
- **Custom palette:** Allows you to load a palette you've created in another program.
- **Transparency:** Makes your page/pasteboard color transparent. Choose this option if your artwork has irregular edges—basically, any shape that's not square or rectangular.

Once you've created (or imported and rasterized) the cels of an animation as a stack of Photoshop layers (see pages 208–209), you can use the Layers palette to preview the action before you take the file into an animation system for final preparation. Set the Layers palette's thumbnails to the largest size (choose Palette Options from the palette's pop-up menu) and shorten the palette until only one layer's thumbnail shows. Then press and hold the palette's up or down scrolling arrow to run the movie as a kind of digital flipbook. If your first frame is in the bottom layer of your file and your last frame is in the top layer, scrolling with the up arrow will run the animation forward; using the bottom arrow will run it backward. If the animation runs too fast, control the speed by clicking an arrow rather than pressing and holding, or grab and drag the scroll box at the speed you want.

— *The Photoshop 4 Wow! Book* (artist Michael Gilmore, CyberFlix)

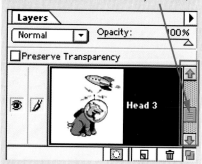

Attributes), then type in the URL that you want to link to in the Attributes palette text field (see pages 212–213 for a Technique applying URLs). Using a web browser, such as Internet Explorer or Netscape Navigator, you can verify if your URL is correct by pressing the "Launch Browser" button on the Attributes palette. Finally, export it using the GIF89a Export Module (see above for details). 🥐

## A SPECIAL ANNOUNCEMENT FOR WEB DESIGNERS

Many people feel overwhelmed by the enormity of technical details involved in designing for the web. Fortunately, there's a great wealth of books covering everything from how to write HTML tags and CGI and Java to designing Cascading Style Sheets and sound. One of the best books about the web is *Designing Web Graphics.2* by Lynda Weinman, and an Illustrator-related excerpt from one of her newest books (*Coloring Web Graphics.2*, co-authored with Bruce Heavin) concludes this chapter on pages 216–217. For additional resources to help you create web-ready artwork, see the Adobe website, suggested readings in the *Resources* appendix and the *Wow!* website (www.peachpit.com/wow.html). 🥐

Here's a quick rundown of some of the GIF89a options:
- **Palette options**: See Tip on the preceding page.
- **Transparency**: Areas not covered by objects will become transparent. Choose this for artwork with irregular edges—any outline not square or rectangular.
- **Anti-Alias**: Smooths the edges of artwork.
- **Dither**: "Blends" colors in a limited color palette. Leave it off if for clean-edged vector graphics. Diffusion dither is usually best.
- **Interlacing**: Displays the entire image quickly, in low-res, allowing the viewer to see the image as it downloads, until the image is full resolution. A non-interlaced image draws to the screen, line by line.
- **Imagemaps & Anchors**: See "Artwork Importing & Exporting" in the *User Guide*, and pages 212–213.

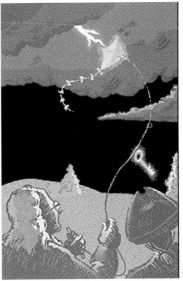

## Gallery: Dave Joly

*Artist Dave Joly created this two-frame animation for the* National Geographic World *website for kids. Joly began this image as a traditional scratchboard illustration, and then scanned the illustration and saved two versions: one scan of the full image, and one cropped detail of the key. Next he then used Adobe Streamline to convert the image to Illustrator objects (see* pages 190–192*). In Illustrator, Joly placed the converted the objects forming the key into position on a layer above (see* Chapter 4 *for layer help). After saving this version as the first frame, he used Rotate on the key object, created some sparkles with the Brush tool, and saved this version as the second frame.*

## Gallery: Dave Joly

*This moon is one of the Joly's animated holiday greet-ings characters. Mouth positioning was achieved by*

*adjusting a few anchor points. Whenever possible, Joly uses masks in order to move objects easily—such as the eyeball. Joly made a mask the shape of the outer eye (see* Chapter 8 *for more on masking), and was then able to select the blue eyeball and move it into position for additional frames.*

# Making Waves

*Transforming and Blending for Animation*

**Advanced Technique**

**Illustrator with Photoshop**

**Overview:** *Create "key" frames with transformation tools; blend to create steps; transform your steps; bring the steps into Photoshop.*

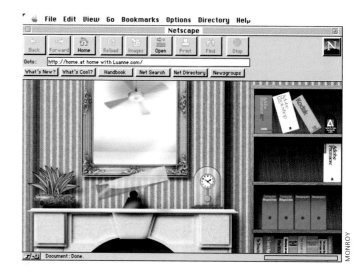

MONROY

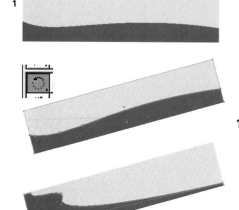

The first key frame; next Rotating a copy; then using the Add-anchor-point and Direct-selection tools to transform the copy into the next frame

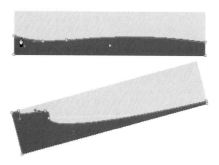

Making certain that the first and last frame have the same number of anchor points in similar alignment for smooth blending (see pages 112-113 for more on preparing objects for smooth blending)

Illustrator's transformation tools, used in combination with the Blend tool, are wonderful animation timesavers. Commissioned by Adobe Systems for a special promotion, Bert Monroy used these techniques to prepare many of the objects within a room for animation.

**1 Establishing the "key" frames.** To create an animation, you must first establish the "key" character positions. How many key frames you'll need will depend on the character, and how it will be animated. Create a character in a neutral position, and if you'll need help maintaining registration, draw an unstroked, unfilled "bounding rectangle" amply surrounding the character. Select the objects making up the character and the bounding rectangle and Option-drag a copy to the side of the original. On the copy of the character (*not* the bounding box), use the transformation tools and Direct-selection editing to create the next extreme position (for more on transformations, see pages 13–14, and pages 38–41). In Monroy's animation, the characters were: fan, clock second hand, clock pendulum, plant, and the "wave." Monroy first drew the wave in horizontal position using a gray rectangle, and a second object for the blue "liquid." He rotated a copy of these two objects to create the left-tilted position, and then used the Add-anchor-point and Direct-selection tools to adjust the liquid anchor points manually.

**2 Using the Blend tool to generate the in-between steps.** Also called "tweening," the secret to the illusion of smooth animation is to create the correct number of steps between the key frames. For video animations, smooth illusion of motion is achieved with 24 frames per second (fps) of animation; for film it's 30 fps; for on-screen animation it's simply as many frames as is needed for your animation to run smoothly. To make the steps between your first two key frames, select each pair of like objects and blend between them (for how to blend, see page 103); because you can only apply a blend between two objects, you'll have to apply the blend separately for each pair of like-objects (including your bounding rectangle), making sure that each pair has the same number of anchor points, and that you select the correlating anchor point in each object when blending. For the wave, Monroy first blended in 12 steps from box to box, and then from liquid to liquid. Since the same number of steps was chosen for each transition, the liquid blends were perfectly registered within the box blends.

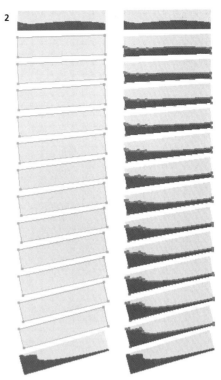

The outer objects after blending (left column), then blending the inner wave (right column)—
**Note:** Selecting the upper right point on the wave gives the smoothest blend

**3 Transforming blends to extend the animation.** Rather than continually starting from scratch, sometimes it's easier to rotate, scale, skew or reflect your blends to extend your animation. Monroy selected his box and wave blend objects, and Reflected them vertically as copies (see pages 35 and 172) to create the right-side rocking motion.

**4 Pasting into Photoshop.** With Illustrator still open, launch Photoshop and create an RGB document larger than your biggest key frame. In Illustrator, copy each character frame and bounding box, and then moving to the Photoshop file, paste "As Pixels" to create a new layer with that step. While that object is still in memory, *also* paste "As Paths" for easy reselection (see pages 184–185). Monroy used his paths to make selections for applying special effects locally—using "Alpha Channels" to create effects such as the darkening on the edges of the liquid, and the bubbles on the surface of the liquid.

The option to "Paste As Pixels" or "Paste As Paths" when pasting from Illustrator to Photoshop; the frames after pasting into layers; the wave after effects using Alpha Channels

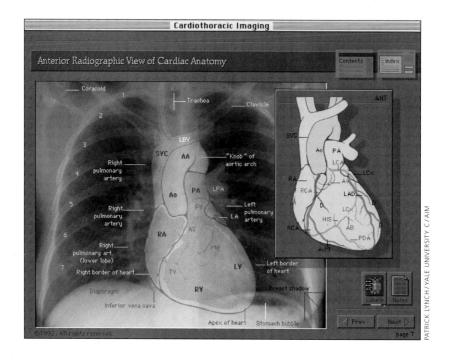

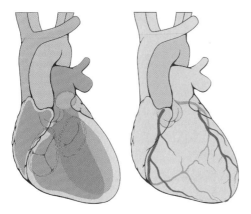

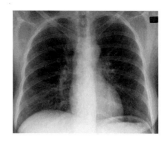

**Gallery (with SuperCard / Photoshop): Patrick Lynch / Yale University C/AIM**

*Patrick Lynch uses Illustrator to create the base illustrations for his interactive CD-ROM development, then uses the Place command from within Photoshop to turn the illustrations into bitmaps. This technique allows him to rasterize fine-lined Illustrator images in much greater detail than would be possible in Photoshop alone (see page 184–186). As a medical illustrator, Lynch uses Illustrator to create detailing in anatomical diagrams, which he can easily adapt by changing colors, adding or subtracting elements, resizing and reshaping, or even overlaying these Illustrator illustrations on top of actual medical films and imaging. For the heart screen above, Lynch rasterized a version of the heart in Photoshop at exactly the correct size and resolution (it had to be scaled slightly horizontally in Illustrator first), and then transparently combined the heart with a scan of an actual chest X-ray. Finally, he brought the individual renderings into SuperCard, where he implemented full interactivity and animation.*

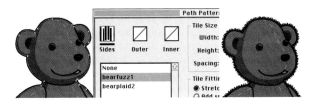

## Gallery: d'JAXN

*Artist d'JAXN doesn't use any high-tech methods when preparing images for multimedia. He began this teddy for the PrintPaks "KidGear" CD by taping his sketch to a Wacom tablet and tracing it with the Pencil tool. After converting those objects into guides (⌘-5, see pages 96–98 and 164), in a new layer (see Chapter 4) he outlined each of the shapes as discrete closed objects with the Pen tool. The floor and the wall were filled with radial gradients (see Chapter 5) and overlaid with objects representing wallpaper pattern and floor texture. d'JAXN then separately rasterized (Object menu) in RGB at 72 ppi, then filtered each with various Gallery Effects filters to create texture. All background objects were then merged using Rasterize again, and then filtered together. Teddy was rasterized, filtered and then masked using a copy of the original paths (see page 140). For detailing, d'JAXN created a plaid pattern for the footpads (which were rotated and scaled individually—see Tip on page 74). To create the teddy's fuzz, he applied a pattern of irregular hatches to copied sections of the outline using Filter: Stylize: Path Pattern to the outline path (see pages 124–128). He then framed all with a solid-filled rectangle before exporting it in GIF "Anti-Alias" format. Using LemkeSoft's GraphicConverter (on the* Wow! *disk for Mac), he was able to crop it, and converted it to JPEG format at 180 ppi as specified by the client (**Hint:** GraphicConverter can batch Trim too).*

# Tabs for the Web

*Preparing Navigational Web Maps*

**Overview:** *Design your background tile; Create your tabs; design variations on the tabs for each web page; assign URLs; Export as GIF89a*

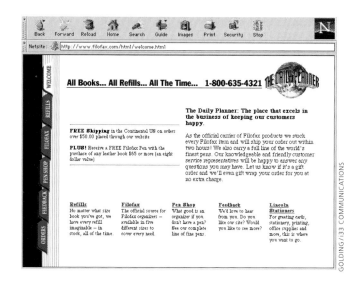

GOLDING/i33 COMMUNICATIONS

1

*The background tile (yellow added for contrast)*

*A detail of the background tile at actual size*

*The background tiled to fill the entire screen*

2

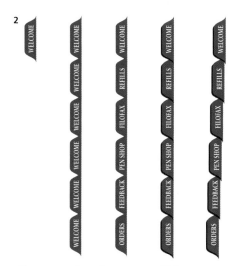

*The process of creating one row of tabs*

Since Filofax organizers rely heavily on tabs, Mordy Golding of i33 Communications decided to use tabs as a navigation tool for one version of their Filofax product-ordering website. Illustrator 7 introduces features that make it simpler to design these web navigation objects.

**1 Designing your background tile.** To create a website background image, design a tile that will repeat to fill your visible screen. Basically anything that works as a simple pattern tile should work as a web tile (see the *User Guide* for tips on pattern making). To save download time, Golding created the "page edges" in the left part of the screen as part of the background image tile, which is the exact width for their screen design, so it only repeats vertically.

**2 Creating your tabs.** Design your first tab using the drawing tools (for help with drawing and tracing, see pages 50–51, 80–83), and with the Type tool, label the tab, center-aligned (see *Chapter 7* for help with type ). Since his tabs were vertical, Golding rotated his text 90° (specified by double-clicking the Rotate tool). Next, Option-Shift-drag your first tab and label to make a duplicate, and then ⌘-D to repeat the duplication for a total of as many tabs as you have pages in your website. Correct the labels with the Type tool. Golding created six tabs representing the six pages on the website. If you wish, add more detailing to the tabs. Golding added shadow, then staggered the tabs to give the illusion of depth.

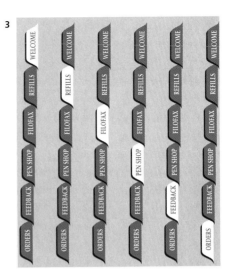

**3 Creating different versions of the tabs for each web page.** To make it easier for viewers to tell which page they are on, create separate versions of your tabs, each highlighting the current page. Golding duplicated his line of tabs six times (one for each web page), then restyled one tab in each group to appear highlighted.

Creating versions of the tabs for each web page (grey added for contrast)

**4 Assigning web addresses (URLs) to each tab.** When users click on your tabs in the actual website, you want them to be taken to the correct web address, so you'll need to assign web addresses (URLs) to each non-highlighted tab (since highlights indicate your *current* address, these don't need URLs). With your first tab selected, open the Attributes palette, and in the text field labeled "URL," type in the appropriate web address (use the ← and → cursor-keys to scroll), and repeat this for all tabs in this first set. For the next set of tabs, you'll be able to choose the appropriate URL from the pop-up menu to the right of the URL text field.

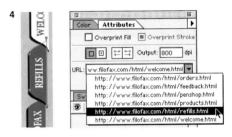

Assigning URLs to each non-highlighted tab

**5 Exporting the files for your web design program.** Select, Copy (⌘-C) and Paste (⌘-V) each set of tabs into their own new document. Save each document separately. Next, to save a rasterized version of each file (for placement in your HTML editor) choose File: Export and select "GIF89a" from the format pop-up. Golding set the following GIF89a options: Adaptive Palette (see Tip "Adapting to GIF palettes" on page 204 for Golding's suggested approach to using this option), Interlace (allowing the image to load gradually), Anti-Alias (for smooth, non-jaggy edges), Transparent (to allow the background image to show through where there aren't fills), and since his images had embedded URLs, he chose Imagemap (this created a separate text file that was included in the actual HTML document).

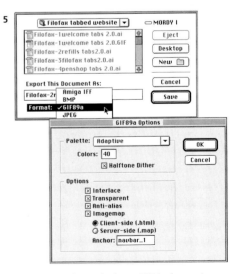

Exporting each set of tabs as GIF89a for use in an HTML editor

### Gallery (with Photoshop): Randy Livingston / White Bridge Communications Inc.

*Read USA Online Mailorder Bookstore (with virtual bookstores on America Online, CompuServe, and the Web) needed a logo to use in print and online. Randy Livingston designed the logo by moving elements between Photoshop and Illustrator. Beginning in Photoshop, he created the shiny red sphere in RGB using KPT Vector Effects' Glass Lens Bright filter (the sphere will revolve in an animated version). After converting the file to CMYK (for print), he created a circular selection, which he made into a "clipping path" (to mask the ball), saved it in EPS to maintain the mask (see pages 180, 183) and switched to Illustrator where he placed it as a linked file. He added the type, which he then converted into objects (Type: Create Outlines, ⌘-Shift-O). Two rectangles filled with gradients formed the "raised panel" (see Chapter 5 for more on gradients). He then used the Pen tool to create the bevel on the right side of the panel. In the first version that Livingston submitted to the client, he created a recess for the ball by filling a circle behind the ball with a linear gradient. For the final version of the logo, the background was changed to resemble that of an old leather-bound book spine; he scanned a book and leather textures and pieced them together to form the spine in Photoshop where he created a new recess in the spine for the red ball shape. Then using his clipping path to select the ball, he pasted it in place as a part of the Photoshop document. This image was saved as a 300 ppi CMYK TIFF and placed as an embedded image object into the Illustrator page. In Illustrator, he applied Filter: Stylize: Round Corners to a copy of the type shapes and then used Paste In Back to place two copies of the "Read USA" behind (one lighter, one darker) to create the embossed effect. The illustration, directly above left, shows the client-approved RGB version of the logo (rasterized in Photoshop—see Chapter 9) for Read USA's opening screen in America Online's Marketplace.*

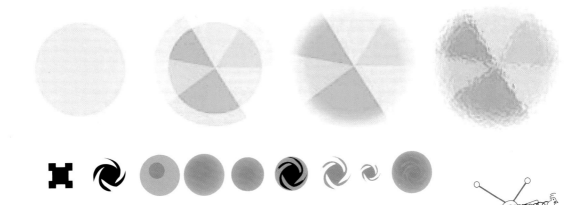

## Gallery: Pamela Drury Wattenmaker

*In this miniature illustration for an* Infoworld *calendar spot Pamela Drury Wattenmaker re-created her initial sketch using the Pen tool to draw separate enclosed objects so they could be filled with different colors. For the background, she created two nested circles with intersecting lines drawn over the circles, and chose Object: Pathfinder: Divide. She recolored and then created blends for each pair of "pie-wedged" objects, selected all the shapes and chose Object: Rasterize at 190 ppi RGB. To this new embedded image object she applied Filter: Gallery Effects, Classic Art 3: GE Glass, with a Distortion of 5, and Smoothness at 3. Although only an RGB image object can be filtered by Photoshop-compatible filters, Drury Wattenmaker re-applied Object: Rasterize so she could convert the object to CMYK for printing. To create the twirling in the clock face, she created a checkerboard of rectangles, chose Object: Pathfinder: Unite, then experimented on the resulting object with the Twirl tool. Variations of this twirled shape were used as masks over nested sets of blends. The final illustration was saved and sent to the client in EPS format.*

# Web-safe Color

*Special Supplement by Weinman / Heavin*

To load exclusively browser-safe colors into Illustrator 7.0, directly open the Web Swatch Library that ships with the program (and should be in your Illustrator folder). Choose File: Open then locate the Web file in the "Swatch Libraries" folder (Web.ai for Windows).

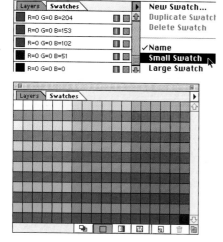

The Web library displayed by name, then shown in an expanded palette viewed by Small Swatch

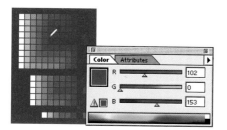

An aesthetically organized GIF format browser-safe palette for color picking, from Lynda Weinman and Bruce Heavin's book and CD-ROM **Coloring Web Graphics.2** (for help storing colors as Swatches, see Chapter 3)

This section of *The Illustrator 7 Wow! Book* was written by Lynda Weinman and Bruce Heavin, and was excerpted in part from their book *Coloring Web Graphics.2*. This book and accompanying CD-ROM include invaluable information about screen-based color issues on the web, as well as hundreds of aesthetically organized browser-safe color combinations and palettes for web graphics authoring. Be sure to check out Lynda Weinman's website for more information about web graphics and her book series on this subject: **www.lynda.com/books/**

## RGB and web-safe colors

One of the best features of Illustrator 7.0 for web graphics is its brand new ability to work with RGB color. Like many other computer graphic programs, Illustrator was originally engineered to generate artwork for print projects, and only functioned in CMYK. With the popularity of the web, and so many Illustrator customers using this product for web graphics, the latest version finally supports the RGB color space. Woo hoo! So, the next question is…how do you use Illustrator 7.0 with "browser-safe" colors?

Browser-safe colors (also known as "web-safe colors"), for those of you not "in the know," are the 216 colors that will not dither unexpectedly (create unwanted arrangements of colored dots) within web browsers on systems with 8-bit video cards (256 colors). If you think your web audience doesn't have this color limitation, you might be wrong. Since you are a designer and work with graphics, it's likely that you have a high-end system that includes the ability to view graphics in 16-bit or 24-bit color. Most of the rest of the world use their computers for more mundane tasks, such as spreadsheets, word processing and database work. The majority of web surfers are using Wintel machines in 8-bit mode.

Unfortunately, the swatch interface differs from that of Photoshop, so you can't automatically load Photoshop palettes into the Illustrator Swatches palette. If you want to make or use custom browser-safe color palettes, the workaround is to create browser-safe artwork in

Photoshop and save it as a GIF. You can then Open or Place the GIF inside Illustrator, and use the Eyedropper tool to select any of the browser-safe RGB colors within the image. Once you've picked up a color with the Eyedropper tool, click on the New Swatch icon in the Swatches palette to store that browser-safe color as a swatch. Save the Illustrator document and the new swatch color will be stored permanently with that file. This is a useful technique if you have web artwork you've already made in Photoshop, and you want to create vector artwork that shares the same colors.

## CMYK versus RGB color selection

If the values are CYMK then change them to RGB (choose RGB from the Colors pop-up menu). The color readout will now be from 0–255, instead of in percentages. (To change colors you've already used, see *Chapter 3*.)

The 216 browser-safe colors are constructed from combinations of six red, green, and blue values: 0, 51, 102, 153, 204, 255 ($6^3 = 216$). If you use the Color palette to mix colors yourself, round off each color value to the nearest number to achieve a browser safe version of them.

## A few last things to keep in mind:

- Illustrator 7 will rasterize your images to RGB within the program; however, the artwork will come out cleaner and crisper if rasterized with the Place function into Photoshop (see *Chapter 9*).

- Gradients between browser-safe colors *aren't* browser safe.

- If you are using the Eyedropper to pick colors from a GIF file, Illustrator will not let you recolor a stroke. You must transfer the color you've picked into the Illustrator Swatches palette first, using the methods described on this page, and then you can change the stroke color. This seems like a bug, or maybe it's a feature <grin>.

### Make sure RGB is not CMYK!

Make sure the colors you pick with the Eyedropper tool are RGB! If the colors are CYMK, they will shift into non-browser-safe colors once the image is rasterized in RGB. Check your color palette to see if your values are in CYMK (see below). One clue that the colors are CYMK is that color values are in *percentages*. Also make sure to check both the Fill and Stroke, and check every object when changing colors so that your colors don't stray. (To update stored colors, see *Chapter 3*.)

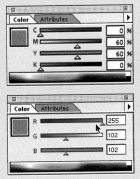

**Hint:** You can type browser-safe color values into the RGB palette.

# Technical Notes

## Book Design

Barbara Sudick is the artist behind the *Illustrator Wow!* design and typography. Using Jill Davis's layout of *The Photoshop Wow! Book* as a jumping-off point, she designed the pages in QuarkXPress, using Adobe fonts Frutiger and Minion, and, on the front cover, Sabon and Univers.

## Hardware and Software

My primary computer configuration was a PowerMacintosh 8500 180c with 192 MB of RAM, an AppleVision 1710 monitor, APS and Zip drives, SupraFax/Modem, and an APS Archive Python DAT backup using Dantz's Retrospect archiving software. Color proofs were made on a Tektronix Phaser 140 printer. TIFF Export (Vision's Edge) creates thumbnails for the Wow! website.

For software, in addition to Adobe Illustrator I used: Adobe Photoshop, QuarkXPress, QuicKeys (CE Software), Captivate (Mainstay), XPert Tools II (ALAP), Day-to-Day Contacts (Day-to-Day Software) to maintain my database, DropStuff and Stuffit Expander (Aladdin), and Dantz's Retrospect for archiving. I communicated with testers using Claris Emailer, sending pages in Acrobat PDF format.

## Pre-press (Color Separations and Proofs)

High Resolution, Inc., based in midcoast Maine, led by Peter Koons and Sandy Soards, produced the color-separated composite film and final color proofs for this book and for its cover. The photos in the book were drum-scanned on an Optronics ColorGetter and imported using Kodak Precision Color Management. Many illustrations were trapped using Island Trapper (Island Graphics Corporation). Screen captures were separated in Photoshop using a GCR with maximum black generation. To track updated placed files and convert spot colors within illustrations, HighRes used PictAttributes (Markware), and Spot (ALAP), respectively. Individual pages were spooled through Helios Ethershare to a Sun Microsystems Sparc Workstation, swapping FPO scans for full resolution images via OPI as served by Kodak Prophecy. Pages were rasterized by Adobe PostScript RIPs and many output using Panther imagesetting technology employing ESCOR screening from Pre-press Solutions. Color proofs of each page were made using the Kodak Contract proofing system.

## How to contact the author...

Sharon Steuer, c/o Peachpit Press, 1249 Eighth Street, Berkeley, CA 94710, or via Internet e-mail: *wowartist@bigfoot.com*, or via the Web: *http://www.peachpit.com/meetus/authors/sharon.steuer.html*

# Acknowledgments

My most heartfelt gratitude goes to the more than 100 artists and Illustrator experts who generously allowed me to include their work and divulge their techniques.

Thanks also must go to those folks at Adobe who went out of their way to help me chase down answers to zillions of questions. Special thanks to Therese Bruno and Eric Hess.

This revision required a major team effort, and would not have happened if not for an amazing group of people. Robin Olson co-authored the text-heavy portions of the Illustrator 7 revisions with humor, patience, and friendship. Diane Hinze Kanzler meticulously updated screenshots, rerouted menu commands, updated the Training materials, and kept me giggling. Peg Maskell Korn did everything I asked of her (and then some) with unsurpassed loyalty and dedication. Elizabeth Rogalin edited cheerfully at all hours. Paul Rauschelbach patiently assembled and mastered the CD from items sent and e-mailed from all over. Marjorie Maggenti created the new index, Zelda Edelson was the on-site proofreader. Mordy Golding was the Illustrator 6 revisions co-author, and contributed this edition to the web portions of the book. Gary Pfitzer edited the first two editions, and prepared the stylesheet that we all lived by. Barbara Sudick expertly designed the layout of this book. And as always, thanks also goes to the stellar team of testers and consultants: Adam Z Lein, Lisa Jackmore, Phil Runquist, Whitney Stevens Miller, Richard Marchessault and Terry Sisk Graybill. Sandee Cohen's role defies categorization, but some of the things she did were: take frantic calls from me at all hours, ensured me that I wasn't losing it altogether, and prepared some essential trouble-shooting information in the book and CD.

Thanks to: A.J. Rogers, with Jennifer Jones and Sally Lampe (Tektronix), Aladdin Software and Dantz. Thanks also to the Adobe Type department, ALAP, Aridi, Avenza, BareBones, BeInfinite, Cartesia, CE Software, Chronchart, Day-to-Day Software, Design Tools Monthly, Dynamic Graphics, Extensis, Hot Door, Image Club Graphics, Macromedia, MetaCreations, Photoshpere, Ultimate Symbol and Vertigo Technology for their special *Wow!* offers.

High Resolution Inc. (Peter Koons, Sandy Soards, Chris Cunningham and John Higgins), a phenomenal prepress facility in midcoast Maine, expertly produced *all* the PostScript color separations for this book. And just for the record, there is no way that a computer separation option would come close to getting the separations that High Resolution got. High Resolution wishes to thank: Island Graphics (Jeff Guns and Mark Alan Cirino), and PrePRESS Solutions (Bob Trenkamp and Irene Schrader).

Thank you Lynda Weinman and Bruce Heavin for adapting the Illustrator section of their *Coloring Web Graphics.2*, and for allowing us to include this material.

And of course, thanks to Linnea Dayton (the *Wow!* series editor) and to everyone at Peachpit (especially Corbin Collins, Cary Norsworthy and Kate Reber) for helping pull this book together.

# Artists

Note: *E-mail and Web addresses will be posted on the* Wow! *website:* **www.peachpit.com/wow.html**

Acme Design Company
*see also* Michael Kline
215 North Saint Francis #4
Witchita, KS 67201
316-267-2263
**84–85, 123, 188** Kline

Erik Adigard, *see* M.A.D.

Adobe Systems, Inc.
345 Park Avenue
San Jose, CA 95110-2704
408-536-6000
*see also* Laurie Szujewska
**141, 145** Laurie Szujewska
**140** Min Wang
**139, 142–144** James Young

Agnew Moyer Smith, Inc.
503 Martindale Street
Pittsburgh, PA 15212
412-322-6333
**56–57, 101** Kurt Hess
*Wow!* **disk**
**58** Rick Henkel & Kurt Hess
**60–61** Bob Whitehouse

Bjørn Akselsen, *see* Ice House Press

Jen Alspach
4197 E. Rancho Caliente Dr.
Cave Creek, AZ 85331
602-585-5341
**70**

Jeff Barney
Barney McKay Design
425 E. 1070 S.
Orenn, UT 84058
801-225-9949
**67, 94**

Kevin Barrack
3908 Pasadena Drive
San Mateo, CA 94403
415-341-0115
**128**

Rick Barry
DeskTop Design Studio
1631 West 12th Street
Brooklyn, NY 11223
718-232-2484
**82–83, 116**

Kenneth Batelman
407 Buckhorn Drive
Belvidere, NJ 07823
908-475-8124
**160**

Eliot Bergman
362 West 20th Street
New York, NY 10011
888-COOLPIX
**198**

BlackDog
Mark Fox
239 Marin Street
San Rafael, CA 94901
415-258-9663
**52, 53**

Christopher Burke
4408 Chad Court
Ann Arbor, MI 48103-9478
313-996-1316
**64, 92–93,** *Wow!* **disk**

California State Automobile
Association
Cartographic Department
150 Van Ness Ave.
San Francisco, CA 94102
415-565-2468
**54–55, 90–91**

Ron Chan
24 Nelson Ave.
Mill Valley, CA 94941
415-389-6549
**130–131, 132, 152,**

K. Daniel Clark
3218 Steiner Street
San Francisco, CA 94123
415-922-7761
**175,** *Wow!* **disk**

Sandee Cohen
33 Fifth Avenue, #10B
New York, NY 10003
212-677-7763
**15, 99, 119, 128,** *Wow!* **disk**

Dan Cosgrove
203 North Wabash Ave.
Suite 1102
Chicago, IL 60611
312-527-0375
**193**

Scott Crouse
59 Coleman Road
Winter Haven, FL 33880
941-294-8146
**173,** *Wow!* **disk**

Michael D'Abrosca, *see* California
State Automobile Association

d'JAXN
Portland, OR 97229-7609
503-526-9573
**211**

Rob Day & Virginia Evans
10 State Street, Suite 214
Newburyport, MA 01950
508-465-1386
**146–147**

Vince DiFabritus
Procter & Gamble
10200 Alliance/Room BA3000
Cincinnati, OH 45242
513-626-6524
**192**

Pamela Drury Wattenmaker
17 South Plomar Drive
Redwood City, CA 94062
415-368-7878
**188, 215,** *Wow!* **disk**

Linda Eckstein
201 W. 70th St. #6G
New York, NY 10023
212-721-0821
**107**

Eve Elberg
60 Plaza Street East, Suite 6E
Brooklyn, NY 11238
718-398-0950
**12, 120**

Virginia Evans, *see* Day & Evans

Gary Ferster
756 Marlin Ave., Suite 4
Foster City, CA 94404
415-577-9696
**105, 121**

Mark Fox, *see* BlackDog

David Fridberg
Miles Fridberg Molinaroli
4401 Connecticut Ave., NW
Suite 701
Washington, DC 20008
202-966-7700
**193**

Guilbert Gates
145 West 12th/Apt 2-5
New York, NY 10011
212-243-7853
*see also* Jared Schneidman Design
**104, 164**

Kerry Gavin
154 East Canaan Road
East Canaan, CT 06024
203-824-4839
**110**

Mordy Golding
320 Leroy Avenue
Cedarhurst, NY 10001
516-239-2083
**206, 212–213,** *Wow!* **disk**

Steven H. Gordon
136 Mill Creek Crossing
Madison, AL 35758
205-772-0022
**59,** *Wow!* **disk**

Caryl Gorska
414 Jackson Street/Suite 401
San Francisco, CA 94111
415-249-0139
*see also* MAX
**109, 149**

Laurie Grace
310 West 93rd St. /5K
New York, NY 10025
212-678-6535
**154–155**

Adele Droblas Greenberg
AD. Design & Consulting
202 Sixth Ave. Suite #2a
New York, NY 10013
212-431-9132
**121**

Wendy Grossman
355 West 51st Street
New York, NY 10019
212-262-4497
**120, 129, 195**

Steve Hart
Time/Editorial Art Dept
1271 Sixth Avenue/Rm 2440 D
New York, NY 10020
212-522-3677
**101, 102–103**

Pattie Belle Hastings, *see* Ice House
Press & Design

Bruce Heavin
www.stink.com
**216–217**

Rick Henkel, *see* Agnew Moyer Smith

Eric Hess
All Things Illustrator
206-545-0218
**14**

Kurt Hess, *see* Agnew Moyer Smith

Lance Hidy
Harvard Business Review
230 Western Avenue
Allston, MA 02134
617-495-6802
**187**

Wendolyn Hill
Biocomm., Yale Med. School
I-E93 SHM/333 Cedar Street
New Haven, CT 06520
203-785-4088
**101**

Diane Hinze Kanzler
15 Carrington Road
Bethany, CT 06524
203-393-1634
**128**

Ice House Press & Design
Pattie Belle Hastings
Bjørn Akselsen
135 West Elm Street
New Haven, CT 06515
203-389-7334
**148**

Lisa Jackmore
13 Joann Drive
Barrington, RI 02806
401-246-2061
**54,** *Wow!* **disk**

Lance Jackson
LSD
1790 Fifth Street
Berkeley, CA 94710
415-777-8944
**190**

Jared Schneidman Design
16 Parkway
Katonah, NY 10536
914-232-1499
*see also* Guilbert Gates
**104** Guilbert Gates
**164** Gates & Schneidman

Javier Romero Design Group
24 East 23rd Street, 3rd Floor
New York, NY 10010
212-420-0656
**138, 149, 150**

Dave Joly
15 King St.
Putnam, CT 06260
860-928-1042
**108, 207,** *Wow!* **disk**

John Kanzler
15 Carrington Road
Bethany, CT 06524
203-393-1634
**166**

Andrea Kelley
17755 Big Basin Way
Boulder Creek, CA 95006
408-338-2616
**98, 114–115, 158–159, 167**

Michael Kline
Michael Kline Illustration
1106 S. Dodge
Wichita, KS 67213
316-264-4112
*see also* Acme Design Company
**84–85, 123, 188**

Lyuda Lavrentyeva
1314 46th Street #E2
Brooklyn, NY 11219
718-633-7143
**70**

Adam Z Lein
P.O. Box 705
2 Bird St
Sterling, MA 01564
*Wow!* **disk**

Joseph Lertola
Time/Editorial Art Dept
1271 Sixth Avenue/Rm 2434
New York, NY 10020
212-522-3721
**156, 199**

Randy Livingston
Bona Fide Design
206 Ernest Street
Washington, IL 61571
309/745.1126
**214, *Wow!* disk**

Patrick Lynch
Yale University C/AIM
47 College Street/Suite 224
New Haven, CT 06510
203-737-5033
**50–51, 210**

M.A.D.
237 San Carlos Ave.
Sausalito, CA 94965
415-331-1023
**36–37** Patricia McShane & Erik
Adigard

Paul Magliari
World Wrestling Federation
Titan Tower-1241 E. Main St.
Stamford, CT 06902
203-353-2853
**199**

Richard Marchesseault
35 Locust St.
Naugatuck, CT 06770
203-432-3905
**3, *Wow!* disk**

Elizabeth Margolis-Pineo
margolispineo concept, copy &
design
138 Glenwood Avenue
Portland, ME 04103
207-773-8447
**121**

Rob Marquardt
Benyas AD Group
126 North Third Street/Suite 300
Minneapolis, MN 55401
612-340-9804
**120, *Wow!* disk**

MAX
246 1st Street/Suite 310
San Francisco, CA 94105
415-543-1333
*see also* Caryl Gorska
**149**

Scott McCollom
P.O. Box 6132
Kaneohe, Hawaii 96744
808-263-8505
**8, *Wow!* disk**

Patricia McShane, *see* M.A.D.

Bert Monroy
11 Latham Lane
Berkeley, CA 94718
510-524-9412
**184–186, 208–209**

Cheryl Moreno
746 17th Ave.
Menlo Park, CA 94025
415-473-9597
**71**

Christopher Morris
9828 Smoke Feather Lane
Dallas, TX 75243
214-690-1328
**160, 189**

Bradley Neal, Thomas Neal
*see* Thomas • Bradley Illustration

David Nelson
Admap Custom Maps
721 Grape St.
Denver, CO 80220
303-333-1060
**179, *Wow!* disk**

Gary Newman Design
2447 Burnside Rd
Sebastapol, CA 95472
***Wow!* disk**

Robin AF Olson
Ultra Maroon Design
63 Osborne Hill Road
Sandy Hook, CT 06482-1544
203-426-5455
**18, 78, 99, 181**

Charly Palmer
TP Design
7007 Eagle Watch Court
Stone Mountain, GA 30087
770-413-8276
**95**

Daniel Pelavin
90 Varick Street, Suite 3B
New York, NY 10013-1925
212-941-7418
**96–98, 154–155**

Paul Rauschelbach
273 Green Street, #10
San Francisco, CA 94133
415-544-0654
***Wow!* disk**

Dorothy Remington
Remington Design
632 Commercial Street
San Francisco, CA 94111
415-788-3340
**65**

Romero, Javier, *see* Javier

San Francisco Examiner
*see* Lance Jackson, Chris Morris,
Joe Shoulak

Ulrik Schoth
Brunnenhof 30
Bochum, 44866
GERMANY
+49-2327-939811
***Wow!* disk**

Schneidman, Jared, *see* Jared

Max Seabaugh, *see* MAX

Charles Shields
Shields Design
415 East Olive Ave.
Fresno, CA 93728
209-497-8060
**120, 121**

Joe Shoulak
5621 Ocean View Drive #2
Oakland, CA 94618
415-777-7974
**106, 172**

Bill Snebold
2416 5th Street, #102
Santa Monica, CA 90405
310-452-0668
**165, 200**

Chris Spollen
362 Cromwell Ave.
Staten Island, NY 10305
718-979-9695
**191**

Nancy Stahl
470 West End Ave, #86
New York, NY 10024
212-362-8779
**86–88, 89, 121, 194**

Sharon Steuer
c/o Peachpit Press/1249 Eighth St.
Berkeley, CA 94710
800-283-9444
wowartist@bigfoot.com
**42–46, 68–69, 72–75, 80–81, 121,**
**124–127, 182, 183, 196, 200–201**

Barbara Sudick
Bethany Wood
Bethany, CT 06524
203-789-8529
**138, 200–201, all pages**
*(Book Designer)*

Dan & Darlene Swanson
Van-garde Imagery
903 S. Second Street
St. Charles, IL 60174
708-686-5320
**197**

Laurie Szujewska
11747 S. Bell Ave.
Chicago, IL 60643
312-238-5581
**141, 142–144, 145**

Clarke W. Tate
Tate Studio
P.O. Box 339/301 Woodford St.
Gridley, IL 61744-0339
800-828-3008
**98, 168–171**

Dorothea Taylor-Palmer
TP Design
7007 Eagle Watch Ct.
Stone Mountain, GA 30087
770-413-8276
**95**

Thomas • Bradley Illustration & Design
411 CenterStreet/P.O. Box 249
Gridley, IL 61744
309-747-3266
**112–113** Brad Neal
**122, 162–163** Thomas Neal

Kathleen Tinkel
MacPrePress
12 Burr Road
Westport, CT 06880
203-227-2357
**5, 138**

Jean Tuttle Illustraton
145 Palisade Street, Suite 406
Dobbs Ferry, NY 10522
914-693-7681
**62–63, 157**

Victor von Salza
Digital PhotoGraphic Arts
6903 SW 54th Avenue
Portland, OR 97219-1338
503-245-9382
**119**, *Wow!* **disk**

Min Wang, *see* Adobe Systems. Inc.

Alan James Weimer
67 Bliss Street
Rehoboth, MA 02769
518-828-0141
**176, 177,** *Wow!* **disk**

Lynda Weinman
www.lynda.com
**216–217**

Bob Whitehouse
*see* Agnew Moyer Smith

Hugh Whyte
Lehner & Whyte
8-10 South Fullerton Ave.
Montclair, NJ 07402
201-746-1335
**66, 111, 120**

Lester Yocum
274 Jay Jay Court
Glenburnie, MD 21061
410-766-3694
**174**

James Young, *see* Adobe Systems, Inc.

# Resources

**Adobe Systems, Inc.**
345 Park Avenue
San Jose, CA  95110-2704
408-536-6000
http://www@adobe.com/

**AGFA**
200 Ballardvale Street
MS 200-4-9-B
Willmington, MA 01887
508-658-5600 x5170

**Aladdin Systems, Inc.**
*Stuffit*
165 Westridge Drive
Watsonville, CA 95076-4159
408-761-6200

**ALAP**
*XPert Tools*
see XChange

**Alien Skin Software, LLC**
*Plug-ins*
800 St. Mary's Street/Suite 100
Raleigh, NC 27605-1457
919-832-4124

**Allegiant Technologies**
*SuperCard*
9740 Scranton Road/Suite 300
San Diego, CA 92121
619-587-0500x106

**Apple Computer**
800-767-2775

**APS Technologies**
*Hardware*
6131 Deramus/P.O. Box 4987
Kansas City, MO 64120-0087
800-874-1427

**Aridi Computer Graphics**
*Digital Art*
P.O. Box 797702
Dallas, TX 75379
214-404-9171
972-404-9171

**Avenza**
*MAPublisher*
3385 Harvester Rd, Suite 205
Burlington,
Ontario  L7N 3N2  Canada
905-639-3330

**Bare Bones Software, Inc.**
*BBEdit*
P.O. Box 1048
Bedford, MA 01730
781-778-3100

**BeInfinite, Inc.**
*InfiniteFX Filters*
4651 Woodstock Rd./
Suite 203, #210
Roswell, GA 30075-1686
404-552-6624

**Cartesia Software**
*MapArt Designer*
5 South Main Street/P.O. Box 757
Lambertville, NJ 08530
800-334-4291

**CE Software, Inc.**
*QuicKeys*
1801 Industrial Circle
P.O. Box 65580
West Des Moines, IA 50265
515-221-1801

**Chronchart**
4640 Edgewood Ave.
Oakland, CA 94602
510-482-3576

**Claris Corp.**
*Emailer*
Santa Clara CA
800-544-8554/408-987-7000

**Dantz**
*Retrospect*
4 Orinda Way/Bldg C
Orinda, CA 94563
510-253-3000

**Day-to-Day Software**
*Contacts*
244 Westchester Avenue/Suite 310
White Plains, NY 10604
800-329-8632
914-686-1018

**Dynamic Graphics Inc.**
*Clip art, etc.*
6000 N. Forest Pk. Drive
Peoria, IL 61614
800-255-8800

**Extensis Corporation**
*Vector Tools*
1800 SW 1st, Suite 500
Portland, OR 97201
800-796-9798/503-274-2020

**High Resolution, Inc.**
87 Elm Street
Camden, ME 04843-1941
207-236-3777

**hot door**
*CADtools*
P.O. Box 3841
Long Beach, CA  90803
562-438-0377

**Illom Development AB**
*LogoCorrector, Toolbox I*
Box 838, Strandgatan 21
Ornskoldsvik, S-891 18
+46-660-786-57

**Image Club Graphics**
729  24 Ave SE
Galgary, AB  T2G5K8

**IRIS Graphics, Inc.**
Six Crosby Drive
Bedford, MA 01730
617-275-8777

**Island Graphics Corp.**
*IslandTrapper*
4000 Civic Center Drive
San Rafael, CA 94903
415-491-1000

**LemkeSoft** *GraphicConverter*
Erics-Heckel-Ring 8a
31228 Peine, Germany
+495171 72200

**Letraset**
40 Eisenhower Drive
Paramus, NJ 07653
800-343-8973 x7210

**Macromedia**
*FreeHand, Director, Flash 2*
600 Townsend Street
San Francisco, CA 94103
800-989-3762

# Publications

**Mainstay**
*Capture*
591-A Constitution Ave.
Camarillo, CA 93012
805-484-9400

**MetaCreations Corporation**
*KPT, Painter, RayDream Designer*
6303 Carpinteria Ave
Carpinteria, CA  93013
800-846-0111

**Microsoft Corp.**
*Excel, Windows*
One Microsoft Way
Redmond, WA 98052
206-882-8080

**Pantone, Inc.**
590 Commerce Blvd.
Carlstadt, NJ 07072
201-935-5500

**PhotoSphere Images Ltd.**
*Preview Pac*
380 West First Avenue, Suite 310
Vancouver, BC  V5Y 3T7
800-665-1496

**PrePRESS Solutions**
*Panther*
11 Mount Pleasant Avenue
East Hanover, NJ 07936
800-443-6600

**Strata, Inc.**
*StudioPro*
2 West St.George Blvd. / Suite 2100
St. George, UT 84770
800-787-2823 / 801-628-9756

**Tektronix Inc**
*Graphics Printing & Imaging*
MS 63-355
P.O. Box 1000
Wilsonville, OR
97070-9980

**TruMatch, Inc.**
331 Madison Ave.
New York, NY 10017
212-351-2360

**Ultimate Symbol**
*Design Elements*
31 Wildertness Drive
Stony Point, NY 10980
914-942-0003

**Vertigo Technology**
*3D Dizzy, 3D Words, 3D HotText*
1255 Pender Street
Vancouver, BC  V6E 2V1
604-684-2113

**Vision's Edge**
*TIFF Export*
3491-11 Thomasville Rd. / Ste 177
Tallahassee, FL 32308
800-983-6337
904-386-4573

**WACOM**
*ArtZ Tablet*
115 Century Road
Paramus, NJ 07652
800-922-6613

**XChange**
*XTensions for QuarkXPress*
800-788-7557

Design Tools Monthly
400 Kiowa, Suite 100
Boulder, CO  80303-3633
303-543-8400

Hayden Books
Indianapolis IN 46290
317-581-3833
**Web Designers Guide to Color**
by Mordy Golding and
Dave White

IDG Books Worlwide, Inc.
San Mateo, CA
415-312-0650
**The Illustrator 7 Bible**
by Ted Alspach

New Riders Publishing
Indianapolis IN
**Designing Web Graphics.2**
**Color Web Graphics.2**
by Lynda Weinman and
Bruce Heavin

Peachpit Press
Berkeley, CA
800-283-9444 / 510-548-4393
**Illustrator Illuminated, 2nd ed.**
by Clay Andres
**The Painter 5 Wow! Book**
by Cher Threinen-Pendarvis
**The Photoshop 4 Wow! Book**
by Linnea Dayton & Jack Davis

Step-by-Step Publications
Peoria, IL
800-255-8800 / 309-688-8866
**Step-by-Step Electronic Design**

Yale University Press
New Haven, CT
203-432-0948
**Manual of Ornithology**
by Patrick Lynch & Noble Proctor
**The Shape of Time**
by George Kubler

# General Index

3-D with Illustrator
  *see also* Dimensions; Streamline
  exporting paths  180, 185
  using 3-D programs  179,
      198–199
  gallery: 197, 200

## A

Acme Design  84–85, 123, 188
Acrobat  25, 178
adding
  *see also* techniques
  Add Anchor Points (Objects)
      filter  33, 35, 119, 171
  Add-anchor-point tool  7
  anchor points  7, 35, 171
  colors to line drawings  85
Adigard, Erik  36–37
Adjust Colors (Colors) filter  118,
      124, 127, 131
Adobe Dimensions  *see* Dimensions
Adobe Systems, Inc. (art department)
      139–145
Adobe Illustrator  *see* Illustrator
advanced techniques  72, 96, 130,
      (Chapter 8) 156–177
Agfa
  PostScript Color Process Guide
      23, 60
Agnew Moyer Smith  56–57, 58,
      60–61, 101, *Wow!* disk
airbrush  112, 199
Akselsen, Bjørn  148
Align palette  9, 117
alignment
  *see also* Align palette; Average;
      techniques
  ensuring with Paste in Front/Back
      78
  of palettes  9, 15, 47, 117
alphabet  *see* type
Alspach, Jen  70
anchor points
  *see also* Bézier curves; handles
  adding  7, 33, 35, 119, 171
  converting smooth curve to/from
      corner  7
  deleting  7
  hiding  19
  redrawing  6
  stray  6
  term definition  3–5
angle  *see* isometric; shear;
      Constrain  21, 56–57, 137

animation
  *see also* techniques; web graphics
      Chapter 10;
  gallery: 207, 208, 210, 211
  timesavers  208
      to create  208
      using the blend tool  209
      with other programs  202
      using for the web  206
      video and,  209
antialiasing  23, 124, 178
  *see also* bitmapped images;
      rasterizing; GIF 89a
  exporting  182
  type  134
architecture
  *see also* isometric; techniques
  creating,
      linear shading  104
      repeating elements  172
  filter use  123, 168
  multiple layers as guides  98
  rendering with gradients and
      filters  168
archiving (backing up)  2
Area Type  133, 134, 135, 144, 147
  *see also* type
Arrange menu
  Average  9
  Hide/Show All  79
  Join  9–10
  Lock  52
  Lock/Unlock All  79
  Transform  14
  Send to Back  12
art  *see* Artists appendix; bitmapped
      images; illustrations; line
      drawings; placed images;
      techniques; templates
Artboard  20
artists  *see* Artists appendix and
      individual  names
Artwork mode
  *see also* Preview mode
  advantages of  4, 49
  changing between Preview and
      18, 77
  selecting paths from  7, 30
assembling  *see* creating; editing
Attributes palette  23, 55, 64,
      205–206, 213
Average (Object Menu) Path  10
  exercises with  33, 34, 35
Average Joining  *also* Average-Join
      *33–36, 52*

## B

backgrounds  *see* layers; templates
backing up  16
  *see also* troubleshooting
Barney, Jeffrey  67, 94
Barney McKay Design  67, 94
Barrack, Kevin  128
Barry, Rick  82–83, 116
baselines  135, 142–144
  *see also* type
basics (Chapter 1)  1–27,
      (Chapter 2) 28–46
  *see also* Zen Lessons on the *Wow!*
      disk
Batelman, Kenneth  160
Bergman, Eliot  198
bevel  198, 214
beveled lines  49
Bézier curves
  *see also* anchor points; curves;
      handles; paths; Pen tool;
      Zen Lessons on the *Wow!*
      disk
  adjusting to fit a template  81
  characteristics  4
  editing  6–7
  making  *see* Pen tool
  rules, recommendations for use  5
  shaping type around  145
bitmapped images
  *see also* graphics; importing;
      placed images; scanning;
      tracing
  antialiasing  23, 180, 178
  gallery: 95
  handling with Illustrator  4
  rasterizing into Photoshop  178
  placed in Illustrator  4, 181
BlackDog  52, 53
bleeds  146–147
  *see also* techniques
Blend Front to Back (Colors) filter
      99, 163
Blend Horizontally (Colors) filter  99
Blend Vertically (Colors) filter  99
blends (Chapter 5)  99–116
  *see also* filters; gradients; masks;
      techniques
  automatically updating  103
  Blend tool  99
  contoured, *see* masks
  creating glowing objects  165
  designing  103
  duplicating for other colors  163
  gallery: 101, 105, 174

Outline Path (Object: Path) filter 64,
131, 132, 163, 170, 171;
gallery: 106, 198, 199
outlines
*see also* Artwork mode
characteristics 4
converting type to 138, 140, 149
ovals 36–37, 41, 51, 83, 130–131, 132
*see also* polygons; rectangles;
ellipses
drawing with 52, 53, 155, 157
Oval tool 8, 41
overlapping
*see also* layers; Paste in Front;
transparencies
objects, joining 52
Overprint Blacks (Colors) filter 23, 55
overprinting
*see also* printing; Attributes palette
as trapping technique 64
overriding
default
color organization 62
styling 16
startup file 22

## P

page
*see also* rulers, guides
Artboard 21
layout, Illustrator use for 146
margins, resetting 19
Page Setup (File menu) 19, 81
scaling with 81
setting up 19–20
Page tool 19
PageMaker program xi, 25, 27, 133
(gallery 139, 146–147, 182)
Paintbrush tool *see* Brush tool
paint styles
*see also* palettes
locating objects with the same 61
*see also* palettes; attributes; colors;
stroke; swatches; tool box
103, gallery: 149
gradients 103, 100
off setting colors 156
Overprint 21, 55
patterns 74
Paint-bucket tool 48
Painter program 23, 180, 194
painterly images
*see also* graphics; illustrations;
techniques

with gradients and filters
168–171
with Brush tool 68, 69, 70, 71, 64,
75, 81, 183, 207
with Painter 194
with Streamline 190
palette
*see also* Align palette; Character
palette; Color palette; Info
palette; Transform Palette;
elements; gradients,
Gradient palette; Layers
palette; paint styles,
Paragraph palette;
Shortcuts palette; Swatches
palette; tools
colors, organizing 62
docking 15, 47
creating new layers with 83
files, accessing colors from 62
layer basics 78
working with 14–16
Palmer, Charly 95
Pantone (PMS) 3, 22, 62, 65, 148
paper
*see also* doc setup; page; Page tool
setting custom size 20
Paragraph palette 134
Parse *see* embed
Paste in Back (Edit menu) 78, 166
Paste in Front (Edit menu) 54, 73,
78, 131, 140, 166
Paste Into (Photoshop) 185
Paste Inside *see* masks
Paste remembers layers 77–79, 92,
94, 152
Pasteboard (Artboard) 21
path editing tool *see* paths
Pathfinder (Object) filter *formerly
under* Filter menu
(Chapter 6) 117–123
*see also* filters
Crop 121, 123, 131–132, 170
Divide 120, 122
Exclude 122
gallery: 123, 132, 173
Hard 121
Intersect 120, 169
masks compared with 153
Merge 121
Minus Back 118, 120
Minus Front 118, 120, 169, 171
photorealistic design with 122
Soft 121, 123, 131, 132
gallery: 70, 123
tips for working with 119

Trap 21, 64
Trim 121
Unite 120, 122, 163, 169
gallery: 70, 129, 172, 198
Path Patterns 124, 125, 126;
gallery: 183, 200
*see also* patterns
paths
*see also* Artwork mode; Bézier
curves; compound paths;
creating; cropping; line;
object; Path Patterns;
stencils; stroke
changing 7
clipping 151, 180–181, 214
closing, with Join command 9–10
corners, setting Caps and Joins 49
cutting 7
editing 7
filters
*see also* Pathfinder
Compound Paths (Objects)
118, 137, 153, 154, 155
Offset Path (Objects) 106,
121, 131, 132
Outline Path (Objects) 64,
106, 131–132, 162–163,
170–171, 198
flowing type around 135
hiding, with Hide Edges 19
importing 115, 180, 194
line endings, specifying 49
offsetting 131
outlining 131
Path Type, creating 136
selection lines, hiding and
showing 54
term definition 4
Path Type tool 135, 144
patterns
*see also* techniques; Path patterns;
swatches palette
Adobe 86
complex, creating 72
control repeat with boundary
rectangle 77
controlling 74
converting to objects 74
creating 72
filling type with 138
manual trapping of 64
realigning 21, 74
retrieving 72
testing 74
tiling, realign 72, 74
transformations 13

# T

Tab Ruler 135
tabs
    setting up for Area Type 135
Tate, Clarke W. 98, 168–171
Taylor-Palmer, Dorothea 95
techniques
    actions, *see* antialiasing; applying;
        assembling; contouring;
        cropping; customizing;
        digitizing; drawing; filling;
        grouping; importing;
        joining; layering;
        lengthening; locking;
        organizing; overprinting;
        posterizing; printing;
        program interactions;
        proofing; rasterizing;
        reducing; rendering;
        reordering; resizing;
        rotating; saving; scaling;
        scanning; selecting;
        sketching; tracing;
        transformations; trapping;
        troubleshooting;
        unlocking
    effects, *see* brush strokes; collages;
        lighting effects; painterly
        images; perspective;
        repeating patterns;
        resolution; special effects
templates 76–98 130
    *see also* techniques
    color images 80–83
    digitizing logos with 82
    gallery: 52, 187
    graphs use as 12
    PICTs opened as 80–83
    placing artwork 87
    preparing 80—83
    rasterizing 124
    reduction of use 78, 80–83
    swatch styling 55
    techniques with 68, 80–81, 89,
        98, 130–131
    tracing 83, 98
        relief with 83
text
    *see also* type
    filters 136–137
    objects 136
textures *see* Ink Pen; Path Patterns;
    patterns
Thomas•Bradley Illustration & Design
    112–113, 122, 162–163

TIFF (TIF) images
    *see also* file(s), formats
    importing 25–26
    bitmapped 182
    coloring 1-bit 82
    supported file formats 178
    *see also* formats
    template 83, 97
    tracing 88
tiles
    retrieve 72
    Transform pattern tiles 74
    in Path Patterns 125–126
Time magazine 102, 156
Tinkel, Kathleen 5, 138
tints
    filling objects with 51
    of colors 63
    with Pathfinder Soft/Hard filters
        121
    specifying percentages 63
    tint slider 51
toggles
    *see also* Glossary on pull-out card;
        tools
    palette underlines 15
Toolbox *see* individual tool names
tools
    *see also* elements; filters; menus;
        palettes; techniques; also
        under individual tool
        names
    basic, exercises in using 41
    mastering techniques 27
tools:
    Add-anchor-point 7
    Area-Type 133, 134
    Convert-direction point 7
    Direct-selection 6, 9
    Ellipse (Oval) 8
    Group selection 9
    Knife 7
    Paintbrush 68–69
    Pen 2, 5
    Polygon 7
    Reshape 14
    Rectangle 7
    Rotate 13, 14
    Selection 9
    Spiral 117
    Star 7
    Twirl 14
    Type tools 133–135
    Zoom 18
Toyo
    CMYK process color models 65

tracing
    see also layers; templates
    geometric tool use 83
    reliefs 82
    scanned art 68
    Streamline use for 179
    as technique for coloring line
        drawings 85, 95
    template 83
    true horizontals and verticals 98
tracking 137, 146
training x
Training folder *Wow!* disk
Transform palette 13, 14
transforming 13–14
    *see also* copying; creating;
        deleting; editing; moving;
        reflecting; reshape;
        rotating; scaling; skewing;
        twirl; Transform palette
    combining 64, 162, 172
    gradients into masked blends 159
    patterns 74
    perspective lines into guides 97
    power 13–14
    reflecting 13, 41, 172
    reshape tool 14, 214
    rotating 13, 117
        documents 26
        lesson 38–39
    scaling
        for placement in other
            programs 27, 83, 182,
            185
        lesson 38–39, 41
        line weights 182
        objects 12–13
        Page Setup options for 20
        patterns 74
        Scale-line-weight enabling
            106, 182
        smooth blend use 113
    stretching 56
    tools for 13–14, 117
    views 56
transparencies
    creating shadows 51
    cropping as technique for 131
    cut-away 175
    with filters 51, 122, 130–131, 132
    glowing 165
    GIF options 205
    with value 51
    Web 204, 213
    X-ray 210
transparency 207

View menu
   Artwork 3
   Lock Guides 97
   Make Guides
   New View 18, 19, 91, 93
   Preview selection 79
      Snap to Grid 22
   tracing template 83
   zooming commands 18
   Show or Hide:
   Edges 18–19, 54
   Grids 18
   Page Tiling 19
   Rulers 21, 30
views 90, 93
   see also printing; Wow! disk;
            Viewing Details
   custom, creating 18
   of images, at actual size 18
   isometric perspective 56–57
   layer 78
   multiple images 18
   organizing with 90, 93
   saving 91
   viewing ratio, high-resolution
            scanning 80
visibility
   anchor points 3
   layers, see Artwork/Preview
            modes
   objects 79
volume
   see also techniques
   gradient used for 111 (gallery)
von Salza, Victor, 119, Wow! disk


# W

WACOM
   ArtZ tablet use 68, 70, 71, 75,
Wang, Min 138–140
warnings see troubleshooting
web exporting 202, 204–206, 212
Web palette 24, 203, 204, 206
Web Ready 204
Web Safe Colors 204, 216
Web Swatch Library 216
weaving
   see also techniques
   elements, in repeating patterns 73
   woof/warp 197
Weimer, Alan 176, 177, Wow! disk
Weinman, Lynda 216–217
What's New in Illustrator 2
Whitehouse, Bob 60–61

Whyte, Hugh 66, 111, 120
widening
   see also transforming
   objects, in a constrained manner
            57
Window menu
   New Window 18
   Swatch Libraries 23, 24, 47, 48
   Show or Hide:
   Attributes 206
   Gradient 100, 102
   Info 30, 56
   Layers 152
   Plug-in Tools see under tool
            name
   Toolbox, see individual tool
            names
windows
   finding lost 18
Windows commands see Chapter 1
            and the FInger Dance
            Summary on pull-out card
World Wide Web
   creating art for, with Illustrator
            Chapter 10
   Peachpit's address x
   Illustrator Wow! Book address x
   Sharon Steuer's address 218
working environment
   recommendations 30
Wow! disk  back pocket of this book


# X Y Z

X-ray transparencies 210
Yale University 50–51, 101, 143, 210
Yocum, Lester 174
Young, James 139, 142–144
Zen of Illustrator 28–46
   Lessons on the Wow! disk
   scaling exercises 35
zero point (origin) 22
Zig Zag filter 118
Zoom tool 18

**Revision Production Credits**

*Author & Curator:* Sharon Steuer

*Copyeditor:* Elizabeth Rogalin

*Book Designer:* Barbara Sudick

*Revisions Co-author:* Robin AF Olson

*Step-by-Step and Gallery Updating:* Diane Hinze Kanzler

*Wow! CD-ROM Mastering:* Paul Raushelbach

*Assistant to the Author:* Peg Maskell Korn

*Contributing Writers:* Mordy Golding, Sandee Cohen

*Wow! Testers:* Lisa Jackmore, Terry Sisk Graybill, Phil Runquist, Whitney Stevens Miller, Richard Marchessault, Adam Z Lein

*Proofreader:* Zelda Edelson

*Midnight Proofreader/Copyeditor:* Peg Maskell Korn

*Index:* Marjorie Maggenti

*Cover Art-direction:* Barbara Sudick

*Cover Illustrations:* Sharon Steuer

*Kibbitzer:* Sandee Cohen

*Caterer:* Jeff Jacoby

*Comedy relief:* Puma and Bear

# Windows Finger Dance Summary *from "The Zen of Illustrator"*

## Object Creation — *Hold down keys until AFTER mouse button is released.*

| | |
|---|---|
| `⇧ Shift` | Constrains objects horizontally, vertically or proportionally. |
| `Alt` | Objects will be drawn from centers. |
| `Alt` click | Opens dialog boxes with transformation tools. |
| | Spacebar turns into the grabber Hand. |
| `Ctrl` | Turns cursor into the Zoom-in tool. Click or marquee around an area to Zoom in. |
| `Ctrl` `Alt` | Turns cursor into the Zoom-out tool. Click to Zoom out. |
| `Caps lock` | Turns your cursor into a cross-hair. |

## Object Selection — *Watch your cursor to see that you've pressed the right keys.*

| | |
|---|---|
| `Ctrl` | The current tool becomes the last chosen Selection tool. |
| `Ctrl` `Alt` | Current tool becomes Group-selection to select entire object. Click again to select next level of grouping. To move selection release Alt key, then Grab. |
| `Ctrl` `Tab` | Toggles whether Direct-selection or regular Selection tool is accessed by the Ctrl key. |
| `⇧ Shift` click | Toggles whether an object, path or point is selected or deselected. |
| `⇧ Shift` click | With Direct-selection tool, click on or marquee around an object, path or point to toggle selection/deselection. **Note:** *Clicking inside a filled object may select the entire object.* |
| `⇧ Shift` click | Clicking on, or marqueeing over objects with Selection or Group-selection, toggles selection/deselection (Group-selection chooses objects within a group). |

## Object Transformation — *Hold down keys until AFTER mouse button is released.*

| | |
|---|---|
| `⇧ Shift` | Constrains transformation proportionally, vertically and horizontally. |
| `Alt` | Leaves the original object and transforms a copy. |
| `Ctrl` `Z` | Undo. Use Shift-Ctrl-Z for Redo (*see page 17 for more on Undo/Redo*) |

To move or transform a selection predictably from within dialog boxes, use this diagram to determine if you need a positive or negative number and which angle is required. (*Diagram from Kurt Hess/Agnew Moyer Smith*)

# Mac Finger Dance Summary *from "The Zen of Illustrator"*

| **Object Creation** | *Hold down keys until AFTER mouse button is released.* |
|---|---|
| `⇧ Shift` | Constrains objects horizontally, vertically or proportionally. |
| `Option` | Objects will be drawn from centers. |
| `Option` click | Opens dialog boxes with transformation tools. |
| [ ] | Spacebar turns into the grabber Hand. |
| `⌘` [ ] | Turns cursor into the Zoom-in tool. Click or marquee around an area to Zoom in. |
| `Option` `⌘` [ ] | Turns cursor into the Zoom-out tool. Click to Zoom out. |
| `Caps lock` | Turns your cursor into a cross-hair. |

| **Object Selection** | *Watch your cursor to see that you've pressed the right keys.* |
|---|---|
| `⌘` | The current tool becomes the last chosen Selection tool. |
| `Option` `⌘` | Current tool becomes Group-selection to select entire object. Click again to select next level of grouping. To move selection release Option key, then Grab. |
| `⌘` `Tab` | Toggles whether Direct-selection or regular Selection tool is accessed by the ⌘ key. |
| `⇧ Shift` click | Toggles whether an object, path or point is selected or deselected. |
| `⇧ Shift` click ▹ | With Direct-selection tool, click on or marquee around an object, path or point to toggle selection / deselection. **Note:** *Clicking inside a filled object may select the entire object.* |
| `⇧ Shift` click ▸ ▸₊ | Clicking on, or marqueeing over objects with Selection or Group-selection, toggles selection / deselection (Group-selection chooses objects within a group). |

| **Object Transformation** | *Hold down keys until AFTER mouse button is released.* |
|---|---|
| `⇧ Shift` | Constrains transformation proportionally, vertically and horizontally. |
| `Option` | Leaves the original object and transforms a copy. |
| `⌘` `Z` | Undo. Use Shift-⌘-Z for Redo (*see page 17 for more on Undo / Redo*) |

To move or transform a selection predictably from within dialog boxes, use this diagram to determine if you need a positive or negative number and which angle is required. (*Diagram from Kurt Hess / Agnew Moyer Smith*)

# Mac Wow! Glossary of Terms

| | |
|---|---|
| ⌘<br>**Option / Opt** | The Command key (this key may have a ⌘ or a ⌥ on it).<br>The Option key can be used to modify many of the tools. |
| ←↑→↓ | The keyboard Cursor-keys: Left, Up, Right, Down. |
| **Toggle** | Menu selection acts as a switch: choosing once turns on, again turns it off. |
| **Marquee** | With any Selection tool, click-drag from your page over object(s) to select. |
| **Hinged curve** | A Bézier curve that meets a line or another curve at a point. |
| **Direct-selection**<br>**Group-selection**<br>**Selection** | *Direct-selection* tool selects points and paths.<br>*Group-selection* tool. The first click always selects the entire object, subsequent clicks select "next group-up" in the grouping order.<br>*Selection* tool (selects the biggest grouping which includes that object— if an object is ungrouped, then only that object is selected).<br>**Note:** *See page 9 and Chapters 1 & 2 for help with selection tools.* |
| **Select object(s)** | Click on or marquee with Group-selection tool to select entire object.<br>Click on or marquee with the regular Selection tool to select grouped objects. |
| **Deselect object(s)** | To Deselect *one* object, Shift-click (or Shift-marquee) with Group-selection tool.<br>To Deselect *all* selected objects, with any selection tool, click outside of all objects (but within your document), or press Shift-⌘-A. |
| **Select a path** | Click on a path with the Direct-selection tool to select it.<br>**Note:** *If objects are selected, Deselect first,* then *click with Direct-selection tool.* |
| **Select anchor points** | Click on path with Direct-selection tool to see anchor points. Then, Direct-select marquee around the points you want selected. Or, with Direct-selection tool, Shift-click on points you want selected.<br>**Note**: *Clicking on a selected point with Shift key down deselects that point.* |
| **Grab an object or point** | After selecting objects or points, use Direct-selection tool to click and hold down mouse button and drag to transform entire selection.<br>**Note:** *If you click by mistake (instead of click-and-hold), Undo and try again.* |
| **Delete an object** | Group-select the object and press the Delete (or Backspace) key.<br>To delete grouped objects, use the Selection tool, then Delete. |
| **Delete a path** | Direct-select a path and press the Delete (or Backspace) key. If you delete an anchor point, both paths attached to that anchor point will be deleted.<br>**Note:** *After deleting part of an object the entire remaining object will become selected; therefore, deleting twice will always delete the entire object!* |
| **Copy or Cut a path** | Click on a path with Direct-selection tool, then Copy (⌘-C) or Cut (⌘-X).<br>**Note:** *See the Finger Dance Summary for more ways to copy paths.* |
| **Copy or Cut an object** | Click on an object with Group-selection tool, then Copy (⌘-C) or Cut (⌘-X).<br>For grouped objects, Click on one of the objects with the Selection tool, then Copy (⌘-C) or Cut (⌘-X).<br>**Note:** *See page 19 for more ways to copy objects.* |

# Windows Wow! Glossary of Terms

| | |
|---|---|
| ⌘ **Option/Opt** | Use **Ctrl** in place of this symbol.<br>Use **Alt** in place of this key. This key can be used to modify many of the tools. |
| ←↑→↓ | The keyboard Cursor-keys: Left, Up, Right, Down. |
| **Toggle** | Menu selection acts as a switch: choosing once turns on, again turns it off. |
| **Marquee** | With any Selection tool, click-drag from your page over object(s) to select. |
| **Hinged curve** | A Bézier curve that meets a line or another curve at a point. |
| **Direct-selection**<br>**Group-selection**<br>**Selection** | *Direct-selection* tool selects points and paths.<br>*Group-selection* tool. The first click always selects the entire object, subsequent clicks select "next group-up" in the grouping order.<br>*Selection* tool (selects the biggest grouping which includes that object— if an object is ungrouped, then only that object is selected).<br>**Note:** *See page 9 and Chapters 1 & 2 for help with selection tools.* |
| **Select object(s)** | Click on or marquee with Group-selection tool to select entire object.<br>Click on or marquee with the regular Selection tool to select grouped objects. |
| **Deselect object(s)** | To Deselect *one* object, Shift-click (or Shift-marquee) with Group-selection tool.<br>To Deselect *all* selected objects, with any selection tool, click outside of all objects (but within your document), or press Shift-Ctrl-A. |
| **Select a path** | Click on a path with the Direct-selection tool to select it.<br>**Note:** *If objects are selected, Deselect first, then click with Direct-selection tool.* |
| **Select anchor points** | Click on path with Direct-selection tool to see anchor points. Then, Direct-select marquee around the points you want selected. Or, with Direct-selection tool, Shift-click on points you want selected.<br>**Note**: *Clicking on a selected point with Shift key down deselects that point.* |
| **Grab an object or point** | After selecting objects or points, use Direct-selection tool to click and hold down mouse button and drag to transform entire selection.<br>**Note:** *If you click by mistake (instead of click-and-hold), Undo and try again.* |
| **Delete an object** | Group-select the object and press the Delete (or Backspace) key.<br>To delete grouped objects, use the Selection tool, then Delete. |
| **Delete a path** | Direct-select a path and press the Delete (or Backspace) key. If you delete an anchor point, both paths attached to that anchor point will be deleted.<br>**Note:** *After deleting part of an object the entire remaining object will become selected; therefore, deleting twice will always delete the entire object!* |
| **Copy or Cut a path** | Click on a path with Direct-selection tool, then Copy (Ctrl-C) or Cut (Ctrl-X).<br>**Note:** *See the Finger Dance Summary for more ways to copy paths.* |
| **Copy or Cut an object** | Click on an object with Group-selection tool, then Copy (Ctrl-C) or Cut (Ctrl-X). For grouped objects, Click on one of the objects with the Selection tool, then Copy (Ctrl-C) or Cut (Ctrl-X).<br>**Note:** *See page 19 for more ways to copy objects.* |